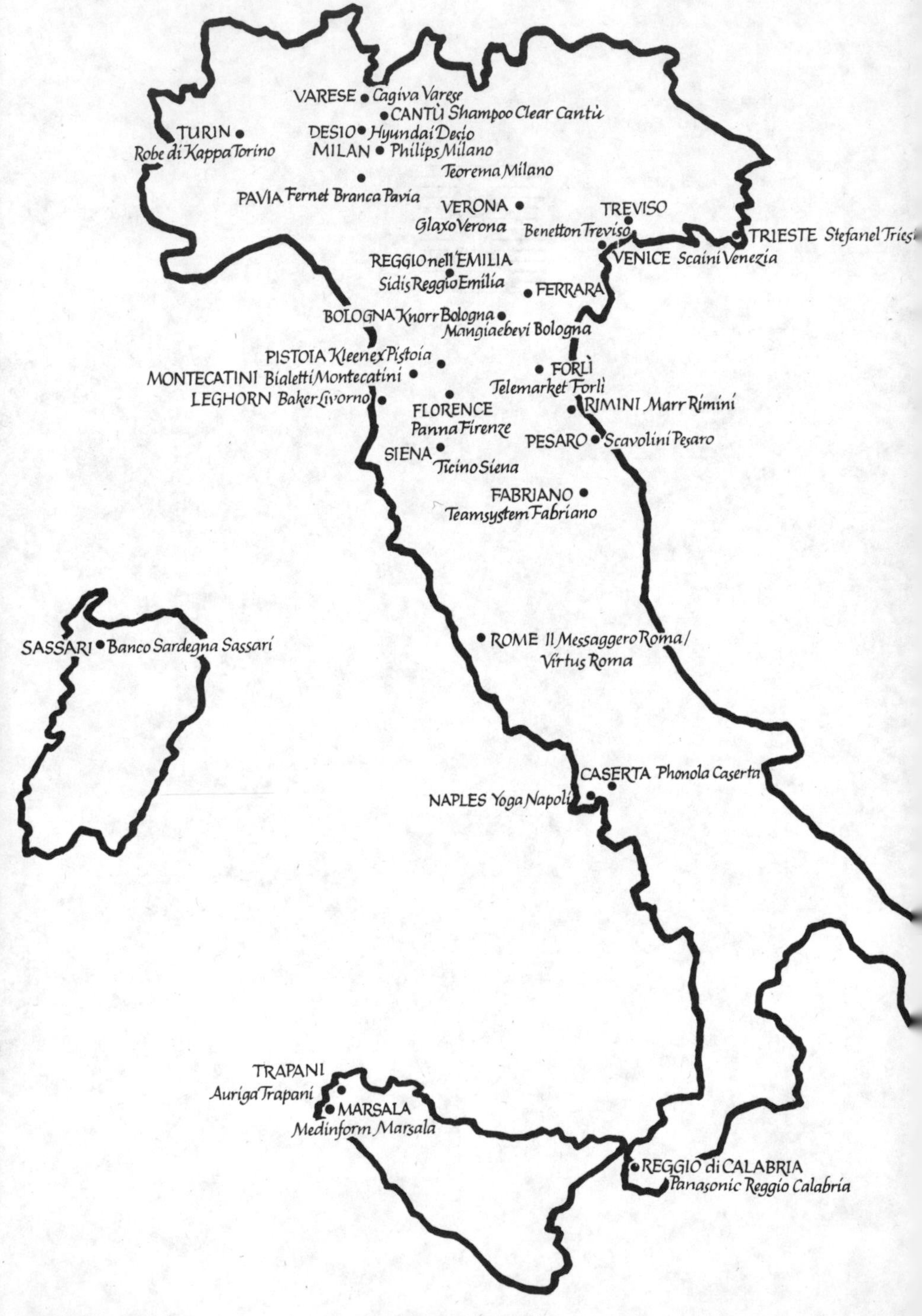

VARESE Cagiva Varese
CANTÙ Shampoo Clear Cantù
TURIN Robe di Kappa Torino
DESIO Hyundai Desio
MILAN Philips Milano
Teorema Milano
PAVIA Fernet Branca Pavia
VERONA Glaxo Verona
TREVISO Benetton Treviso
TRIESTE Stefanel Tries
VENICE Scaini Venezia
REGGIO nell'EMILIA Sidis Reggio Emilia
FERRARA
BOLOGNA Knorr Bologna
Mangiaebevi Bologna
PISTOIA Kleenex Pistoia
MONTECATINI Bialetti Montecatini
FORLÌ Telemarket Forlì
LEGHORN Baker Livorno
FLORENCE Panna Firenze
RIMINI Marr Rimini
PESARO Scavolini Pesaro
SIENA Ticino Siena
FABRIANO Teamsystem Fabriano
SASSARI Banco Sardegna Sassari
ROME Il Messaggero Roma / Virtus Roma
CASERTA Phonola Caserta
NAPLES Yoga Napoli
TRAPANI Auriga Trapani
MARSALA Medinform Marsala
REGGIO di CALABRIA Panasonic Reggio Calabria

Il Basket d'Italia

A Season in Italy
with Great Food,
Good Friends,
and Some Very
Tall Americans

Jim Patton

Simon & Schuster
New York London Toronto Sydney Tokyo Singapore

SIMON & SCHUSTER
Rockefeller Center
1230 Avenue of the Americas
New York, New York 10020

Designed by Paulette Orlando

Manufactured in the United States of America

1 3 5 7 9 10 8 6 4 2

Library of Congress Cataloging in Publication Data
Patton, Jim, date
Il basket d'Italia: a season in Italy with great food, good friends, and some very tall Americans/Jim Patton.
p. cm.
1. Basketball—Italy. 2. Basketball players—United States—Biography.
I. Title.
GV885.8.I8P38 1994
796.323'64'0945—dc20 94-16163
CIP

ISBN: 0-671- 86849-7

To my nephew, Gus Phipers
1977–1987

Acknowledgments

I owe particular thanks to my mom Grace and my dear departed dad James D. Patton, for everything; my sister Sarah and her husband Chuck Mills, for blind faith and limitless generosity; my dear former wife Jenelle; Dave Marlin, the genius behind my genius; Terry Ross, a great editor and friend in Portland, Oregon; Cam Stauth ("Author"); Richard Pine, my hotshot agent; and Jeff Neuman, editor grandissimo.

I couldn't have written the book I did without the help of many people in Italy. I'm particularly grateful to Tom Federman, Dan Peterson, Flavio Tranquillo, Antonio Ricciotti, Bob Morse, Rudy Hackett, and "Lucky" Luciano Capicchioni. I'll always have a special feeling for Darryl Dawkins, Dino Meneghin, and Roberto Brunamonti, who were invariably accessible and engaging and generous. I'll always appreciate the hospitality and friendship of Bill Wennington and his splendid wife Anne.

Above all, I'm indebted to the special six from *basket*world, who not only provided the best possible company but took my phone calls at all hours, went out of their way to help me (usually without my asking), and generally made me feel like family: Ettore Messina, Lou Colabello, Mark Crow, Alberto Bortolotti, and Mike and Laurel D'Antoni. Friends for life.

Finally, my profound thanks to my unofficial sponsors, who more or less adopted me the first day and were there for every little thing until the last: Italo and Rosita Nicoletti, their son Luca and daughter Mariagrazia, Rita Pozzi (Rosita's sister), and her daughters Daniela and Raffaella. Words can't explain.

To all, *molte grazie.*

Contents

Home on the Riviera 11
Rick Mahorn Is Gone 24
"Il Monumento Nazionale" 39
Life After Death for "Chocolate Thunder" 55
"Grandi Coglioni" 70
Bortolo and Friends 81
League's Leading Scorer—*Cut!* 89
"C'è Solo un Brunamonti" 96
Thanksgiving at the D'Antonis' 107
Sugar 124
"Killer Myers" 137
I Say a Little Prayer 146
Lou Colabello Sweats 153
A Toast to the *Stranieri* 159
Oscar 169
Not Looking for Love (in All the Right Places) 178
Movers and Shakers in the Long-Body Bazaar 188

"Sky" Walker Comes to Fabriano 198
Dino Revisited 203
D'Antoni Floating 217
"Welcome, Chris, the Future Is in Your Hands" 228
Toni Wins 236
McAdoo's Back 250
Looks Like Curtains for Philips 260
Getting Very Near the End 264
The Kiss 278
Loose Ends and Endings 292
Afterword 311
Postscript 317

Home on the Riviera

So I've popped through the looking glass. It's midnight and I'm finally at rest in the deserted bar in the Hotel Vittoria in the little resort town of Riccione, Italy, after a two-days-in-one haul that started back in Portland, Oregon, U.S.A., and took me through five airports and nine time zones before I landed at Milan's Malpensa airport this morning. I spent the afternoon driving my EuroDollar Rent-A-Car all over the countryside, having stupidly agreed to deliver an old guy I met on the plane to his relatives' home down around Florence, which turned out to be well *past* Florence and way up miles of muddy, potted, twisting roads into the mountains. Then it was another four hours on the crazy *autostrada* to make it to Riccione, where I stopped in a bar and called Marina, a woman whose name I was given by the Italian League PR director (by way of the NBA office). Marina told me to get directions to the Hotel Vittoria down by the sea, spend the night, and come see her tomorrow at the Palazzo de Turismo, the tourism bureau.

I found someone who could speak enough English to direct me to the Hotel Vittoria, and I parked in the street out front and checked in, and now here I am at midnight, sitting at a table near the bar. *In Italy*. On the Adriatic Riviera. The ocean is out there in the dark, not far; I could smell it as I got out of the car.

I'm just hoping for the best. It's strange to be in a place where you can't count on communicating. I don't know *anything*. I don't know how much I paid for this Jack Daniel's; I just knew the barman would understand my order. Five thousand lire? Five thousand anything sounds like a lot, but who knows?

I can't worry about it. I'm elated to be here, that's all.

The deal to write a book on Italian basketball came just in time.

As recently as two weeks ago I was nothing but an underachiever in my late thirties, a failed novelist and failed husband living alone and working three nights a week in a private mental ward, taking deranged little old ladies to the potty and wondering, as I stood in the hall listening to them tinkle at four in the morning, what had become of my life.

For three years I'd stayed sane writing a sports column for a weekly newspaper, but then jockworld itself started to seem less than sane. I mean Blazerworld and the NBA, which are all that matter in Portland.

The first year I was a fan, and I wanted the Trail Blazers to win. (They lost to Detroit in the finals.) The second year, disillusioned by the arrogance I saw in the players and in certain pockets of the organization, I wanted them to lose. (They started out 19–1 and won the most games in the league, but pleased me in the end by getting knocked off by the L.A. Lakers.) Last year, crying over my divorce, I didn't care either way. (Chicago crushed Portland in the finals.) I started wondering why I paid any attention at all. Football lost me years ago, baseball more recently; was the inconceivable now coming to pass?

Because the Blazers had done so well, I saw more than games—I saw the business of the NBA. I didn't simply tune in the finals on TV and savor the action and drama as I'd always done; I was picking up press credentials at league headquarters (where we also received T-shirts, caps, yearbooks, candy, and passes to a twenty-four-hour hospitality room), shoving my way into intimate media sessions of five hundred, going to parties. It was big business.

I pitied the beat writers and the TV reporters who had to stay on civil terms with the players, especially with the stars. How many times did I see Clyde Drexler shrivel someone with a look when he didn't like a question? How often did I hear Jerome Kersey and Terry Porter and Kevin Duckworth, considerably less PR-conscious than Clyde, wantonly insult people? The poor reporters had no choice but to take it. They could laugh and pretend it wasn't happening—or at least, that it wasn't degrading—or they could let it eat them up, but either way they had to stay on speaking terms with Jerome and Terry and Duck, and they definitely had to get Clyde-quotes after every game.

I didn't. There was no one I *had* to talk to, so if someone was rude to me, I could be rude right back. "Where do you get off acting like you're *better* than me?" I snarled at Clyde one time after he tried to embarrass me in front of his teammates. "You're a big basketball player, but that doesn't make you better than anyone else. Where do you get off acting that way? These other guys might have to take it, but I don't."

I was on a self-righteous roll. It was fun seeing Clyde, the master of controlled situations, floundering in uncharted waters. "I . . . no . . . don't . . . I resent that," he stammered. "I don't think I'm better than anyone else. I never have."

"You *do*, Clyde. All you guys do, and you don't even realize it, because you've been treated like gods since the seventh grade. I understand it. The miracle would be if you *didn't* think you were better than guys like me."

My disillusionment peaked when the ballyhooed Dream Team debuted in Portland at the Tournament of the Americas in July. I'd had my fill of the Team before the first game, before the first *practice*, but I knew things were out of hand when the tournament started and NBA security forces started bouncing people around like Hell's Angels "body-guarding" the Rolling Stones at Altamont.

Before one game, when I was trying to take some pictures for a friend's book on the Dream Team, one goon almost threw me out of the Coliseum when I asked him why he was pushing me back while allowing a couple of leggy teenagers to hang out up near him. Words. Backsass. Threats. "Let it go," said one of the Coliseum security guards. "They've been assholes all week. There's nothing you can do."

Because the League is *big*.

It was all too much. Dream Team. Team Dream. The Dreamers. The Twelve. The greatest team ever put together. The greatest show on earth. The greatest thing ever in the history of the world. Bigger than that.

How big is infinity?

Too big for me. But not too big for Nike: the shoemakers put on the most shameless spread I've ever seen out at the campus in Beaverton for the Dreamers and a few thousand VIPs like myself. They could have fed entire countries in high style for weeks. A band. A comedy act. Fireworks. There's Chris Mullin. David Robinson. We found Michael inside. The Dreamers. Nike. Big business. It was all one.

My friend Cam Stauth, who was writing the Dream Team book *The Golden Boys*, took me along to Barcelona as a research assistant. It was more of the same—more hype, except now you couldn't get anywhere near the Team. Now that they were busting the *world's* chops by fifty points a game, they were *way* too big.

We couldn't wait for it to be over. Then it was, and I didn't know what to do.

In a couple of months it would be Blazer time again. Was I ready for another year?

Deliver me, Lord. It was too depressing. Not only the jocks, but my *life:* three nights a week debating with schizophrenics and changing wet beds and putting up with Big Girl, the nurse; writing an unremunerative column (Mr.

Seventy-five-per, to my friends) for an embarrassing weekly newspaper; ruminating over everything my ex-wife said during our split and believing most of it; taking too many intoxicants, whether to salve my various pains or punish myself further.

Another year of the same? Maybe I'd just cut my throat instead.

The first thing I did was quit the newspaper when the editor-owner insulted me once too often. I made sure my letter of resignation burnt that bridge forever.

Without even a penny-ante writing gig, I had no excuse not to pursue my idea for a book on the wild and woolly (or so I'd heard) Italian pro basketball league. I got together with Blazer executives Bucky Buckwalter and Brad Greenberg, who'd been scouting in Europe for years and knew everyone. I met with longtime NBA forward and Portland resident Mychal Thompson, who was getting ready to go back for his second season in Italy.

I got stories, I got yarns. It sounded lawless and crazy. Fans threw things at players, coaches, and referees so often that the courts had protective shields for the benches and portable roll-out tunnels so everyone could escape safely after the final buzzer. Fanaticism.

And the personalities. It sounded like a basketball *Casablanca*, peopled with forgotten stars, foreign legends, faded vets, young comers, drug fiends, dropouts, vagabonds, mercenaries, mental cases, wheeler-dealers, and string-pullers—all kinds of characters in all kinds of circumstances dropping in, dropping out, every man for himself.

I made contacts. I talked with former Pistons bad boy Rick Mahorn, who was heading back for his second year with Il Messaggero Roma. Mahorn agreed to be a contact throughout the season if I actually wound up in Italy; this seemed like a coup.

I threw it all into a proposal and sent it to an agent, who called back saying he thought he could sell it.

And I come in one day and there's a message on my

recorder: Call this editor at Simon & Schuster. Simon & Schuster! I call, we spend forty-five minutes getting acquainted, it seems to go well. He says he or my agent will get back to me.

My agent does, a couple of days later, saying Simon & Schuster is buying. My advance is forthcoming.

I'm gone. Good-bye to the graveyard shift, my body out of whack all the time; good-bye, Big Girl; good-bye, little old ladies ringing your bells and asking me to potty you and wipe your shriveled bottoms afterward. Good-bye, small town. Hello, my new life.

I'm gone *now*. It's early October; NBA teams aren't even in camp yet, but in Italy they're already playing regular-season games. But what do I *do?* I don't have a clue. Italy? Where they speak Italian, which might as well be Martian to me, and where I don't know a soul?

I throw myself on the mercy of the NBA's international PR department, where a woman named Barbara Colangelo—Barbara Bottini from Milan, it turns out, now married to the son of Phoenix Suns president Jerry Colangelo—kindly offers to make a couple of calls on my behalf.

Twenty-four hours later the Italian League PR director not only knows I'm coming over to spend the season but is asking, through Barbara Colangelo, whether I'd be interested in living on the Adriatic coast while I'm there; he's got a friend, Marina, who works in the tourism bureau in a little resort town and can probably help me find something at off-season rates. . . .

Gone. Suddenly I'm booking a flight to Milan, Italy, packing up, closing my apartment, calling in sick my last weekend at the hospital, saying good-bye to my friends, picking up a couple of books on Italy, and, well, getting a ride to the airport.

Winging it, completely. Wondering, as we wing across the Atlantic, what I've gone and gotten myself into.

• • •

But I survive the first step. Finishing my Jack Daniel's in the Hotel Vittoria bar at midnight, I'm fading fast, but I'm here.

I'm awakened in the morning by the sun shining through the big, east-facing windows, right into my eyes.

Italy!

The sea is out there, across the street and a block beyond. Waves rolling in, the sun rising in the blue sky above.

I yawn, stretch, brush my teeth, and take a leisurely shower, tingling with a sense of well-being.

I'm out on the balcony, flossing my teeth and sucking in the salt air and marveling at my good fortune, when I notice a half-dozen people clustered around a little white car down in the street. Realizing it's my EuroDollar rental, I fly down three flights of stairs to find the Italians jabbering and exclaiming about a punched-in window on the driver's side, where someone let himself in and helped himself to the radio.

Worse, the printer I dragged through all those airports is gone, along with my suede jacket and a bag containing my return airline ticket and checkbook and bank card.

What have I gotten myself into?

When the crowd disperses, there's nothing to do but sweep the glass off the seat and, cursing Italy and Italians, drop off the car at the EuroDollar office in Rimini, two or three miles up the beach. The two guys working the office, who can't speak a word of English, come outside and gape at the damage as if they've never seen the like, and since I didn't pay for insurance when I rented the car, they won't let me leave until I not only pay for the rental but sign a blank order, stamped with my Visa card, to repair the damage and replace the radio. I know I'm getting shorn, but there's nothing I can do. They can't understand my protests; they just keep pushing a pen into my hand and pointing at the work order on the counter.

Finally, helpless, I sign and storm out. *Nice place, Italy. . . .*

And yet, five minutes later I'm down at the bright, breezy, exquisite Rimini beach, and with my feet in the sand, sandals in my hand, and my face lifted toward the sun, I stroll south, marveling again that I'm here when everyone I know is going about business as usual back home. I feel like a kid out running free while everyone else is in school—except that this is legit, and will go on for months.

I stroll all the way back to Riccione. It turns out to be a good three miles and takes almost two hours, but hey, I'm dawdling. Why not?

I got ripped off, okay, but it's not going to ruin Italy for me. I've got everything to be happy about.

In mid-afternoon I find my way to the Palazzo de Turismo and meet Marina, a petite, exuberant blonde in her early forties who's helping me out as a favor to the fellow Alberto in the league offices in Bologna, an old friend.

Marina speaks very little English, but with both of us gesturing and pulling words out of my Italian-English dictionary we establish that I'm at the Hotel Vittoria, that I've been robbed and have gone to Rimini since we talked late last night, and that I like it here nevertheless and could certainly tolerate living here if I could find an affordable place.

Marina makes a call. "Signora Nicoletti?" She jabbers for a minute; I can't pick out anything except *americano* and *libro* (book) and *lega* (league). She covers the phone and asks me what I can afford. I've been dreading this part. I know things are expensive in Italy, and I've been seeing numbers like one thousand dollars a month in my head, which is double what I want to spend.

"Six hundred *mille*," I reply pathetically after some quick calculations on a pad. Embarrassing. Six hundred thousand lire, or about $460. Good luck.

Marina relays my message, listens a moment, says "Okay, *ciao*," and hangs up. "Signora Nicoletti come here," she says.

A few minutes later there's a knock and an energetic middle-aged woman pokes her head in: "Marina, *ciao!*" She comes in, a gust of good cheer, looking me in the eye and shaking my hand exuberantly. "*Buon giorno!* You are *ameri-*

cano? Jeem, your name is? I Rosita." She's the wife of Marina's boss, Italo Nicoletti, and she's going to show me an apartment in a building the family owns nearby.

We walk a few blocks to an apartment house rising above a pharmacy on the corner of Via Puccini and Viale Dante. Rosita's parents, eighty years old, live on the first floor; her sister, Rita Fabbri, and Rita's twenty-one-year-old daughter, Rafaella, on the second; Rita's twenty-six-year-old daughter, Daniela, on the fourth. The other five apartments go to tourists during the summer and apparently sit empty the rest of the time.

Rosita shows me one of the two third-floor apartments. It's huge: three bedrooms, two bathrooms (a bath *and* a shower). It's completely furnished in the peculiarly tacky style of beach rentals everywhere, with bad art on the walls and tasteless vases and ashtrays and knickknacks everywhere. In compensation, an incredible balcony runs the length of the building and looks down to the Adriatic a block and a half away.

Rosita lets me have it for six hundred thousand lire a month. I'm flabbergasted. Tomorrow I'll be settled in this outrageous place, a shout away from the ocean, for less than I was paying in Portland.

It's the off-season now, Rosita explains. In the summer, when the 31,000 citizens of Riccione are overrun by 150,000 tourists, she rents this place for 3 million lire a month (around twenty-five hundred dollars), but from October to May it brings in nothing. She's glad to have me.

I'm ecstatic. And aglow, when Rosita invites me to dinner. They're eating at her sister's, the apartment below mine; I can come any time after seven.

I pass the late afternoon wandering around my new hometown of Riccione (re-CHO-neh), Italy. It's a pretty well-known resort town (Mussolini had a summer place here), and though it's quiet now, almost sleepy, there's a leftover sense of crowds and noise and activity and laughter. Vacation season in Italy ends promptly on October 1, and now, a week later, I see shopkeepers emptying their windows down at "the Center," an open-air mall of shops and cafes and a supermarket, pharmacy, movie theater, and post office. Most of the restaurants and hotels along the tourist strips are already closed, out of business until spring. The people out and about are clearly locals, waving to each other and stopping to chat as they shop and do errands. It's peaceful.

A bunch of teenaged girls in Levi's trip by, looking in shops and chanting, "Na, na na, na-na-na-na . . . na-na-na-na . . . hey-ey Jude" as the Beatles tune issues from speakers that rise out of the cement like giant mushrooms. The Beatles are big: a few minutes later it's "Let It Be," and then "Here, There And Everywhere."

I walk down to the beach and head back to the hotel that way—sandals in my hand, feet in the sand. It's a beautiful, wide beach, a long way from the water to the endless line of boarded-up concession stands and padlocked *bagni* (where people rent umbrellas and chairs during the season). Beyond the *bagni* the Via D'Annunzio runs north to Rimini and south to Cattolica; on the other side of the Via D'Annunzio are the backs of the huge hotels that run as far as the eye can see.

The Adriatic Riviera.

Home.

It's one of the nicest dinners of my life, if dinner means everything from food and drink to camaraderie and goodwill.

I walk over from the hotel and ring the buzzer outside the building at 7:15. Rosita's sister Rita picks up, apparently, and she can't understand me at all. I don't get much farther with the young female voice that comes on next. I hear giggling. "Mama!" someone calls.

Finally Rosita gets on. "Jeem? You arrive?"

Up in Rita's second-floor apartment a moment later,

earthy, energetic Rosita greets me with a European kiss-kiss on both cheeks.

"Jeem . . . *Pat*-ton?" she asks, double-checking my name before making introductions, and then presents me to the others: her son, Luca, a softspoken guy of thirty-one, and her daughter, Mariagrazia, twenty-six, who looks extremely lithe in her stirrup pants and has big brown eyes and a charming little shy smile; her sister Rita, fiftyish, and Rita's daughters, Rafaella and Daniela. She says her husband will be along, but they never know when. "My father, he only work," Luca says. "Always."

Luca speaks a little English and usually gets my drift if I speak slowly and simply enough. Mariagrazia speaks a wee bit, Rita and her daughters virtually none. I immediately get out my little Italian-English dictionary. Rita's got another one on her shelf, and they're both being passed back and forth as we happily struggle to communicate.

Luca fills the wineglasses, and as Rita and Rosita work in the kitchen and lithe Mariagrazia watches me with her big, soulful brown eyes, he asks me all about my project, my trip, my impressions of Riccione. With a lot of help from the dictionary and his cousin Rafaella, who does speak some English but needed to be coaxed, he manages to answer my questions. His father, Italo, is a big shot at the Palazzo de Turismo and the head of Riccione's sports association as well as a member of all sorts of associations and societies and boards, a go-getter still at sixty-three—always gone to meetings, which is why the family never sees him. During tourist season all four of them—Luca and Mariagrazia and their parents—work the three-star hotel they own a couple of blocks over. Off-season, at least this year, Luca and his mother and sister will be leading work crews on renovations over at the hotel. Luca, an architecture student, will be going back and forth to Firenze (Florence) for some classes and exams.

He and Mariagrazia have always lived with their parents,

like most unmarried Italians. The family is in a long process of finishing and moving into a new house, which is why they've been coming over to Rita's for dinner every night.

Rita and her daughters also own and operate a hotel a few blocks over. (Who doesn't, here? A pamphlet I saw in Marina's office said there are 440 hotels in this little place, not to mention 1,600 in Rimini.)

The doorbell rings and Signor Nicoletti lets himself in, a handsome but somewhat harried-looking man who, however, brightens as they all greet him and then clamor to introduce the *americano*.

Signor speaks not a single word of English; we can't even begin to communicate. But he's tremendously good-natured, cutting up with everyone as he quickly drains a couple of glasses of wine. He has Luca ask me if everything is going okay, if there's anything I need.

For the next two and a half hours I'm plied with food and libations and good cheer. This is dinner in Italy: *piadina*, a thin pita-like bread, with prosciutto; a huge bowl of spaghetti with fish sauce; fresh fish; fried onions; spinach; and a couple of things I can only guess at. Rita's up and down, removing platters and wine bottles and bringing more. Luca keeps asking me about America. Mariagrazia keeps looking at me, though she's said she has a boyfriend. (I keep looking at her, apparently, or I wouldn't have noticed.)

I must join them every Thursday, Rosita says.

I can't believe my great luck. So what if I lost my printer, my suede jacket, my airline ticket and checkbook and what all? It's just stuff. *This* is priceless.

We finish, long after we started, with liqueurs from a well-stocked cabinet in one corner of Rita's living room. Signor quaffs a couple straight off before abruptly saying goodnight and heading off for some important meeting or other. "Always he have meetings," Luca says. "Always he work."

The rest of us stay, sampling liqueurs and cutting up. Rosita gets loose, telling stories and singing songs. Mariagrazia, amused but a little embarrassed, tries to button her up, but Rosita's having a good time. We all are.

Eventually Rosita's got me up and doing a turn across Rita's living room with her.

I can't believe I'm here.

Every Thursday, Rosita reminds me as I finally take my leave.

I spend Friday morning strolling around town and up and down the beach in the early-autumn sunshine. I sit on my balcony at the Hotel Vittoria, studying my Italy books, trying to learn to say more than *grazie* and *ciao*. At lunch I try a restaurant down in the Center, where I play it safe with pizza and *birra*, and for dinner I stop at the Savioli, a comfortable neighborhood restaurant-bar across the street from where I'll be living; this time I play it safe with spaghetti and *birra*. Late at night I stop near the Center for a cone of gelato, Italy's famous soft ice cream, and wind up making a mental note that I *cannot* let myself get hooked.

Saturday morning I meet Rosita at the Nicolettis' old house, a couple of blocks over, to pick up the key to the apartment. A half hour later I've checked out of the Hotel Vittoria and moved my stuff over.

I clear the knickknacks from a couple of shelves in the living room and prop up some snapshots of family and friends. There. I'm in. I'm really here.

To make it official, I walk down to the market and buy some crackers, bananas, yogurt, and bottled water. Three days in Italy, I've got a place at the shore with food in the refrigerator.

Hello, my new life.

Rick Mahorn Is Gone

A few days later I make my first trip to the league's eighteenth-floor offices in Bologna to meet PR director Alberto Bortolotti, who's responsible for my getting the great place in Riccione and who told me over the phone that he's at my disposal. Sounds great to someone who was answering little old ladies' call-bells a couple of weeks ago.

Alberto, in his mid-thirties, is a big, good-natured, Spanish-looking guy with olive skin and straight black hair. A journalist for fifteen years, he came to work for the *lega* only this season. Fortunately for me, one reason he got the job was his excellent English.

The offices are modern and roomy, but after meeting Daniela, Loretta, and Tiziana, the three beautiful secretaries out front, I hardly see anyone else around. Not many people work for the league, Alberto says. This is surprising to one accustomed to the gargantuan NBA, but I'm beginning to understand the difference in scale here. The *lega* has thirty-two teams, more than the NBA, but that's the only way it's bigger.

Most of the organizations, Alberto says, employ only a few people beyond the players and coaches—president, general manager, accountant, PR man, secretary, maybe a team manager—and even some of these have other jobs. NBA clubs have more people than that making coffee.

But then, it's something of a part-time league, in an *americano*'s view. Although the regular season lasts seven months, longer than the NBA season, it's only a thirty-game schedule—a game every Sunday, October through April, the only variations being midweek games before Christmas and in the last week of the season. The playoffs are brief: a couple of two-out-of-three series and a best-of-five championship round.

In addition—and I've got to write all this down as Alberto explains—several teams each season are playing in various cup competitions, meaning they'll play a dozen or so weeknight games against other top European pro teams. The only thing bigger than the league championship is the Euroclub Championship, known until recently as the European Cup, in which the top teams in the various European leagues in the previous year compete for a title to be decided near the end of the current season. Toni Kukoc's Yugoslavian clubs won three in a row until last year, when Kukoc came to Italy and another Yugoslavian team stepped up, Partizan Belgrade, led by a kid named Danilovic. Danilovic, Alberto tells me with a fan's partisanship, not only followed Kukoc to Italy this past summer but signed right here with Knorr Bologna and is tearing up the league in the early going.

You've got the Korac (CORE-otch) Cup, named after a Yugoslavian player who was killed a few years ago, which includes the previous season's third, fourth, fifth, and sixth finishers in each of the major European leagues and two teams from several others—sixty-four in all. It's not prized like the league title or the Euroclub Championship, Alberto says, but there is some prestige attached to the Korac Cup throughout Europe.

Then there's the Cup of Cups, the one people *now* call the European Cup—but to understand that, I've got to understand the Italy Cup. I'm scribbling. As near as I can tell, all the teams in the Italian League—the Lega Pallacanestro

Italiano—take part in an early-season round-robin tournament to determine the participants for the Italy Cup Final Four in March. The Italy Cup is about bragging rights more than anything. The winner does participate in the next season's Cup of Cups (European Cup) against the winners of Spain's and France's and the other countries' versions of the Italy Cup.

Even the *lega*'s no cinch to understand. All I can grasp right now is that there are thirty-two teams in all—sixteen in A-1, sixteen in A-2—and that besides the playoffs for the championship there's what they call a play*out* between the A-1 also-rans and the top A-2 clubs to determine who moves up and who moves down the next season. I figure I'll pick it up as time passes.

Naturally the league wants to look good in a book published in the U.S.—the clubs are allowed two foreign players each and vie with Spanish and French teams for top Americans—and Alberto couldn't be more accommodating. He answers my questions and loads me down with league guides, media guides, magazines, and statistics. When I ask about a guy named Dino Meneghin who, according to Bucky Buckwalter and the few Italians I've talked to, is Italy's greatest player ever, he says, "Ah, the monument," and not only tells me about him but gets on the phone and, just like that, arranges for me to meet this icon on Friday in Rimini, where Meneghin will be spending a few days with his team. It was never like this in the NBA.

The bad news comes when I mention that I need to call Rick Mahorn, who's agreed to be my big contact over here.

Alberto looks at me like I'm hopelessly out of the loop. "You didn't know? Il Messaggero cut Mahorn a few days ago."

He locates the fax the team sent out and gives me a rough translation. Il Messaggero contends that Mahorn violated his guaranteed contract with a *grave intemperanza* in the locker room after a Korac Cup game last week. "Given the legal aspects of the case," the brief message concludes, "the organization considers it inadvisable to say any more."

A *grave intemperanza?*

"Cursing at his teammates, cursing at the coach," Alberto says. "The newspapers say he throws a chair. We don't know this, but"—he shrugs, pointing at the fax with the Il Messaggero letterhead—"they send Rick away."

I'm shaking my head. My big contact is gone. Amazing.

Not so amazing, according to Alberto. He says Mahorn was a two-million-dollar pain in the butt to Messaggero last season, his first on a two-year contract, even though the team won the moderately prestigious Korac Cup and reached the semifinals of the league playoffs. Mahorn looked down on the Italians, only played hard when he felt like it, etc.

Apparently he showed up this season with the same attitude plus fifteen extra pounds around his middle, and was so interested in dropping the weight that he managed to miss about a third of Messaggero's preseason workouts for one reason or another. In short, he never endeared himself, and he didn't get much sympathy when he blew a gasket last week.

This is bad news for me. Mahorn's probably back in the U.S. by now. Even if he's still in Rome, he probably won't want to talk, under the circumstances. But I get on Alberto's phone and dial the Rome number Mahorn gave me a couple of months ago.

"Yeah?" It's Rick; I remember the surly grunt he issues when he answers the phone. It puts you off. Maybe it's supposed to.

I plunge in, reminding him that we talked back in August and he agreed to help me with my book.

"Oh yeah, Jim, how ya doin'?"

His breezy response alerts me. After three years around the NBA I know that most of these guys consider writers a lower species, and when they're friendly with one they hardly know (using your first name is a giveaway) it's because they want sympathetic treatment.

"I'm fine," I tell him, "but I hear you've had some kind of trouble."

"Yeah," Rick says casually, "there's been some bullshit . . ."

"Can we get together and talk about it?"

No problem. Nice as can be, the bad boy offers to pick me up at the train station any time I want to come to Rome; he'll be around a little longer.

I tell him I'll be there tomorrow.

A little before noon the next day, after a picturesque five-hour train ride down to Falconara and then all the way across Italy, I call Rick from Rome's immense Termini station. He says he'll pick me up at one o'clock, in a "dirty-as-hell gray Mercedes," in front of the McDonald's a couple of blocks away.

From 12:45 to 1:30 I stand out on the curb in the warm October sun watching the lunchtime traffic whoosh around the Piazza della Repubblica, a big traffic circle with an elaborate fountain in the middle. I can't believe there are so many dirty gray Mercedes on earth. Waiting, waiting—knowing NBA types show up late for appointments even when they want to be nice, because they figure they're being nice by showing up at all—I take in the teeming life: people heading in and out of cafes and restaurants, beautiful girls lolling around the fountain, gypsies and Third-World types selling watches and belts and sunglasses out of briefcases on the sidewalks, brave traffic cops trying futilely to impose some order on the anarchy. I can't believe I'm in what my dad used to call "RomeItaly."

Finally the right dirty-as-hell gray Mercedes pulls up. As I get in, Rick, wearing shades and talking on a cellular phone, shakes my hand and says, "How ya doin', Jim," then resumes chatting on the phone as he wheels the car casually, one-handedly into the insane traffic. My single day with the EuroDollar car was enough to persuade me to get around for the next few months by train, bus, taxi, metro, or on foot—any way but driving—and now, with Rick gabbing away as the midday crush assaults us from all directions, I'm afraid

I'm going to have a nervous breakdown before we're even out of the piazza.

We make it out, but then things get even worse. Tiny Italian cars dart in front of us. People make three lanes out of two in both directions, six lanes where there ought to be four. People on the left try to cut across two lanes to turn right (and persist until they can); people on the right insist on turning left. Death-defying teenagers and geriatrics alike swerve in and out of traffic on *motorinas*, little motorized scooters. Horns blare and fists with middle fingers extended fly out of windows everywhere.

"Takes balls to drive over here," I remark when Rick finishes his conversation.

"No big deal," he says, spinning the radio dial. "You just gotta do like they do. It's like a game of chicken."

Rick takes a few more calls, punctuating his talk with blasts on his horn and muttered epithets: "Fuckin' Italians," "Fuck you, buddy," "Wha'choo gonna do, fool?" At one point he skirts a tangle by wheeling the right-side tires up onto the curb and going around. "Ain't my car," he chuckles when I give him a look. The organization provided him with the Mercedes and is letting him keep it for as long as he's in Rome.

So how long will he be here?

"Until my lawyers settle the contract with Messaggero."

"I thought it was guaranteed, two million dollars or something."

"It is," Rick says, "but 'guaranteed' don't mean shit here. You can be guaranteed and they'll tell you"—he makes a universal fuck-you gesture—" 'Have a nice day.' "

I tell him I've heard that Messaggero considers the contract terminated and doesn't intend to pay any of it. How much is he trying to get in a settlement?

"All. All of it."

At last we leave the car in an underground garage and walk to the famous Spanish Steps, a huge three-tiered staircase near the Colosseum, where we're supposed to meet someone or other and go to lunch. Rick, wearing black jeans and a brown shirt with the tail hanging out, looks thick and powerful—a trifle *too* thick, as I've heard, through the butt and thighs; there's a bit of a waddle in his step. He's got a diamond stud in his left ear, a gold chain around his neck and another on one thick wrist. A big leather purse hangs from his shoulder, and he's got the cellular phone in his hand.

Sitting on the Spanish Steps amid dozens of people sunning, chatting, reading, and eating lunch, I broach the subject of Rick's falling-out with Messaggero.

"It was no big thing," Rick says. "Management shouldn't have handled it the way they did. In the NBA they would have just done something within the team, like a fine, and that would have been it.

"In the U.S. we grow up playing basketball; we've got a hoop on every corner. Here, every other corner you see a soccer field. I feel like, 'We started basketball, so I'm more knowledgeable of the game. Having been in the NBA, I feel like I can show you certain things to help the ballclub.' But not here. Here it's like, 'My way, or fuck it.' "

He complains about the way things are done in Italian training camps, which aren't like the NBA's. He disagrees with practice philosophy in general: too much conditioning, too many repetitive drills, too little scrimmaging—not like the NBA. He didn't like being awakened for team breakfasts on overnight trips—they don't do that to you in the NBA.

"There was lots of stuff I disagreed with, but I dealt with it because this is what I get paid to do. I didn't argue with 'em. I did what I was supposed to do.

"I wasn't supposed to speak my mind. But I spoke my mind, and apparently they didn't like it. I guess I was supposed to sit there and shut up and play basketball.

"The way they handled it, I feel like I got a raw deal. They could have settled this in a different way. 'Cause I had an outburst after a game last year. I threw a bottle and it just burst, hit a wall or something, and everybody looks like, What's wrong with *him?* I was frustrated because we lost a game to a team I knew we could beat. But it was like they didn't want to get themselves ready to do that.

"Then this year they didn't throw me the ball but once in one game . . . so I threw a bottle. I was saying, like, '*Pass* the goddamn ball, *pass it!* I'll give it back, but I wanna touch the ball, I wanna be a part of the offense.' "

In other words, they let him get away with tantrums before, so why not now?

I tell Rick I want to hear all the details later, when we're in a quiet place with no distractions. For now, I ask if he would recommend Italy to other American players.

"Guys would really have to think about leaving something that's pretty good like the NBA. They have to be leery, some of the guys that think they'll get a couple of years here in their twilight years. You'll get a couple of years, but it all depends on how these people want to respect you."

As for the off-court experience, he's got mixed feelings.

"You only play thirty league games plus playoffs here, mostly on weekends, so there's no long trips like in the NBA. I was home a lot with my family. The Italian lifestyle is very family-oriented, very laid-back. Even in a metropolitan city it's a slower pace. And we liked the historic aspect of the country and of Rome.

"But you have to be very open-minded, level-headed enough to deal with a lot of different personalities, things of that nature. You have to deal with a lot of unnecessary bullshit: the driving, everybody smoking, all kinds of things. You have to just shut your mind to it.

"Not knowing anybody was a big change. All my friends are in America. You've got the telephone, but you get tired of the telephone. You want to see people, you want to be around them. That's why you tend to cling to any Americans you know. I was lucky I had my wife. We hadn't been married that long when we came here, but I really learned that I can live with her for the rest of my life."

Finally our lunch companions show up: a couple of lawyers, one American and one Italian, from the firm that's handling Rick's contract settlement with Messaggero. As we wander around looking for the right place to eat, Rick takes a couple of calls on the cellular phone (one from his agent in the States), then joins me in chatting with the lawyers about Rome, soccer, the NBA. I'm convinced that Rick, at least away from the colliding-egos basketball world, can be as pleasant as people around the NBA used to say he was.

After lunch we walk the lawyers to their office, go back to the car, and head for the other side of the city, where Rick's got some errands to do. We land in a stupendous traffic jam: gridlocked Romans leaning on their horns, thrusting middle fingers out their windows, inaudibly—but visibly—swearing behind their windshields. Rick seems preoccupied and emits only a few indifferent oaths, as if out of habit: "Kiss me, bitch," when a lady flips him off; "*Go,* fool," when a man starts to butt in front of us and then hesitates.

He gets a call from Croatian star and Celtics draftee Dino Radja, Messaggero's other foreign player—its only one, now—and Rick's best friend here. They chat for a few minutes and make plans to get together tomorrow.

Eventually we escape the traffic, Rick makes his stops, and, as I've been invited to dinner, we start for the Mahorn place on the outskirts of Rome. After a stop to pick up some food at a *rosticceria*—something like a delicatessen, where Rick orders with a little bit of Italian and a lot of pointing—we drive a little farther out before passing through a gate manned by a uniformed guard into what Rick calls "our complex." It's something like a vast, high-class subdivision in the States. The residences—"villas and town houses," Rick says—are back off the road, obscured by big trees and darkness.

The road goes on and on. I tell Rick I'm looking forward to seeing his place; back in the States it always sounded impressive when we heard about players going to Italy and being provided with *villas*.

"A villa ain't shit," Rick snorts. "When you see it, it's not nothing like what you think it would be. It's nothing but a house on some land with a fence. It's nice, it's a beautiful house, but it's just a house."

Finally we pause in front of some big iron gates. Rick pushes a button to open them and we're there.

In a bright, spacious, modern kitchen I meet Rick's gracious wife, Donyale, who's wearing a robe and holding their three-month-old daughter, Jordan. (A surprising name, considering that Rick was the chief villain in all those muggings of Michael in the late-eighties Detroit-Chicago rivalry.) Rick kisses Donyale and takes the baby. Even as he listens to happy chatter from Moyah, his ten-year-old daughter from a previous liaison, and squats to check on year-old Alexandra, who's crawling on the floor, he's cooing and mugging for Jordan like Bill Cosby. Millions of fans who have him pegged for a thug wouldn't believe it.

Rick shows me around the main floor. Maybe the villa's not a castle, but it's roomy, carpeted, and nicely furnished. There's a two-car garage (containing a little Fiat they bought for Donyale) and a huge enclosed backyard, the patio lights showing the first fallen leaves on the lawn. Messaggero owns the place (Michael Cooper lived here before Rick, in his single season in Italy) and pays electricity, water, everything but the phone bill.

Moyah proudly shows me the upstairs, her (and the nanny's) part of the spread, and tells me about her first few weeks of fifth grade at the American school ("*hard*, a lot harder than fourth"). Then we all share dinner around the kitchen counter: chicken and potatoes from the *rosticceria*, green beans, bottled water. Alexandra sits beside me in her high chair, scarfing bits of chicken that Rick puts in front of her; in between bites she gapes at me, grabs the finger I hold out and says "Hi, hi, hi" over and over. It's all very pleasant, very American. I'm feeling sentimental, breaking bread with fellow Americans all the way over here, talking about "back home."

Afterward, Rick and I retire to the living room. I want the lowdown, start to finish, on the fateful locker-room incident. I turn on my recorder.

Rick settles back and then starts out *so* casual, so exaggeratedly mellow—considering he's just been thrown off the team and stands to lose most of $2 million he would have received for playing some fifty ball games—that it feels like he's faking it.

"Basically," he drawls, "a few things happened at the beginning of the season. The ball wasn't being passed inside. I went from averaging sixteen points a game last year to seven points. To me it was like, 'What do you want me to do this year—post up, or what? Just . . . *be here?*' So it ended up where I went in there after the game last week and asked the coach, 'What's going on? What do you want me to do? What do I have to do for this damn team?'

"So it went from there," Rick segues—nothing about cursing anyone, nothing about throwing anything. "That was last Wednesday night, and Thursday we had the day off anyway so I didn't hear from 'em."

That night someone from the organization called and asked him to come to the gym an hour before Messaggero's Friday morning practice. Rick says he figured he was in for a reprimand, maybe even a fine.

"But when I got there, the president of the team gave me a letter talking about 'criminal conduct' and saying our contract was terminated. I was like, '*Damn*, you really *can't* say anything and voice your opinion and be a ballplayer.' Because every ballplayer voices his opinion in the NBA. You speak to the coach; there's a revolving door to the coach. But not in this matter."

"So," I ask, "you didn't go off that night as bad as they're claiming?"

"No, I didn't," Rick replies, exaggeratedly placid again, presenting as the kind of fellow who couldn't possibly do the kinds of things people say. "I threw a chair," he finally allows. Then adds, "At a *wall*," and then—in a muttered aside, as if the fact is scarcely worth mentioning but honesty compels him—"in the coaches' office." Oh.

I ask, "Do you think Messaggero terminated the contract

as a result of that one incident only?"

"Totally that one incident, yeah, because I'd gone off before. I threw a bottle of water one time, and they talked to me, but that was it. I never threw a shoe at a teammate like they said in the letter; I threw two bottles of water in the locker room. And nothing directed at anybody, 'cause if I want to hit somebody, I can hit 'em."

I'm sure I don't have this straight. "They've hassled you for throwing a couple of plastic water bottles?"

Rick shrugs. "I think one broke a window, I don't know. Still, if they want to talk about criminal acts, I'll pay for the chair. I paid for the window.

"And I didn't say anything too derogatory about the team [after the fateful game last week]. I just asked, What do I have to do for this team? You know, I feel like if I'm scoring four points and getting two rebounds, basically I'm not doing shit to get the money I'm getting paid. I think if somebody's getting paid that much money, he should get the basketball just like the other person's getting the basketball."

I tell Rick I've heard he was never in the best condition over here, last season or this.

"I don't know what the team thought. All I know is that when the game starts, I'm going to war. I'm here to play basketball. There's a lot of things they said that I didn't agree with, and things maybe they felt I should have improved. But hey, everybody has their own side."

"Do you have any regrets? Things you would have done differently?"

"I would have done things differently if I was them."

I try not to seem too astonished. "Them?"

"If I was them I would have handled this situation a different way. They should have, you know, just *talked*. I mean, we're all men."

"Any regrets for how *you've* been?"

"I don't really have any regrets," Rick says, ultra-cool again. "I mean, hey, I'm gonna be me, no matter who I'm playing for."

Does he think the Messaggero mess will hurt him in how he's perceived around the NBA?

"No, because people there know me. I've never done anything to disrupt anybody, never burned a bridge that I crossed. I just figure everything that happens is an open door. God leaves an open door for me to walk through."

It's ten o'clock when we start the half-hour drive to Termini station downtown. In the car we chat about Rick's NBA days, various ex-teammates and opponents. Rick's pleasant. He's been pleasant all day, though I know there's been a considerable degree of self-interest in it.

My sense—without even hearing Messaggero's side—is that Rick came to Italy with the wrong attitude. *In the NBA this, in the NBA that. I was an NBA champion; let me enlighten you. I'm a superstar; my salary proves it; give me the ball and watch me*.

But this wasn't the NBA. It wasn't America. Different people, everything different.

And Rick was the same player he always was. He wouldn't find Patrick Ewing or Hakeem Olajuwon waiting in the lane in Rimini or Livorno, but there would be someone there, and the two or three crude moves he used in the NBA wouldn't go a lot farther here. He wasn't a guy you'd design your offense around, especially when you had Dino Radja inside: younger, taller, and quicker than Rick, with post moves and a jump shot. No doubt Messaggero wanted the same things from Rick that NBA teams wanted: rebounding, defense, toughness.

Riding the train back across Italy through the night, I recall something Rick said on our drive back to Termini. When I remarked that his former Pistons teammate Joe Dumars had always seemed like a salt-of-the-earth type, Rick said yeah . . . then added, "But after a few years, when he became a *stahhh*, Joe changed a little bit."

I'm convinced that though Rick had a successful NBA career and made a lot of money, he harbors some resentment about never having been a *stahhh*, about being overshadowed by Dumars and Isiah Thomas and Bill Laimbeer and even coach Chuck Daly in Detroit, then by his pal Charles Barkley in Philadelphia. When he got the huge contract in Italy, he *was* going to be the star. He came over and acted like he was.

A few days after my trip to Rome, the behemoth Ferruzzi Group—which owns, among many other things, *Il Messaggero,* one of Italy's biggest newspapers—announces that it's pulling out of basketball ownership and selling the Rome franchise.

The surprise development raises questions about the Mahorn case. Was the sale of the team dependent on the Ferruzzi Group's dumping Rick's outsized contract?

Of course, you need pretty solid grounds to get out of a guaranteed contract scot-free. The Ferruzzi Group obviously felt that Rick's outburst was sufficient.

Rick and his agent, Aldon Walton, obviously didn't. The lawyers we ate lunch with are working on it.

Meanwhile Rick, after a trip to the States to work out with a few NBA teams, signs a three-year contract to play for New Jersey under his former coach Chuck Daly, who's beginning his first season with the Nets.

According to *USA Today*, the three-year package adds up to some $1.8 million, or about what Rick would have earned for this one season in Rome. Over here, in addition, he was given the villa and the Mercedes, and the organization paid his Italian taxes.

In the next few months I find a few people who say Rick gave Messaggero toughness, wanted to win, knew how to win. And Messaggero did win last year's Korac Cup—largely due to Rick, by some accounts, who subdued Real Madrid's awesome Arvidas Sabonis in the finals—and made it to the league semifinals.

But most people sound more like Ettore Messina, the respected young Knorr coach, who told me, "Rick Mahorn was a disaster in Rome. Last season he was fat and lazy, very lazy. This season he was doing nothing from the beginning.

"In the NBA he was the bad boy, the hard worker. Then he came here and said, 'Now it's time to rest. Fuck you—you Italian guys do the dirty work, I'm Rick Mahorn.' And what happens? He goes back to the NBA and he's again the bad boy: screening, rebounding, working hard."

Mahorn came to be regarded as an example of a bad, bad choice by an Italian club: big money, big ego, little motivation, a bad fit for the team. He's proof that NBA complementary players don't automatically become stars in Italy.

After spending that October day with him, I felt pretty sure that the first piece of advice for Americans coming over should be, Don't expect to find America in Italy. They have their own ways of doing things, and they're not paying you to tell them you know better.

When in Rome, do as the Romans do. If you don't like their ways, say *arrivederci* and catch a plane.

"Il Monumento Nazionale"

The evening after that first quick trip to Rome—after riding the night train back and then sleeping into the afternoon—I take the bus up to Rimini to keep the appointment Alberto arranged for me with Dino Meneghin, who's staying at the Hotel Continentale with his Stefanel Trieste team.

I don't expect it to be much fun. Now nearly forty-three and playing his twenty-seventh season in the league, Meneghin (men-uh-GEEN, as in "green") is one of the most famous people in Italy. Even people who don't follow *basket*, as the game is known here, nod at the mention of his name and say, "Ah yes, Meneghin. The legend."

In America every Alaa Abdelnaby is a legend in his own mind; Barkleys and Drexlers—though unknown outside the rabid but relatively small world of sports fans—are treated like gods, and carry themselves as such. What can I expect of this guy, who's been revered by his countrymen, fans and non-fans alike, for some twenty-five years?

I don't hear the best stories until later: How Dino once whacked a teammate upside the head when he didn't think the guy was playing tough enough defense in a big game.

How he put pornographic magazines in his coach's luggage just before the team went through customs on a trip to Yugoslavia, back when the authorities were hassling people over such things. How he led the Varese dynasty of the seventies to an unheard-of ten consecutive European Cup (now Euroclub Championship) finals, then went to Milan and helped make that club the dynasty of the eighties. How he amused his Milan teammates at the expense of a player who mixed himself a daily post-practice drink of Gatorade, protein, and vitamins, by stirring the concoction with his dong while the hapless player took his shower. How he flattened a referee with a forearm shot and the ref apologized. How he used to cut holes in his teammates' underwear so their privates fell out when they dressed after the game. How, after the opposing team protested a New Year's Eve game in London and a rematch was scheduled for nine o'clock the next *morning*, he got himself ejected with two technicals at the tip-off and ran off the court waving his arms, ecstatic. How he gets standing ovations in Israel and all over Europe, having been voted the greatest European player ever as far back as 1984. How he broke the door leaving the team president's office when Milan unceremoniously let him go after the '89–'90 season, when he was forty years old and had finished his twenty-fourth year in the league.

I know precious little of this when I meet Dino Meneghin this first time. I know only that the magazines call him "*il monumento nazionale*" and everyone says he's the greatest Italian player ever. When you ask how a guy with a 10-point career scoring average could be so great, they shrug and tell you about all the championships. Maurizio, the bartender over at the Savioli, told me, "A team is not the same without him. When he play in Varese, the team is champion. He go to Milano, the team is champion. Maybe it is not all Dino, but it is in the record. When the team have tough times"—he flexes his bicep and growls, *Grrrrrr*—"Dino is there."

I ask for the great man at the Hotel Continentale desk,

they call his room, and five minutes later he steps out of the elevator.

He doesn't look like any legend. I recall Rick Mahorn's assessment: "Dino ain't shit." He's about six-nine and broad-shouldered, but otherwise strictly ordinary-looking. He's wearing a tan sweater, blue jeans, and big low-cut basketball shoes—no fancy duds, no earrings, no gold. The outsized shoes kick out in a splay-footed walk that I would never associate with a great athlete.

He does have a striking face: long, angular, clean-shaven, with a square chin, a sharp jaw, and a long, narrow nose. Short black hair. Rugged—a Marlboro Man, Italian version.

We go sit on a couch off the lobby, and right away I get a good feeling about him. There's no trace of arrogance. When I say, "People tell me you're the Italian Kareem [Abdul-Jabbar]," he smiles and says, "Only because of the years, not the ability."

He speaks pretty good English—heavily accented, naturally, but he has no trouble expressing himself.

He says he was born in Alana de Piave, a village near Venice. When he was six his family moved to Varese, a small town north of Milan, and he was introduced to *basket* at thirteen.

"I was taller than everyone else my age, so in school they say, 'Why don't you play basketball?' And I try, because I was doing swimming, and shotput, and I didn't like them so much because I had to practice by myself—it was no fun. So when they approach me to play basketball, I say okay. And when I arrive at the gym and see all the other guys shouting, yelling, running . . . it was beautiful noise, you know, with all the people together.

"I loved right away the basketball because, first of all, I was with the people, and second"—he laughs—"because it was covered: no rain, no wind. When I practice with the shotput, sometimes I practice in the rain, the cold, and I didn't like it so much."

At thirteen he practiced with Varese's junior team. The

next year he played for it. In the Italian system, you're the property of your local *società* (sports club) unless and until your rights are sold to another one. You play for your *società*'s junior team, then the best players move up to the big team, the professional team, in the *lega*.

Meneghin made the big team at fifteen, when little Varese was in a lower league. The following year Varese moved up to Series "A," and the record book shows that in his first season in the big time, 1966–67, young Dino Meneghin played in twenty-two games for Ignis Varese and scored a total of 28 points.

"I have no experience, no technique, nothing," the legend says of those days. "But I practice hard every day, and I have good teachers. Toby Kimball, an American [previously a six-year journeyman NBA forward], was a great player. I start to learn many things: how to move, how to shoot, everything."

Despite what he claims was an unremarkable start in basketball, it didn't take Meneghin long to become a force as a *pivot*, or center. Beginning in 1969, when he was nineteen, Varese won seven Italian championships in ten seasons and reached the European Cup finals every year, winning it five times. Some people say it was the greatest Italian team ever. "Those were great, great times," Dino says.

One of his teammates for nine years in Varese was Bob Morse, a 6'9" forward who played college ball at Penn and was a third-round draft choice of the Buffalo Braves (now the L.A. Clippers) in 1972. Morse came to Italy instead and put together probably the finest career of any American ever to play here, leading the league in scoring six times in nine seasons in Varese and winning all those championships. "Morse was awesome multiplied by two," says Dan Peterson, the American who became a coaching legend in Italy and still lives in Milan.

"When we started practicing that first summer," Morse tells me, months after this first meeting with Meneghin, "what struck me was Dino's intensity. He just threw himself into the game passionately.

"He was *vocal*. It wasn't always that pleasant: 'Get your ass over here, do this, do that.' You could see that even at twenty-two he had a feel for the game. And that competitiveness . . . he was a *warrior*, that's the best word.

"He was an inspiration. As long as he was there, we were a great team. Without him, we would have been competitive, but not great."

By all accounts except his own, Meneghin was also the soul of Italy's national team for twelve years, playing in the first of four Olympics in 1972 and spending every summer in international competition.

By the late seventies the Varese dynasty had run its course. Meneghin had suffered many injuries over the years and the papers were saying he was finished. "In Italy," Dino says, "when you reach age thirty they say that's all for you." Despite achieving numerous career highs in '80–'81, he was sold to Milan that summer.

If the seventies Varese teams weren't Italy's greatest ever, the eighties Milan teams were. Italians tick off the names in the same tones in which American fans speak of Auerbach, Russell, Cousy, Sharman, Jones, Havlicek, and the rest: *Coach Dan Peterson*, *D'Antoni*, *Meneghin*, *McAdoo*, *Carroll*, *Premier*, *Boselli*, *Ferracini*, *Gallinari* . . .

Beginning in '81–'82, Meneghin's first season there, Milan played in eight straight league finals, winning five championships. Two European Cups. A Korac Cup. Win, win, win.

Dan Peterson, who was head coach at the University of Delaware before becoming the most famous coach (and TV pitchman) in Italy, gushes about Meneghin.

"Dino . . . what can I tell ya? The greatest. Tough? The toughest of the tough. Bad, Bad Leroy Brown was a Girl Scout compared to this guy. *Nobody* mixed it up with Meneghin.

"The greatest athlete you can imagine. He's forty-two now, but imagine that body—about six-nine, two hundred and fifty pounds—when he had speed, jumping ability, the whole thing. The guy was something else, I'm telling you.

"A coach's dream. He'd give you whatever you needed, when it mattered the most. I'll tell you one story, all you need to know about Meneghin: We're in a tough playoff game, Dino's out with a bad muscle pull, he can barely move. We're down nineteen points but start to come back. I tell him, 'Dino, I'm gonna need you. I don't know when, I don't know what for, but I'm gonna need you.' So we come back and finally go up by two, it's the end of the game, we have to stop 'em. I put Dino in. We're in our famous one-three-one zone, they run a play, and a little six-three guard, *quick*, comes off a screen with the ball. Looks bad. But Meneghin switches out and takes him, he misses the shot, we win. One play.

"Whatever had to be done, he'd do it. He'd step in front of a locomotive. Listen, in the States they say a guy's a 'winner.' In Italy we've got a word, *campion*, used very sparingly: 'He's a *champion*.' That's Dino. In the States they say Karl Malone is a winner. Bullshit—he's a talented player. Meneghin is a winner, a *campione*."

I ask Dino to describe himself as a player.

"I have fun to play defense," he says. "If I see a player who scores generally twenty points, I should like to make him score ten, eight—that's a good job for me."

He's bullshitting, right? Even the gunners say things like that. Dominique Wilkins probably says he enjoys passing above all.

But everyone else will tell me the same. Mike D'Antoni is an American who played two and a half years in the NBA before coming to Milan in 1977 and becoming, by consensus, the league's greatest point guard ever; today he's Milan's head coach.

"Dino didn't score a lot when he came to Milan," D'Antoni tells me a few weeks later, "he just did the right thing all the time. And played some defense. One reason we were successful was that most of the Americans playing over here, the stars, were big men, and since Dino could neutralize one of them we had an extra American, in effect, to kill the other team."

Dino: "Since I was sixteen, eighteen, I play for teams with big shooters. So I have to set picks, get rebounds, play defense; I have no time for scoring. If they put a weak player on me I can score twenty points, like anybody, but I never ask for twenty points. When I was twenty-four to thirty years old I score eighteen, twenty, twenty-four, I had highs of forty-four, thirty-six, but it's not the most important thing to me. If they ask me to do it I do it, but I'm not going to get mad if they don't give me the ball. I don't care. I like much more to make a good assist than to score two points, because an assist is togetherness-work . . . how you say? . . . *Teamwork*."

NBA teams weren't scouting Europe much until the 1980s, but Marty Blake, now the League's scouting director and once the general manager of the Atlanta Hawks, heard about Meneghin and drafted him for the Hawks back in 1970, when Dino was a raw twenty-year-old. Dino says he never even knew about it. (Blake says he never bothered calling because Atlanta's owners, it turned out, wouldn't let him sign a European.) He was, however, invited to the New York Knicks summer camp in 1974.

"I wanted to go," Dino says, "even if I don't make it . . . to play with them, learn from them." But he had knee trouble, his future was uncertain, and when Varese offered him a three-year contract he figured he'd better take the sure thing.

"It's a pity I didn't try. The NBA is like a dream to us here. But you can't have everything in life." Dino smiles. "Maybe in the next life I will try."

Could he have played in the NBA? Probably not as a center, not at 6'9"—although Dave Cowens starred in Boston during the seventies at that size, largely on the strength of his own ferocity. Dan Peterson has no doubt that Meneghin could have helped any NBA team as a power forward. Mike

D'Antoni thinks he would have been a Kurt Rambis type, a banger who would have had to be with the right team. Bob Morse, who played alongside him during Dino's heyday, likens him to Maurice Lucas—that is, a banger with skills. "He had a hook shot with either hand, a half-hook, a drop-step move, a turnaround. No question in my mind that at twenty-five, given a year or two to adjust to the NBA, he would have been a good player."

Marty Blake declares, "He was a great rebounder, a great defensive player. Anybody who says he wouldn't have been a great power forward in the NBA doesn't know what he's talking about."

Ask Dino how it feels to be Italy's most famous player, and the response is revealing.

"First of all, I'm famous because I always play for winning teams. I was nineteen when we won my first Italian championship—a very young team, and nobody expected we could win it. After that, many other championships, many cups. That's why I am famous, for sure." As if he just happened to be passing through.

"But you were a great player, *sì?*"

"Yes, yes, but I am first famous because I played for the big teams, and *then* because I play good. I play good for the national team, play good for my club, because I always want to win. Many times I fight with the opponents, I argue with the referees . . ."

I remind him that a little earlier he said something about how well he gets along with the refs.

He laughs, a little sheepishly. "Now I try to be different, but before, this was my big problem. Many times I was out with technicals. Maybe now I am better because there is less pressure. Before, I played for big teams, we have to win every game, and I was like Charles Barkley—I heard he has many problems.

"But I'm completely different on the court and outside.

On the court it's a job, and I'm paid for winning, not just for playing. Since I was young they teach me, Give your best on the court—for yourself, for your teammates, for the *società*, and for the people who come to watch the game."

He's away from the pressure now. Dan Peterson retired from coaching after Tracer Milan won the Grand Slam in 1987: Italy Cup, league championship, European Cup. The team won a last title in '89 under Franco Casalini, Peterson's longtime assistant, before falling to tenth place in '90, when D'Antoni and Bob McAdoo were thirty-nine and Meneghin forty. Milan management, figuring the run was over, named D'Antoni head coach and sold Dino and McAdoo.

Dino's a part-time player now, but he seems content. In Trieste, a city of 240,000 on the border of the former Yugoslavia, he lives in an apartment overlooking the Adriatic with his de facto wife, Caterina, whom Dino claims he'll actually marry next summer. Three or four times a year his parents, both seventy-one now, come from Varese to spend a couple of weeks.

And it seems fitting that since he's old enough to be the father of half the players in the league, he *is* the father of one of them: Andrea, nineteen, who's in his third season with dad's former team in Varese.

Money? Dino came up before the big lire of recent years and says he's not nearly the highest-paid Italian player now, although others estimate his salary at around five hundred thousand dollars, which would certainly place him near the top. (Benetton Treviso *pivot* Stefano Rusconi, purchased from Varese prior to last season for a record $15 million, is said to earn some $1 million a year; then there's a considerable drop to the next level.)

"Money is important," Dino says, "but not *so* important. I cannot stay on the chair for the rest of my life, but I have enough money to live in a nice house, have a nice car, have a nice life even if I'm not a multimillionaire. I don't care about such big money. I don't need much more.

"Bob McAdoo, Joe Barry Carroll, they told me that in the

States the players always talk money, money, money. Here, we never talk about money. You can live well on what we make: nice hotels, a big house, a nice life. I think the first thing is to be happy. The people that go to the factory or the office every day, all the year—that is work. Our work is only to be in shape. Get up, eat, practice, go back home, eat . . .

"Here, the big money is for the soccer players. That's the big sport, and the soccer players think about money, contracts, big cars with phones. Most of them think they're superstars, better than anybody else, because they can kick a ball, because they go out on the field with eighty thousand people watching them. Sometimes it's their ruin."

While we're talking about arrogance, I ask him about the American players who come to Italy—former NBA players, many of them, even if they come over only when they're washed up in the League. Has Dino ever resented them, since some are paid several times what even an Italian national monument makes?

"I don't resent them. It's okay that they make the money, because first, they are for sure better than us. Second, because for sure they help us to grow up. Since I was young, I look at them like teachers: I'm the pupil, they're the teacher. I think they are very important for our kids who watch them play.

"And people like them. When the people see a fast break, a dunk, a great shot, they have fun, so they come much more to our games. The sponsor becomes bigger, so there is more money—for the Americans, but for us too. And the newspapers and television always speak much more of the Americans, and this makes our *basket* movement bigger and bigger."

Dino says American players are most noticeably superior to Italians in size, agility, and ballhandling. He's always been a center here, one of the biggest, but in the NBA he'd have been a mid-sized power forward. An NBA shooting guard such as Terry Teagle is a small forward here; an NBA small forward such as Mike Mitchell is a power forward; an NBA power forward, a Cadillac Anderson, plays center; and a true center, a Darryl Dawkins, is Gulliver among the Lilliputians. And height isn't the only difference. Some of the Italian centers are so scrawny they wouldn't survive their first Karl Malone pick.

"We see some Americans so powerful . . ." Dino says, shaking his head. "They go so fast, dunk so easy. But the first thing is how they handle the ball. We like to fast-break, but never so fast like NBA. We don't have such players like K.J. [Kevin Johnson], [Michael] Jordan, [Scottie] Pippen—they come like from outer space."

The twenty-seven-year veteran watches the NBA on television every chance he gets. "There's always something to learn. I watch how they move, how they play defense. And for sure I go crazy when I see fast breaks, like Pippen or Isiah Thomas, Michael Jordan, Magic Johnson—it's like going to a movie."

It's eight o'clock, time for me to go. Dino's youthful teammates are passing through the lobby on their way to the dining room for the group dinner. Dino and I will get together again later in the season.

"One more question: How long will you keep playing?"

Dino laughs. "Everybody ask me, but I don't know. I'd like to play until 2000, but I know it's not possible. I see after the season. If I feel in shape, if I can still give the team something special, I go on playing.

"Since I was thirty, I never wanted even a two-year contract. I say, 'I make a one-year contract. At the end we sit together, and if you are not satisfied with my job, you tell me; I don't have a problem with it, I'll quit or go to another team. If I'm not satisfied, I'll tell you I don't think I can do another season with you.' From 1980 until now, only when I go to Trieste two years ago I ask for a two-year contract, because I have to change my life, leave my parents, everything.

"I like to be free. Even in '74, after a knee injury, when Varese give me a three-year contract, as soon as I sign I think, 'Now I have to stay here three years.'

"Maybe," he adds, "that's why I never get married until now—because it is hard to be free.

"So I don't know how long I play. I realize I'm a lucky guy. I do a job I love and they pay me. I play now because I love it. Money is important, but it is not what pushes me."

We finally adjourn. As Dino goes into the dining room, the huge sneakers splaying out in front of him, his teammates and coaches, seated down both sides of a long table and already eating, erupt in a mix of clapping, laughing, and good-natured jeering. I don't know what it's about—maybe about the old man being late due to an interview with a *giornalista americano*—but Dino, grinning, just gives them a wave and takes a seat.

Sunday evening, October 18, I see my first Italian League game: Trieste at Rimini. Or, as Italians say, Stefanel (a clothing manufacturer) at Marr (a grocery wholesaler).

Rimini is a small-fry operation for an A-1 team—this is its first season in A-1, and Alberto tells me the club will probably be back in A-2 next year—and the Palasport Flaminio looks like a high-school gym to me: old, dark, with a capacity of only thirty-five hundred. There's no pregame feast for the media as in the NBA; I'm simply directed to an eight-seat courtside press table, where I find a warm bottle of water and a stack of paper cups.

On the sides of the court—behind signs for LA Gear, Società Gas Rimini, Rigamonti, Butler Pommes Frites, Salmonfette, Coalma, Centrone, and other products and services—plastic seats run all the way up, but at the ends there's nothing but folding bleachers, high-school–style, with numbered spaces.

Still, there's an excitement I've rarely felt at an NBA game—even seventy-five minutes before game time, even at an early-season game between a middling team, Stefanel, and 0–4 Marr. The bleachers at one end are filled with a youthful Marr cheering section, hooting and chanting in the otherwise empty "arena."

Fans filter in, and finally Stefanel jogs out onto the floor. There's Dino, massive in his team's burgundy warm-ups, with a bunch of kids—none over twenty-four, I note in the program, average age twenty-one and a half. They huddle briefly at the foul line and, breaking with a clap, wave to the fans before forming layup lines. A nice gesture: they at least pretend to notice the people who pay their salaries.

A reporter from the *Trieste Oggi* sits down beside me. His English is pretty good, fortunately, and before the game starts he gives me the book on Dino.

"He only plays a few minutes each game now, but he is very important to the team because he is a monument and the referees are afraid of him. He can push and hold, anything he wants. He gets tremendous respect all over Italy, but when he plays outside Trieste, people get mad because he plays rough and gets on the refs and they don't do anything."

Stefanel has had some injuries, and Dino's in the starting lineup. Though he moves with the stiffness of age it's immediately clear that he's not only the fiercest player out there, he knows how to play the game, and I begin to imagine what he was like in his prime—when, as Dan Peterson and Bob Morse will tell me, he was not only brawnier than he is today but could outrun most guards.

I do know that few men his size in the last twenty years, in any league, have been able to pass like Dino. Besides drilling a jumper from the key, he makes three sweet assists in the opening minutes, including a blind opposite-direction number that Larry Bird would have been proud of.

He doesn't overtly hassle the refs, but when a ball is slapped out of his hands and no foul is called he gives the nearest one a look, smiling and shaking his head, and keeps on staring at the poor guy as play heads the other way. A purist would say he should be hustling back, but like the aging Kareem, he's not going to go end-to-end every time anyway, so why not throw some guilt into an official who was still in grade school when the Legend came into the league? It might help later.

The 2,600 spectators are raucous from the opening tip, making more noise than I usually heard from the inevitable 12,888 in Portland's Memorial Coliseum.

The game features lots of outside shooting—partly because of the zone defenses, which are illegal in the NBA; partly because there are no dominant inside players to go to; partly because the three-point line is so close, slightly longer than our college distance but much shorter than the NBA's; and partly because the two best players on the floor, Stefanel's Albert English (formerly of the Washington Bullets, where he was known as "A. J.") and Marr's Larry Middleton, are quick, eager-to-fire guards, hoisting up bombs whether they're open or not.

Just before halftime, after a call goes against Marr, I realize why the benches and scorer's table are protected by long, high sheets of Plexiglas: debris showers the court, cups and wadded-up paper and candy and various other stuff. Of course, the Plexiglas does nothing for the players out on the floor. Last year Benetton Treviso star Toni Kukoc got hit in the eye with a coin, and later I'll hear about the controversial playoff game in Pesaro a few years back when Dino himself got hit in the head with a coin on his way off the court at halftime and didn't play the second half; Milan lost, but was later awarded the game on a forfeit, which paved the way to that last championship.

Impromptu halftime entertainment is provided by eight raggedy kids, none more than seven years old, who bound out of the stands with a junior-sized ball the moment the buzzer sounds and play a roughhouse game until the big guys return. No one stops them; the *carabinieri*, laughing and applauding, watch them right along with everyone else.

Dino, who missed Stefanel's first four games with a shoulder strain, doesn't start the second half. He's on the bench for ten-plus minutes as the lead repeatedly changes hands.

Returning with 9:30 to go, creaky with age though he is, he's the obvious difference as Stefanel gradually pulls away. Here's *il monumento nazionale*, who'd been in the league for a couple of years before any of his teammates were even conceived and who's won everything in sight, looking like the hungriest guy out there. In a small gym in a tight game, twenty-six hundred rabid Italians make a deafening noise, but in the closing minutes you can hear the frantic, red-faced Meneghin over it all, bellowing instructions and encouragement at the kids.

His left shoulder is hurting; at breaks in the action he massages it or simply leans over with the arm dangling as if it's about to fall out of the socket. His age shows when either team fast-breaks: he takes a couple of steps, realizes he can't help, and then waits for the game to come back his way. He doesn't jump much for rebounds.

Yet he grabs them. And when he gets the ball, he knows what to do with it. Three times in the final minutes he snags rebounds, whirls, and flings perfect floor-length passes leading to hoops.

Yes, he works the refs a bit, but there's nothing abusive in it. He gets away with a couple of blatant hacks, but when he's finally called for his first foul with seven minutes left he reacts as he did in the first half when he felt he'd been hammered. Hands on hips, shaking his head, a little smile on his face, he gives the ref a long look that says, "Okay, you're human and I won't make a fuss"—with the implicit, "*but*, I want the next call."

It works. A minute later someone nudges Dino and the official sends him to the foul line. Dino sinks the first pair of four straight down-the-stretch free throws.

At the final buzzer—as the unhappy Marr fans torment the new coach by chanting the name of his predecessor, "*Piero Pasini! Piero Pasini! Piero Pasini!*"—Dino runs off the floor looking as if he's just won another championship.

Like everything else, the Italian postgame scene is different from what I'm used to. There are only a half-dozen or so writers here anyway, and because there's no locker-room access these few are just milling around in the hallway downstairs, waiting for the coaches to appear for brief Q-and-A sessions.

I almost miss Dino on his way out. I walk up just as he finishes with one of the reporters.

As when I saw him at the hotel, he's decidedly not stylin': blue jeans, a red nylon jacket, and the gargantuan sneakers. He shakes hands, smiling, and when I compliment him on his game—and his passing in particular—he smiles and says simply, "You're a friend."

I say I'll call him in Trieste down the line.

"The afternoon is the best time," he says. "Two o'clock I'm usually at home." Like a regular guy.

A *campione*.

Life After Death for "Chocolate Thunder"

I've got to see Darryl Dawkins, of course, especially as he's playing right over in Forli, forty minutes by train on the way to Bologna.

Darryl Dawkins.

He fell out of sight a few years ago. Like even the most flamboyant of players and personalities, he might as well have died when he left the NBA.

I did see him on a brief clip on an HBO "History of the NBA" special, in a segment called "Characters of the Game," telling most amusingly how he'd fooled people by lasting so long in the NBA. He smiled, mugged, and rolled his eyes, and even I, who had never been a big Dawkins fan, had to admit he was cute.

Sometime last season I heard he was playing in Italy—still among the living, after all. And now we're almost neighbors.

Last week Alberto gave me his phone number, I called, and Dawkins, accommodating as could be, agreed to hang out with me this Monday afternoon. He'll pick me up at the Forli train station at one o'clock.

• • •

He came on the scene in 1975, the fifth pick in the NBA draft straight out of Maynard Evans High School in Orlando, Florida, a monstrous 6'10½" and 275 pounds at age eighteen. The year before, a slender 6'10" prodigy named Malone had entered the pros—the American Basketball Association—directly from high school and started scoring and sweeping the boards right away, so what was *this* awesome kid going to do? He was not only more powerful than Malone (and almost every other pro, even then), but he could run and jump and had a nice little shot; let him smooth out the rough edges, develop maybe a hook shot, and he'd be Wilt-Plus, tearing the roofs off arenas around the NBA. The Philadelphia 76ers were in for a long run of championships, right? Lucky for Wilt he'd retired, right?

You know the story. The beanpole Malone filled out and became Moses, no last name required, three-time NBA Most Valuable Player and a shoo-in Hall of Famer.

And Darryl Dawkins became the self-styled "Chocolate Thunder," best known for his occasional fearsome dunks and the colorful names he gave them—including, after he threw one down over Bill Robinzine that shattered a backboard, the "Chocolate Thunder Flyin', Robinzine Cryin', Teeth-Shakin', Baby-Makin', Rump-Roastin', Bun-Toastin', Wham-Bam Glass-Breaker I-Am Jam."

The 76ers, despite rosters including Julius Erving, George McGinnis, Doug Collins, Steve Mix, Henry Bibby, Lloyd Free, Bobby Jones, and Maurice Cheeks, won a single championship—in 1982–83, the year they let Dawkins go after seven seasons and brought in, ironically, Malone.

Dawkins served the New Jersey Nets for the next four years. He quipped, he livened things up, he made a lot of friends.

Some years he even made the starting five. In 1983–84 he averaged nearly 17 points per game. A serviceable player, but the only time he was mentioned in the same sentence as Malone was when someone was talking about teenaged prodigies going straight from high school to the pros.

In the fall of 1986, six games into his fifth season in New Jersey, twenty-nine years old, Dawkins needed back surgery, and his NBA career was essentially over. In the fall of '87 the Nets traded him to Utah. In mid-season Utah traded him to Detroit, and Dawkins, beset by personal problems (his wife of a few months had committed suicide while he was in Utah), decided to pack it in for the year. He started the '88–'89 season with the Pistons and played in fourteen games before being released in favor of the forgettable William Bedford.

"I figured that was enough basketball," Dawkins tells me in his Forli living room in the autumn of 1992.

Almost thirty-six years old now, the erstwhile Chocolate Thunder is in his fourth season in Italy, shooting a preposterous .770 from the field for Telemarket Forli in the A-2 division.

Preposterous, maybe, but not a fluke. He shot .775 and .837 in two seasons in Torino, and .808 last year in Milan. (To put that in perspective, the NBA single season record is .727.) Yet he still breaks coaches' hearts, just like he did in the NBA.

Before going up to see Dawkins, I spend Monday morning drinking cappuccino with Lou Colabello at a sidewalk cafe in Rimini. It's sunny and blue, salt air drifting up from the sea a couple of blocks away.

Alberto at the *lega* suggested I might want to meet Colabello, an American who lives right here in Rimini and is the new team manager for Dawkins's team, Telemarket Forli.

He's lived here for most of the past fifteen years. Now in his early forties, Colabello grew up in Boston, and though slight of build he played both basketball (point guard) and baseball ("curveball pitcher") at UMass. A couple of years later he got a call from a guy he'd grown up with, who was playing professional baseball in Italy and said the teams were looking for Italo-Americans.

"I didn't even know they had pro ball in Italy, but once I did I figured it beat working, you know? So one day I'm over there scrapin', and the next I'm over here living at the beach. Didn't make a lot of money, but who cared?"

He got Italian citizenship and even pitched for Italy in the 1984 Olympics in L.A., though he'd seen his best days by then. He married an Italian woman, Silvana. A son came along, Chris, now eight years old. Colabello the family man fretted about what he was going to do when baseball was over for him.

The family ended up in the States in the late eighties, where Lou worked at a sales-rep job he loathed. They went back to Italy, but he couldn't find anything. Back to the States—nothing but crappy entry-level jobs. So last spring they decided to try Italy again.

Nothing.

But just a couple of months ago, when they were out of money and ready to go back to the U.S. (and Lou back to the hated sales job), a friend saw a want ad for someone fluent in both Italian and English. Colabello called. The Forli *basket* team had a new owner who wanted a "team manager": someone to deal with the press, make travel arrangements, purchase equipment, help American players adjust, etc.

Lou had never done anything like it, but Giorgio Corbelli, the new owner, remembered him as a famous baseball player, and that was enough.

"I'm not making much money," Lou says, "and I have to take the train to Forli and back every day, but I love it. I'm back in sports, and hopefully this job will lead to bigger things."

He thinks the world of Darryl Dawkins, who also joined the team this season. He's spent a lot of time with Dawkins and his wife: getting them into an apartment, helping them secure a washing machine, providing some American company. His son Chris idolizes Dawkins, though he'd never heard of him until two months ago—the simple result, Lou says, of how Dawkins treats people. He assures me I won't have any trouble this afternoon.

Lou's a good guy himself, and as he leaves me at the train station a little before noon we agree to meet again next Monday morning; the team has Mondays off, and Lou's free once he drops Chris at school.

Then I'm on the train, and marveling again. My life! On Monday mornings as recently as a month ago I was dragging home after yet another three-night stretch with Big Girl and the schizophrenics and the demented little old ladies—down on myself, bored, hopeless. Now I spend Monday morning (after sleeping all night, like a real human being) drinking cappuccino and eating croissants at a sidewalk cafe in Italy, on the Adriatic Riviera—because it's my *job*. I'm riding the train over to find out what ever happened to Darryl Dawkins *because it's my job*.

Milan bought Dawkins from Torino prior to last season, thinking he was the one piece they needed to win the championship, maybe even the Euroclub Championship. Says Mike D'Antoni, star point guard for the great Milan teams of the eighties and now in his third year as head coach, "I was like coaches all through Darryl's career—I thought I could get him to give that little bit extra. He'd never won anything in the NBA or over here and I thought he would see that here was his chance. But it never happened. Darryl is concerned about his shooting percentage, that's about all.

"It's sad. He's got that body and all that talent, but a guy like Kurt Rambis, who played on championship teams, has a satisfaction that Darryl will never have.

"I *like* Darryl," D'Antoni assures me. "But you can't win with Darryl. He doesn't think about other people. He never looks around and says, 'Okay, I'm gonna get *you* a championship' or 'I'm gonna make *you* a great coach.' "

Johnny Rogers, a pale, red-haired, sharp-shooting forward who played two seasons in the NBA, was the "other American" in Milan last season. He emphasizes that he likes Darryl and all, great guy, and he's never been quoted on this, but, uh . . .

Yes, Johnny?

"Well," says the soft-spoken Rogers, hedging, "he's at an age where he can't go all-out all the time like other players do . . ."

And it was a problem?

Rogers nods, reluctantly. "We just kept waiting for Darryl to get in shape, but it never happened. It was a shame, because we had a great team. We were in the Euroclub Championship Final Four and we lost that. Then we lost in the league playoffs the same week, and all of a sudden we were done for the season.

"It was a little strange, because everyone liked Darryl as a person. He's always clowning around, always gets a laugh out of the guys. And he gave a lot to the team—like, the defense always sagged on him, so we were open for jump shots. But we were unhappy because we couldn't run as a fast-break team, because Darryl wouldn't run. After the other team scored he wouldn't get the ball out of bounds quick. We weren't as good as we could have been and it was frustrating, because you want to win. Yes, it got a little old."

Darryl's version of his unhappy year in Milan, as we sit in his Forli living room a few weeks prior to my talks with D'Antoni and Rogers, is a little different.

"I had been lucky for two years in Torino, playin' with a great bunch of guys. They wanted to win, they didn't care who got how much money. In Milan, a bunch of guys were like, 'He's makin' this amount, or that amount, and I should be gettin' this.'

"My wife, Robbie, and I [he remarried in 1988] didn't like the big city. The people weren't friendly. The team didn't pay me on time. And I didn't get the ball like they promised I would. Mike [D'Antoni] would say, 'Darryl, you're doin' your job, you're doin' what you're supposed to do. These guys are gonna get you the ball or they're gonna come sit by me.' But they never got me the ball, and they never went to sit by him. Then he came to me with a different story: 'Darryl, it's not that they don't *wanna* pass you the ball, it's that they don't know *how*.'

"I was used to playing in the NBA. When I got a guy in front of me and locked him, the ball was *there*. You get to Italy, they don't have that mentality. You get that guy locked and they're holding the ball, looking like, 'Should I?' I'm saying, 'Throw it *now*.' Then when they finally do, it's too late."

D'Antoni's version: "Darryl has to accept that he's not playing with as talented players over here. That's just an excuse not to go all out.

"Darryl would come down the court and just be bumping around, not really looking for the ball. Then the guards have to do something else with the ball. By the time Darryl turns around, it's too late. Then he complains that he doesn't get the ball.

"And he'd say it to the papers. He *destroyed* Piero Montecchi as a point guard, saying he didn't get him the ball enough. Now he goes to Forli and he's in the papers saying, 'Now I've got a point guard, but the other outside players are suspect.' "

Who knows?

Darryl feels he took disproportionate blame for Milan's failure to win anything last season. "After we lost in the [Euroclub Championship] Final Four last year—after I had about eighteen points and nineteen rebounds—the general manager said, 'If you'd'a did more, we'd'a won.' They always blame the Americans. Very rarely do they blame their own people."

Darryl moved on to Forli, where the team, having finished last in A-1 last season, dropped to A-2 this year.

Last year the team was called Filanto Forli; now it's Telemarket, having been acquired by the bald, rotund thirty-six-year-old Giorgio Corbelli, who's made a fortune in, yes, telemarketing, and knows absolutely nothing about *basket*. Corbelli had already signed Rob Lock, a 6'10" *pivot* who played at Kentucky and briefly with the L.A. Clippers, but he couldn't resist when the one and only Darryl Dawkins became available.

It's a bad fit. The big guys get in each other's way inside. There's not enough outside shooting. Telemarket flounders, and the fans stay away in droves. Only a thousand or two straggle in for each home game.

Maybe more would come if Darryl were putting on the kind of mind-bending displays Corbelli expected, but even in A-2 he isn't dominating. Sometimes his teammates don't get him the ball very often, but sometimes they get it to him plenty—it's just that Darryl, unless he's got a layup or a dunk, won't take a shot. Against competition in the lower end of the Italian League, he's averaging just 15 to 20 points per game and 8 or 9 rebounds. He puts up only 9 or 10 shots per game, sometimes fewer. You recall Dino Meneghin saying, "He's so big and strong—too much for anybody here if he feels like playing. Lucky for us, he doesn't always feel like it." You realize how Darryl has compiled these otherworldly shooting percentages, and you wonder what meaning he attaches to them.

Darryl doesn't shed much light on the issue. When I tell him, later in the season, that some people think he's obsessed with his field-goal percentage, he says, "I don't shoot a shot that I don't think I can make. I refuse to be one of those guys out there just shooting and hoping it goes in."

Of course, Kevin McHale doesn't take shots he doesn't think he can make, but even McHale shoots only .550 or so. If you shoot from more than a foot away, you're never sure it's going in.

Who knows? *Basket*-wise, who could ever figure Darryl?

In any case, Telemarket isn't doing well early in the season, and according to Lou Colabello, Corbelli and his front-office people aren't happy with Darryl. They think he could be doing more.

Some things never change.

• • •

On this October afternoon we sit in the Dawkinses' Forli living room talking for a couple of hours. "Cut me off, man, 'cause I'll ramble," Darryl tells me at the start, and it's true, he doesn't need much prompting to riff for ten or fifteen minutes at a time. He's got a fantastic memory for people, places, events; one story reminds him of another, and another, and it's not long before he's far afield. But he's entertaining, funny, and you just let him go.

He likes Italy more than most of the Americans I meet. For one thing, he gets involved.

"Robbie and I had a lot of fun those two years in Torino," he says. "We helped coach the women's team there. The girls asked me to do it, but it helped me a lot more than it helped them. It got me out of the house and into the community. They also helped me learn to speak Italian.

"Some of 'em still call me, even today. Two came to visit us in New Jersey last summer. And now we got a godchild here in Italy.

"We used to go bowlin' too. It started out five people: me and my wife, two girls from the team office, and one boyfriend. Wind up bein' about twenty people every Thursday night."

Here in Forli, Colabello told me, Darryl helps out once a week in the little kids' "Mini-Basket" program.

"He's the perfect American for Italy," Colabello said, "if he fits in with your team's style. He's a great guy, respected by everyone. He knows he's lucky to still be playing basketball, making good money, and he's grateful. He loves kids, he treats everyone well, he's funny, he signs every autograph—the fans love him."

Chocolate Thunder, a goodwill ambassador? Who woulda thought it?

Rick Mahorn told me Dawkins could still play in the NBA, and Darryl says he still gets calls. "But I don't have any desire to go back to the NBA, especially because I want to play another three or four years. Here we play a few exhibitions, then thirty games and playoffs. In the NBA it's eighty-two games plus playoffs. After two years of that I'd be lucky to be walkin'.

"I get to spend a lot more time with my wife over here too," he says, and grinning over at Robbie, who's joined us, adds, "She likes that." Robbie makes a face at him.

Is there anything he misses about home?

His eyes light up, as if I've actually brought him what he most desires. "Man, the thing I miss over here"—a long pause, as he dreams—"is *soft . . . bray-ed.* The fresh-baked bread here is great, but not the sliced bread. You miss making a sandwich with lettuce and tomatoes on regular sliced bread and biting into it and not having it bite back. This stuff here'll tear the inside of your mouth all up."

Any complaints besides sliced bread that bites back?

Nothing he can't live with. "We've accepted that this is Italy, and things in Italy are not like they are in the States. You know you ain't just gonna drive out at one, two o'clock at night, starving, and go to a Burger King."

Robbie adds, "A lot of Americans forget that this is *not* home. Here, when they promise they'll have something done tomorrow, the expression is, 'I know tomorrow's the day, but what *year?*' The two most important things you need here are patience and a sense of humor, then you'll be fine."

A few minutes later we leave for a trip to a new American-style shopping mall about thirty miles away. Once we're there, it's obvious why Darryl is so popular. Utterly at ease even as people nudge their companions and point, he stops and chats in his elementary Italian with any who approach. He not only signs autographs, he makes sure everyone goes away happy. One man requests an autograph for his little boy, who seems cowed by this black behemoth and is already moving away as his father thanks Darryl; Darryl notices, beckons the boy back, bends down, makes a moment's small talk, and leaves them both beaming.

Someone mentions Telemarket's recent loss, when Darryl missed a big free throw at the end; I can't understand what's being said, but Darryl somehow mimes a ball clanging off a rim and shrugs helplessly, sending the man away grinning. In an hour or so at the mall, he makes a couple of dozen new fans.

"Some Americans," he says later, "don't like to get out and interact with the people. But everywhere we've been we went out in the community, and everywhere we went people have accepted us. Torino was great. Then in Milano—remember?" he asks Robbie. "The little old ladies that used to wait for me after every game? '*Bravo*, Dawkins! *Bravo*, Dawkins!' Win or lose, they'd be waitin' to shake hands.

"I like people. Even in the NBA I'd give a kid a ride home after a game and he'd say, 'Wow, my mom makes the best pasta in the world,' or something. So I'd say, 'Okay, okay, I'll come eat with you sometime.' So you get there and half the neighborhood's there, and his mother has cooked this pasta or fried chicken or cornbread or whatever, and they got their best dishes on the table . . . I got a good feelin' from that. But I've seen some players, I won't mention any names, a kid asks for an autograph and they just walk on by. I don't understand how guys can't take a few seconds to say hello to a kid, sign an autograph. I'll never understand that."

A nice guy, Darryl, and clearly happy with his life here. But the basketball question begs to be asked: Does he feel he reached his potential as a player?

There's an implicit put-down in the question, but I found a roundabout way to ask. "When you look back, are you happy with your NBA career?"

"I had a lot of fun," Darryl replies readily, and I sense he knows what I really mean and wants to let me know what *he* thinks is important. He goes on: "The first thing they holler about me is, Did you 'mount up to your potential? Well, I was around fourteen years and got paid, so I must'a 'mounted up to somethin'."

Sure, it's evasive. Sure, former coaches and teammates from Philly to Forli who feel shortchanged might say, That's Darryl; having fun and getting paid is all that matters.

Maybe it is, in a way. At Thanksgiving I joined Americans from miles around at Mike and Laurel D'Antoni's apartment in Milan. D'Antoni and Johnny Rogers, two who feel shortchanged, were less than kind when Darryl's name came up. But Pace Mannion, a former University of Utah star and NBA journeyman—six teams in six full or partial seasons—told me, "I don't think you can knock Darryl at all. I got to know him when I was with the Nets, and later he was in Detroit when I was there. He's a great guy; he'd do anything for you. In fact, I made the team in New Jersey because of Darryl. I was trying to make it as a point guard, and every time down the floor during training camp I'd pass the ball in to Darryl first thing, because I knew my man would immediately double-team him. Darryl just kept passing it back out to me for open jumpers, and when you make enough of those, they're gonna keep you. Darryl didn't have to do that, he could have worked on his own game, but he knew I was struggling to make the team.

"Maybe some people think he had the potential to do more than he's done, but I don't look at it that way. All I know is that he's been playing professional basketball for longer than I can imagine playing, and he's made a good career, he's made a good living. The way I look at it is, as long as Darryl is happy with himself, that's what matters. And Darryl is a happy person. I'm happy *for* him."

A couple of weeks after our October interview I'm among twenty-five hundred souls watching Telemarket take on Cagiva Varese in a game that's pretty typical, Darrylwise, of the half-dozen Telemarket games I see during the season.

On the first possession, Darryl takes a feed three feet from the hoop, overpowers his defender—Johnny Rogers, ironically, who's giving up four inches and about sixty pounds—and slams it through. The upper-deck rooting section erupts, screaming Darryl's name and sending dozens of rolls of toilet paper streaming to the floor.

A minute later Telemarket takes off on a fast break—except for Darryl, who hangs back. When a teammate misses at the other end and nine players wind up scrambling for the ball, Darryl is conspicuous down at the other end of the floor. He realizes it and takes a step or two—just as Telemarket grabs the ball and scores and the action comes back to him.

He runs the floor the next time, takes a pass on the move, and lays it in.

A moment later he hangs back when Cagiva runs, but after they score, the Telemarket player taking the ball out of bounds spots him and flings it the length of the floor. As soon as the crowd sees it's Darryl down there all alone, the sound starts: they know what's coming. Their "Baby Gorilla" grabs the long pass, flexes his knees, pulls the ball back behind his head with both hands, elevates, and, spreading his legs wide—impressive!—throws it down *whomp!* like they've never seen anyone but Darryl throw one down. They go nuts as he turns and jogs to the other end.

Rogers shakes his head as if he's thinking, *Cherry-picking bastard.*

Sometimes Darryl runs the court, sometimes not. When he doesn't, I don't know whether he can't or simply doesn't want to. He looks to be in good shape, but he is thirty-five years old.

The fans don't seem to care. They're awed when a rebound comes off toward Darryl and, though there's no one within ten feet of him, he sets himself as if he's contending with Moses Malone, spreads his arms, flexes, and explodes—soaring magnificently, snatching the ball like a grapefruit in his huge hands, seeming to hover over the floor and the nine mortals there before finally deigning to alight. They go ape when he grabs a rebound and waves the ball overhead with one hand before zipping a (pointless) long pass; and again when he pulls down another rebound and, with the Cagiva defenders heading to the other end, takes a couple of dribbles in the open court.

Telemarket's going to win, to even their record at 5–5, and there's a standing ovation for Darryl when coach Pasini pulls him with a minute to go. A teammate flies off the bench and into his arms and Darryl, grinning, lifts him up and almost twirls him overhead. As the applause and laughter continue he waves in all directions. The cheering section sings, "Dah-rill, Dah-rill, *Dawkins! Dawkins!* Dah-rill, Dah-rill, *Dawkins! Dawkins!*" As the final seconds run out, fans come down and reach around the Plexiglas for high-fives. Darryl obliges.

Everyone goes home happy.

Darryl finishes with 22 points and 11 rebounds. He "shoots" 9-for-9, raising his percentage to .835.

I chat with Robbie for a few minutes after the game, as the wives and girlfriends wait for the players to shower and dress. Within fifteen minutes most of them—in their blue jeans, sweatshirts, basketball shoes, and nondescript jackets—have come out, met their partners, and left. "Darryl's always last," Robbie says.

When I stroll down a back hall to the locker room a few minutes later, I see why. Darryl may be several years removed from the NBA, but the habit of stylin' on game day remains. Alone in the little room except for Lou Colabello and a couple of adoring ballboys, with whom he's boisterously joking, Darryl is getting himself up in a pleated snow-white shirt (buttoned to the top, no tie), a tailored black suit, and shiny black loafers. Admiring himself in a mirror, he slaps on cologne, needlessly brushes the scant bit of hair remaining on his pate, then goes about applying several pounds of gold: watch, chains, bracelets, rings. The heavy chain around his neck bears a pendant with DD inlaid in diamonds.

A few minutes later I walk out of the arena with Darryl, Robbie, and Colabello. Lou mentions to me that Darryl has been contacted by someone in the States about being part of a series of Legends basketball cards, along with such as Bob Lanier, George Gervin, and Artis Gilmore. I'm wondering how Darryl's NBA career averages of 12 points and 6 rebounds per game, in *anyone's* mind, translate into legend status.

But then, he was a memorable character. No doubt he's more vividly and more fondly recalled—by fans, anyway—than many a more productive player from the seventies and eighties. As Darryl tells me in a later interview, "People liked me because I could talk. I'd give 'em somethin' besides the usual cliches." Lots of it was funny.

Seeing Darryl so content in Italy reminds me of that great moment in HBO's "History of the NBA" special a year or two ago. Darryl mugs for the camera, telling how he "fooooooled 'em, lasted faw-teen years, and now I got that good pension plan comin' and"—making big eyes, the guy who found the golden egg—"I ain't complainin' about *much*."

Out in the parking lot, I ask Darryl if he ever saw it.

"I think I did see that once," he says, resplendent in his suit, fresh off a 9-for-9 and a win, well-paid and a hero in little Forli, Italy. "And you know what? I still ain't complainin'."

"Grandi Coglioni"

October 25: Kleenex Pistoia at Knorr Bologna, a rare Saturday night game. I've come to see Knorr point guard Roberto Brunamonti, whom I heard about from Brad Greenberg, the Trail Blazers player personnel director. Brunamonti is thirty-three now and will never play in the NBA, but he's highly respected in Italy—even more as a man than as a player, it seems, which is saying something, because he's been on the national team for the last fourteen years, captain for the last few.

I called him yesterday and we agreed to meet for a few minutes after this evening's game. After that I'm meeting Tom Federman, the young lawyer I met through Rick Mahorn in Rome, who called the other day saying he'd be spending the weekend in Bologna. Alberto couldn't get him into the game with me—Knorr Bologna games are always packed, apparently—so I'm meeting him afterward at the *Basket* bar near the arena.

I get to the Palasport early, and as soon as I step into the press room I'm thinking, This is more like the big time. It's organized, professional. Friendly, efficient women check me in and assign me a seat in the press area. While there's no NBA-style feast, there's a long table with plates of bite-sized quiches and cakes and other hors d'oeuvres, pitchers of various juices, and a thermos of potent Italian espresso, all attended by comely hostesses in cream-colored jackets and black microskirts.

The gym is more like the big time, too, though I later note that its capacity of sixty-nine hundred is only a little more than half that of Portland's Memorial Coliseum, which is the smallest in the NBA.

There are big signs for the Knorr players all around the stands, black spray-paint on white sheets: FLAVIO FLY, RICKY FOREVER RICKY, MAGICO PREDRAG (for Predrag "Sasha" Danilovic, the touted Serbian who was drafted last summer by the Golden State Warriors but signed to play two seasons here first). And one bigger than the rest, probably forty feet long, nailed to the wall along the top of the bleachers on one side: C'E SOLO UN BRUNAMONTI.

No advertising here except for three red-yellow-green KNORR signs at courtside. (Knorr makes soup.) As in all the arenas, long sheets of Plexiglas shield the benches and the scorer's table.

I hardly notice any of this when I first come in. I'm taken by the fact that though it's forty-five minutes before game time and the lower-deck stands and the upper-deck sides are still nearly empty, at each end the upper deck is packed. The Untouchables and the Forever Boys Virtus are going at it.

The Untouchables are fifty or so guys in their late teens and early twenties who, I soon learn, support Kleenex Pistoia at every game, home and away. They're wearing blue-and-white shirts with UNTOUCHABLES scripted across the front, they've got huge UNTOUCHABLES banners draped over the railings, and they're making serious noise with their chants and cheers and put-downs for the other end.

At the other end: the Forever Boys Virtus, Knorr's crazed rooting section. (Sponsors change, but the official, enduring name of the Bologna *società* is Virtus Pallacanestro Bologna. Many fans refer to the team simply as Virtus [veer-TOOS].) The Forever Boys have their own banners up, one at least one hundred feet long saying VIRTUS PRIDE, with, for some reason, a drawing of Bart Simpson between the words. Waving black-and-white Virtus Bologna towels, they're dishing abuse right back at the Untouchables. I can't understand what either side is saying, but I can tell it's not nice.

Back and forth it goes, one chant answering another, sometimes both sides going at once, creating an echoing din in the otherwise near-empty Palasport.

When the first journalist makes his way into the press section, I ask him what these loonies are saying.

Amused by my innocence, he points toward the Untouchables. "How you say in English? . . . 'Fuck you!' "

And the Bologna side, what are they saying back?

" 'Fuck off!' "

A moment later the Untouchables spring out of their seats, jumping up and down en masse, up and down, pointing at the Bologna end and chanting something. "What's this one?" I ask.

" 'Who doesn't jump comes from Bologna!' "

It's nutty. There's nothing like this in the NBA, I assure my companion. He says all Italian teams have cheering sections like these.

The Forever Boys Virtus, in polished, practiced style, respond with another impassioned impropriety. The Untouchables come back with something along the lines of "The electric current is strong, the blue-and-white of Pistoia can kill you." (I realize something is lost in my friend's translation.)

And so on, and so on. At some point jazz issues from the sound system, but it's drowned out. The Untouchables and the Forever Boys are rocking the joint, long before tip-off, and they won't stop all night.

When the teams come out for warm-ups there's no sign of Roberto Brunamonti. I'm told he's having back problems and won't play tonight. But I assume he'll be in the arena somewhere; I'll try to locate him after the game, as planned.

I focus instead on the twenty-two-year-old Danilovic, who

last season led his Yugoslavian club, Partizan Belgrade, to the Euroclub Championship and then told reporters, "Next year I would like to play in Italy with Brunamonti."

Danilovic signed a two-year contract for around $1.2 million a year, and so far he's been worth it: Knorr's sitting on top of A-1 and Danilovic is fifth in scoring and third in both two- and three-point percentage. But I'm intrigued because of something Alberto, the league PR man, said one day when we were discussing the best players in the league. As far as I knew, the best is Benetton Treviso's Toni Kukoc, the one the Chicago Bulls have been after for so long. But Alberto hedged. "Toni is good, everyone says Toni is the best, but for the NBA I say Danilovic. Because he is a fighter. Danilovic has, as we say in Italy"—and, smiling, he cupped his hands down around his crotch in an illustration that required no elaboration—"*grandi coglioni.*"

A lean 6'6" or so, maybe 190 pounds, Danilovic is a rough-looking kid: dark-haired, unshaven, with bright splotches of acne on his nose and cheeks. He goes through his warm-up routine with a scowl on his face, all business, seemingly oblivious of everything around him. His manner reminds me of a businesslike Yugoslav I knew in Portland who became a 20-points-per-game NBA guard: Drazen Petrovic.

A buzzer sounds, and finally it's game time. No American-style pregame intros; instead, as the teams huddle in front of their benches and the starters shed their warm-up suits, the pumped-up PA man announces the starting lineups, the fans punctuating each name with a collective "Hey!"—or jeers, depending on allegiances. "Morandotti, *numero tredici! (Hey!)* Wennington, *numero dodici! (Hey!)* Danilovic, *numero cinque! (Hey!)*"

The place is packed now, people sitting in the aisles, standing in the exits, everywhere, and they're all part of the show. Players, coaches, referees, fans, even the writers, are loud, emotional, demonstrative. It's theater, thousands of wild Italians riding a wave of emotion for ninety minutes: coaches racing up and down the sidelines, stamping their feet, screaming at the refs and even their own players, flinging their arms up in frustration, jumping up and down, doing anguished pirouettes; refs calling fouls with gusto, hopping on one foot as they point out the guilty party and acting out the misdeed with all sorts of flourishes; players exhorting each other, shouting at their own coaches, acting incredulous at disagreeable calls; the fans and even the reporters carrying on, screaming, shaking their fists, flipping middle fingers, whacking their foreheads in dismay or disbelief.

The Untouchables are on their feet from start to finish. "Pee-stoy-uh! Pee-stoy-uh! Pee-stoy-uh!" they're chanting at first, punctuating it with snappy, practiced clapping, and then it's one taunt after another all night long. "Binelli, change sports!" they sing, to the tune of "When the Saints Go Marching In." A bit later, to the tune of "For He's a Jolly Good Fellow," "Nobody can deny that Morandotti's the son of a whore!"

And every time they start something, the Forever Boys, who never sit down either, try to be louder, lewder, cleverer. They've got drums beating, horns and whistles blowing, and their ringleader inciting them through a megaphone.

Basketballwise, it's a far cry from the NBA. You get some good ball, up and down, the crowd roaring, a fast break coming, three sleight-of-hand passes—and then a huge groan from *both* sides' fans, *basket* fans, as the guy blows the easy layup. Or the Untouchables are going nuts, Kleenex is on a streak, their man's got a wide-open ten-footer—and he misses everything. Or Knorr's threatening to bust the game open, they get the ball inside, the defender even falls down—but the man receiving the pass bounces it off his foot and out of bounds. Or a guy's free throws are so long that it looks as if he's trying to bank them in. You see shots there's no name for, not jumpers or hooks or layups—*prayers* are all you can call them. I've seen it in every game I've attended, even this, the best of them: plays so egregious there's nothing to do but shake your head.

But the biggest difference between this and an NBA game

is that American players are bigger, stronger, faster, and springier than Italians. As Dan Peterson says, Italian pros have the same fundamentals as NBA players; the difference is that the NBA player "does things in half the time and twice as high off the floor."

It's not the NBA, but one guy is headed there. It's not easy to assess a player's NBA potential when you see him against lesser competition, but Danilovic, a shooting guard, looks legitimate. If he's not quite the shooter Petrovic was when he arrived in Portland—not yet, let's say, because he's three years younger than Drazen was at that point—he's much quicker, jumps better, gets to the basket more easily, plays better defense. Like Drazen, he works hard to get open on offense, and knows how. Like Drazen, he's feisty. Remember the name.

He's got 18 points by halftime: a three-pointer, a couple of jumpers, and several gliding finger-rolls. Knorr leads by thirteen, despite the Untouchables' best efforts.

Kleenex never makes a game of it, but you wouldn't know it by watching either team's supporters: they're whistling, cheering, hooting, catcalling, and gesticulating to the very end. (Untouchables: "White-and-blue, you must play with your hearts!" Forever Boys: "Fuck you! Fuck you!")

Danilovic racks up 17 more in the second half. He gets several on uncontested drives to the hoop, but just when I'm thinking I need to see more, he drills a turnaround jumper from eighteen feet that's tough even when you're alone in the gym; few players try it in a game.

He ends up 13-for-18 from the floor and scores 35 points, and when coach Messina removes him with a minute remaining he gets a standing ovation, the Forever Boys and gradually everyone else (save the Untouchables) chanting, "Sa-sha-Da-*nee*-lo-veetch! Sa-sha-Da-*nee*-lo-veetch! Sa-sha-Da-*nee*-lo-veetch!"

He never looks up, never waves, never lets on he's even noticed. Dead serious, though Knorr's got the game nailed down, he says something to his replacement and simply takes a seat, drapes a towel over his shoulders, and swigs water until the buzzer sounds.

Even then he doesn't smile. He just jogs off and disappears down the stairs to the locker room.

Downstairs a few minutes later, the coaches answer questions for the press. Players emerge from the locker rooms, wearing jeans and sneakers and carrying their gym bags, and walk right on by. Reporters hardly bother talking to players over here.

When the reporters are finished with the coaches, Alberto introduces me to Ettore (ETT-uh-ray) Messina. Only thirty-three years old, Messina came to Bologna ten years ago as an assistant and now, in his fourth season as head coach, is on the short list of candidates to take over the national team next summer. (It's been a given that someone is going to replace the legendary Sandro Gamba ever since Italy, last summer, failed to make it to the Olympics.)

Messina's a trim, intense guy who resembles the sportscaster Al Michaels back in the States. He speaks the best English of any Italian I've met.

"Oh, the next Feinstein, eh?" is what he says, shaking my hand after Alberto introduces me and explains my project. He's talking about John Feinstein, who wrote the revealing Bobby Knight book, *A Season on the Brink*, a few years back. "Well, just leave out my bad language."

I'm surprised. "You read many American books?"

"I keep up," he allows with a sly look. I get the impression he keeps up with pretty much everything. It doesn't take a minute to see he's got a quick mind.

More important, he says this: "Let me know if there's any way I can help. We can have lunch someday. You can come watch us practice if you want. I'll talk to our president and see if I can arrange for you to travel with us sometime. It's the behind-the-scenes stuff that makes a good book."

He's right, of course. And he means what he says. "Let me give you my phone numbers at home and at my office. Feel free to call anytime. If you want to get together, just let me know."

Getting this kind of reception from anyone in the high-powered NBA is inconceivable.

One more wonderful person. I don't know what I ever did to deserve all this.

That's what scares me. It's bound to end.

When I meet Tom Federman at the *Basket* bar he's with a statuesque young woman named Monica whom he apparently knew when he spent a year at the university here. Statuesque but bland—or perhaps just uncomfortable speaking English, so that she doesn't say much.

They persuade me to ride out to Monica's family's place in the country, where Tom stayed last night. Her parents are away; she'll call this friend of hers; if nothing else we'll go out to this amazing restaurant Tom knows . . .

It's dark when we get out there, but you can tell by the distance from the gate to the house that this place is an estate. Inside, the stone house feels vast and solid, with rock and tile and heavy wood everywhere. Big fireplaces. Antique furniture. Tom takes me down into a musty wine cellar stocked with dozens of vintages and, according to Tom, a bunch of three hundred-year-old brandies and whiskeys.

We settle for drinking contemporary Chivas Regal at the big kitchen table, waiting for Monica's friend.

Fiona, when she arrives, turns out to be nothing like statuesque. Petite. A wisp. I guess she's my date, and though she's not my type, she's nice—much livelier than Monica, more fun. Speaks excellent English, and of all things she's a *basket* nut. Specifically a Virtus Bologna nut.

Her favorite, she says—clasping her hands in front of her, swooning—is Brunamonti, who else?

Brunamonti! I forgot all about finding him! It's too late now; I'll have to call him next week.

Tom convinces us we should all go out to dinner, then drive to Riccione and spend the night at my place. Monica and Fiona can drive back to Bologna tomorrow, Sunday, and he'll train back to Rome.

We wind up at an old-fashioned restaurant out in the countryside somewhere toward the coast, north of Riccione. There's a big, crowded parking lot, and from the outside the place might be a warehouse. Then you go in and wait in a foyer bustling with people in black and white, with red aprons, working hard—family, by the feel of the interactions.

It's boisterous in the big room. And I do mean a *big* room: sixty feet square, maybe eighty feet, filled with heavy wood tables packed with celebratory Italians. We get a small table in a corner and immediately turn our chairs to take it all in, since it's too loud to talk anyway.

For a minute it seems half the people in the room are in one party, because people on all sides are singing along with a stout, bald man at the big table in the middle who's serenading his group with a guitar and a Pavarottian voice. The big table, actually two long tables together, is covered with wine bottles and glasses; the dishes have long been cleared, but the dozen or so senior citizens are having a great time, not to mention entertaining everyone else, so no one's moving them out to accommodate the line outside.

So un-American, in every way. The raucous good cheer. The whole long meal these people shared. The freedom to sing and be crazy. The way dozens of people who aren't with the group get in the swing. The fact that no one brings the group their bill and chases them out.

I'm thinking, This is Italy.

We order white wine and red, and antipasto, and pasta (I take a tomato-and-peas sauce that's a specialty of the Emilia-Romagna region), and grilled chicken, and sirloin, and vegetables. It just keeps coming. Wine keeps coming. *This* is Italy.

We can't talk over the din of gabbing, laughing, and singing, but we try: shouting, gesturing, leaning ever closer to each other. It's part of the fun.

And it's great fun. It's long past midnight when we leave. Monica's sleepy, so Fiona drives, and I sit in front with her and we gab all the way down to Riccione while Tom and Monica snuggle and then doze off in back.

When we finally make it to my place, Monica, wiped out, says good-night almost immediately. Fiona doesn't last much longer.

Tom, inexplicably revived and apparently inspired by the noise down in the street, wants action, and we walk over to the Savioli, the neighborhood place where I eat almost every day. It's packed, it's loud. November's almost here, but tourists are still coming to Riccione on the weekends, and I've learned that since Italians don't start eating dinner until nine or ten o'clock and don't finish for two or three hours, 2 A.M. isn't all that late. Even on weeknights the Savioli stays open until three or four; I'm awakened often enough by departing revelers down in the street.

We order shots at the bar and talk for a minute with my pal Maurizio the bartender, who's too busy to stop for long, though Tom's expert Italian does remind him to chide me, as usual, for not studying more myself. I'm a little defensive; I know I should be doing more, but then again, I've been here for only three weeks; Tom went to school in Bologna, has lived in Rome for a year or two, and works with Italians. I'll get there.

Or I won't. I'm not sweating it. I'm not sweating anything these days.

Back home, I put on shorts and a T-shirt and get in bed. Fiona's conked out.

She's still conked out when I wake up in the morning. I go out to the living room, walk out on the balcony to check the weather, come back in, and sit in my big chair and make some notes about last night's game. I'm glad Fiona was asleep and there wasn't any weirdness. I'm happy to see her when she appears a half hour later.

I don't know what happened in the other room, but Tom and Monica, when they appear, seem a little awkward with each other. Tom occasionally kisses her like a guy who thinks he should but doesn't really want to.

Still, it's a nice day. We all go out for coffee, I show them around my town a little, we take a long walk on the beach. We eat a delicious lunch at the Savioli, where people are going crazy over the soccer on the TV sets. (*This*—this madness for "football"—is Italy too.)

Fiona and Monica leave in the early afternoon. I'll see them again, at least Fiona: she's got season tickets to Knorr games, plus she's good friends with the seven-foot *pivot* Augusto "Goose" Binelli and his wife and is going to try to arrange a dinner for the four of us.

Tom sticks around until after dinner, when I walk him to the station. I'll definitely be seeing him again; we hit it off, and he says I can crash at his place in Rome anytime.

Great times. Nothing remarkable—just a little bit of real life, with more wonderful people.

Bortolo and Friends

I can see how things don't work out over here for some people—players, tourists, anyone.

A few days later I'm in Rome again. My computer is dead and I can't imagine that I can get it fixed in a little place like Riccione, and when I called Tom he said there's a computer shop a few blocks from his office. Besides, he said, Friday night is Halloween, we ought to party. Partying generally isn't my scene, but why not? I might as well be able to say I partied in Rome one Halloween night.

Long past midnight, after a great dinner at Tom's friend Raphaela's apartment and some barhopping and a costume party at the American embassy, we're tripping through the streets and I'm giddy again about being in RomeItaly: buildings darkened with age rising around me, statues here, sculptures there, music sounding from bars, restaurants in full swing at 2:30 A.M. Rome! The cobblestones under my feet were probably trod by Mark Antony, not to mention Rick Mahorn.

Raphaela wants to show me something, and after we turn a corner I'm suddenly facing the awesome Trevi Fountain. I saw it in my books in sunlight, and here it is in front of me, lit up for nighttime so that I can see the million coins in the water and the sculpted figures that were the lifework of God-knows-how-many artists. You could study it forever, yet at the same time it's simply one more thing in the neighborhood: the Spanish Steps aren't far away, the Colosseum (which I get the willies just thinking about), various other ruins. Reminds me of my visit to the Impressionist museum in Paris years ago: if you had *one* of those paintings at home you could study it forever, but when they're all in one place you cruise a hundred masterpieces in fifteen minutes.

I couldn't be happier as, with 4 A.M. approaching, I fall asleep on a couch in Raphaela's living room.

Mere hours later I'm having a day that makes me see why some people just don't like going outside the familiar, comfortable U.S.A. If my first day in Italy had been like this, I might not have stayed.

I've got to get my laptop fixed this morning and head back to Riccione this afternoon: tomorrow, Sunday, I'm meeting Alberto and some of his Bologna friends for lunch in Rimini, then we're going to a couple of games. Gotta go. I'm up and out Raphaela's door, computer bag in hand, before anyone else has stirred.

The little hole-in-the-wall shop Tom recommended isn't open yet, though it's past nine. It's still dark inside at ten, though the sign on the door says *sabato* is a regular business day.

I'm fuming. Robbie Dawkins and many others have told me you can't count on anything in Italy—shops and offices may or may not open, trains may or may not run, no rhyme or reason to anything—and suddenly I feel like throwing a rock through someone's window. Is this how these people run a business? The loose-ends, live-in-the-moment, do-what-feels-right Italian way that's usually so charming seems like anarchy now when it means, "Take Saturday off if you want, to hell with customers."

The shop never does open up this morning, and according

to the sign it's never open on Saturday afternoons. I try to call Tom for advice, but the pay phone keeps swallowing my money without putting me through.

The next one does the same.

Doesn't anything work in this country? And don't they care? How can they live this way?

Screw it, I say. I just want to get out of here. Rome is too big, too crowded, too loud, too dirty. I head back to Raphaela's; I just want to get my stuff and get on a train home.

I'm tired, hot, sweaty, and *pissed*, and now it's raining and I'm hurrying, but the rain on the cobblestones makes them slick as ice and I'm slipping and staggering and swearing about the blankety-blank cobblestones; why don't they pave this whole godforsaken city with good-old concrete?

And the grime! Buildings and palaces and monuments and sculptures gray or even black with age! Is it too much to scrub things down, say, every few centuries?

Better yet, knock it all down and start over. New buildings, streets wide enough for something bigger than a chariot, *no cobblestones*. History's fine, but the twenty-first century is right around the corner.

And now, when all I want is to ditch Rome and get back to Riccione, I can't even do that! Raphaela calls Termini station about schedules and is told there's a strike today, no trains running until 6 P.M.!

People have told me it happens all the time. They shrug when they say it: it's always been so and probably always will be, those hundreds of twerps in their little blue uniforms and caps deciding every so often to inconvenience an entire country in which most of the population ride the trains. Christ! It goes on year after year, the beefs never solved! Why doesn't the government or somebody *do* something? But *noooooo*—they just *live* this way!

I get to Termini at five o'clock, an hour before they'll start selling tickets and running the trains again all over the country, but there are already two or three dozen people lined up at each of the forty or so ticket windows. Two hours later I've got my ticket, but it's another hour and a half before my train leaves. When the time comes to board it's a mob scene among several hundred of us who couldn't travel all day, and I finally decide to give up and wait an hour for the next train to Falconara.

Even then there's a crush to get on—you could get trampled and no one would know or care—and I still wind up standing, packed in with far too many others at the end of a car. I want to throttle the ones who insist on smoking when we're jammed so tight that their elbows poke others when they lift their cigarettes and half of us are choking. I want to thrash the ones who haven't brushed their teeth this week—half the people in Italy have bad teeth—because I'm catching a lot of bad breath.

It's past midnight when we reach Falconara, another hour before my connecting train comes, and yet another before I get off in Rimini—Rimini because this train doesn't make the Riccione stop, ten minutes back. So it's two-thirty in the morning, long after the last bus from the Rimini station down to Riccione, and I've got a choice between walking for an hour and a half or approaching the bunch of vultures bullshitting over at the taxi stand.

It's two-thirty, I'm miserable, I'm not about to walk to Riccione.

It's three miles straight down the Via D'Annunzio to the corner of my street, four at the most, but by the time we're halfway there it's obvious the twenty-five thousand lire in my pocket (almost twenty dollars) won't cover it. I end up walking the last ten blocks.

If I'd had a day like this within a week of getting ripped off that first night, I'd have been gone for sure.

But I didn't. Nothing but good things happened. The Nicolettis. Alberto. Lou Colabello. Tom. Everyone.

And now, after a few hours' sleep, a shower, and a walk along the beach, I have such a wonderful day that I realize my tribulations are nothing. Less than nothing.

I take the bus back up to the Rimini station, where Alberto, having driven over from Bologna, picks me up at twelve-thirty. When he was growing up his family had a summer place in Riccione (his late father was a good friend of Signor Nicoletti) and he's always looking for a reason to come over to the coast, which affords him the chance to "eat feesh." Today at one we're meeting a bunch of his friends—Knorr fans coming over for the five o'clock game in Rimini—for lunch at one of his favorite restaurants, a few miles west of town.

The place is in another of those buildings that are so unremarkable on the outside that even Alberto, who's been there, drives right by it the first time. I'm reminded of a striking difference between Italy and the States: not only are there virtually no billboards anywhere, but often you can't even tell what's inside a building or behind a storefront without going in. Like the place where I ate last Saturday night with Tom and Monica and Fiona, this one could be a warehouse.

According to Alberto it's some kind of historic building, erected back in the eighteenth century. And it's impressive inside. You walk into a vast room with tables on either side, and straight ahead is a huge open grill with a couple of men in aprons turning fish, chicken, beef, vegetables, and various things I can't identify. Dark, heavy wood beams support the ceiling. A worn, polished staircase takes us upstairs where, being the first to arrive, Alberto and I sit facing each other in the middle of a long, long table set for thirteen, starting on the wine that's already waiting. We're well into some *piadina* and prosciutto by the time we hear noise down below and then the sound of twenty-two feet coming up the stairs.

They're a bunch of old friends, Virtus Bologna season-ticket-holders for years, who travel together to every road game within two hundred miles—which takes in most of the *lega*. Singles, couples, women, men—ranging in age from early thirties to mid-fifties—all they've got in common is that, like nearly all the Italians I've met, they're warm and welcoming, friendly and funny. Any friend of "Bortolo" is a friend of theirs. (Alberto—Bortolotti—explains that he's known thus among this group because his old friend Alberto So-and-so, the garrulous guy sitting beside me, claims the more common " 'Berto.")

A happy group, a happy time, as mealtime always seems to be in Italy. A social time. No hurry—*au contraire*, you drink some wine and loosen up and talk, talk, talk.

Though I've never cared for being the center of attention, I'm something of a novelty over here—more than a tourist, but not your average working American—and I'm getting used to it. Today it lasts a few minutes, until I've explained myself to the ones who speak English and Alberto has explained me to the rest.

By the time my tagliatelle arrives (noodles, with a spicy vegetable sauce that's another Emilia-Romagna specialty), one man has invited me to his restaurant in Bologna, another has invited me to his uncle's restaurant (with its cellarful of centuries-old wine and brandies), and 'Berto, a bachelor, has told me I can stay at his place overnight if I want to come to the city and play *basket* with him, Bortolo, and their friends on Tuesday evenings.

English is a struggle for everyone sitting around me except Alberto, and once the novelty of having an *americano* present wears off, they drift back to talking to each other. Alberto keeps trying to include me until I assure him I'm happy just being here, watching and listening, and that it's perfectly fine if he just enjoys himself with these friends he doesn't see all that often.

Unfortunately, Alberto and I can't stay for the duration; the game these people came to see isn't until five o'clock, but we're going to the three o'clock game down in Pesaro first. A few minutes after two, having hurriedly gorged ourselves, we say our good-byes and take off.

We breeze through Riccione and arrive thirty minutes later at the arena in Pesaro—another "Palasport," like the gym in Bologna and a few others. After squeezing into my seat a couple of rows behind the Virtus Roma bench (the club is no longer "Il Messaggero" since its sale by the Ferruzzi Group) I spend most of the game watching and listening to the "Inferno Biancorosso." This is Scavolini Pesaro's maniac upper-deck rooting section, "Red-and-White Hell," which is extraordinary even for Italy. I've noted in the *lega* guide that Scavolini finished near the bottom in last season's *Coppa Disciplin*, an arcane measure of each club's fans' behavior, and Alberto says the only unusual thing about it is that they weren't dead last as usual.

They're crazed. They're hanging over the upper-deck railing, blowing whistles and horns to support their leader's efforts on his megaphone, cursing the Roma players and the refs, cheering their own. More entertaining than the game.

Throughout, I'm amused by the Italian obsession with soccer, even at the *basket* game. Sunday is soccer day and even Alberto, the moment we sat down, became one of hundreds of people here with a plug in his ear, listening to his team's game on a transistor radio. Whenever there's a goal in the Bologna game he lets the journalists around us know, and depending on which side scored they slap high-fives or commiserate. You see the same reactions all over the arena.

The moment the Roma-Scavolini game ends we're gone, clipping back up to Rimini for Knorr vs. Marr. Bortolo's got soccer on the radio all the way.

In Rimini's Palasport Flaminio we sit at the little eight-seat courtside press table where I sat when I came to see Dino Meneghin in my first Italian game. In the tiny arena it's easy to spot 'Berto and the rest of the Bologna crowd, who come by at halftime and express concern about their team being played even by lowly Marr.

In the second half Danilovic, despite a bruised elbow that requires a quick wrap (which, however, he suddenly rips off before the trainer even finishes applying it, and checks himself back into the game), plays like a man possessed and leads Knorr to an easy win.

I get my first glimpse of Roberto Brunamonti, whom I

stood up in Bologna last week and never did call back; I catch him for a minute after the game and find him to be one of the most normal, regular-guy jocks I've ever met.

The games are great, but the rest is even better. Alberto, his friends, a meal I'll never forget. Alberto, much more than the *lega* PR director who arranges passes for me—a friend—cracking wise all up and down the coast.

That's what I fall asleep thinking about, this night.

League's Leading Scorer—Cut!

At that first Stefanel Trieste–Marr Rimini game—the Dino Meneghin game—a solid-looking young black man in jeans and a black leather jacket entered the arena early in the second half to a big ovation. He leaned against a wall and watched the rest of the game, frequently interrupted by fans coming up to shake his hand and chat for a moment.

It was John "J. J." Eubanks, someone told me, who had played the first month of the season for Marr before being released and replaced by Larry Middleton, despite the fact he was leading A-1 in scoring.

Three weeks later, when Alberto and I were in Rimini for the Knorr-Marr game, the same thing happened: Eubanks appeared, the crowd cheered. The cheering made sense: he'd been a sensation for these fans. But why was he still in Rimini?

I caught him after the Knorr game and asked if I could come see him in a couple of days.

"If I'm still here," he said. "I'm just waiting to get my contract settled, and once that's done I'm outta here."

Three days later he's still killing time in a little hotel near the Piazzale John F. Kennedy, and I catch the bus up to Rimini.

Eubanks is from Louisville, where as a 6'6" guard and small forward he averaged 25 points per game at Sullivan Junior College and was twice a JC All-American. He signed with Marshall University of the Southern Conference but had a conflict with the coach and, before playing a game there, transferred to Tennessee State, where he had to sit out not only that season but part of the next. In the partial season he played, Eubanks led the Ohio Valley Conference in scoring average, but that was the extent of his college career. "I really haven't played all that much basketball," he tells me.

In the summer of 1991 he played in the 6'7"-and-under World Basketball League, where he earned about eight hundred dollars a week over a four-month season and was named rookie of the year. That winter it was the Global Basketball Association, for similar wages. This past summer, 1992, the WBL again.

That's where he was when his coach, Mike Silvester, who played in Italy and maintains his contacts here, told him that Marr Rimini was "looking for a scorer, someone to average twenty-five points a game." Offered a little money to fly over and try out in August, when Italian training camps open, Eubanks jumped at the chance.

Things went well. "We scrimmaged against Messaggero, one of the big teams, and I hit six threes and scored about thirty. They was impressed." Marr signed him for $150,000 (agreeing to pay his Italian taxes), plus an apartment and the use of a car. Guaranteed.

"But it's nowhere *near* guaranteed," Eubanks laments, his voice rising as soon as he touches on the subject. "If I stay here all season they'll still pay on a monthly basis, but if I leave there's a settlement. And I'm going to have to take a settlement, for *way* less than they owe me, because I'm too young to just sit around and do nothing here. We're supposed to talk at eleven tonight to finalize the deal."

I ask him to back up. How does it happen that the league's top scorer gets dropped four games into the season?

Eubanks shrugs. "I did what they asked me to do. I came

and averaged over twenty-five points [32.5], shooting well [.636, eighth in A-1 at the time]. I did not hog the ball, I played with the team. Unfortunately, this is a young team, but they expected you to go out and beat Messaggero and those teams. It's just not gonna happen.

"So we lost a few games [0–4 in league play]. Then we play an Italy Cup game against Siena, Darren Daye's team, and after the game they're telling me, like, 'J., it shouldn'a been you.' *The other team!* I'm like, 'It shouldn'a been me *what?*' They say, 'You didn't hear? You were released today. You were cut.'

"No one from the team, no one from the front office, told me *anything!*" Eubanks still can't believe it. "*No . . . one . . . told . . . me . . . anything!* If my fiancee wasn't there, I probably woulda had a breakdown. I went to talk to Massimo [Bernardi], the coach, and he would not talk to me. He said, '[General manager Ricardo] Cervellini will meet you in the office in five minutes.' Wouldn't even talk to me.

"That's not all. I've got this friend named Tony Zeno, used to play in Italy. He said, 'J., something's fishy. Larry Middleton's in town.' " Middleton played the last three years in Trieste but hadn't been re-signed.

"Middleton was already here, so that meant they were bringing him in. They had told him not to come to the game because they figured I'd know.

"So they already knew, all that day. I felt *terrible!*" For a moment Eubanks looks as if he might cry, reliving it. "The whole crowd and everybody knows, and I'm out there smiling on the court like everything's fine. I didn't know *anything*.

"Finally Cervellini showed up and told me the team decided they needed a point guard. This was true. We'd lost a few games in the last three or four minutes because we didn't have anybody with experience to take care of the ball. He said, 'Your contract's okay, we're gonna pay you,' all that."

But it wasn't as simple as getting paid in full and going home, and unlike Rick Mahorn, Eubanks didn't have the money to hire lawyers to intercede. To make matters worse, Marr refused to deal with his agent back in the States, Elouise Saperstein. ("They didn't like her because after they gave me a bad car when I first got here—the gas gauge didn't work, the dash fell out on me, the brakes wasn't any good—she told me to write 'em a letter saying that if they didn't get it taken care of, I wasn't gonna play that Sunday.")

"So . . . four, five, six days go past, and I hear *nothing* from 'em. Finally they tell me they've got a guy that's trying to get another job for me, another team. But I went and talked to some players and some people around here that know the team, and they said that what Marr does is, they tell you they're looking for another job for you so they don't have to pay you right away. They know they have to pay you off, but they want to compromise with you, so they try to wait you out. The longer you wait and the tireder you get of being here, the more they figure you'll take whatever they offer. Now it's been three weeks, and this is the first week we've made any movement."

I ask him what he's been doing in the meantime, what he's been thinking.

"First—I gotta tell you *this*—I had to move out of the apartment they gave me; that's why I'm in the hotel now. I don't know why, but mold started growing in the place. *Mold! Ev-ry-where!* I mean, the walls were white when I moved in, and in a couple of weeks they were *green!* My fiancee is allergic to mold, so I had to send her home."

Apparently Eubanks thinks I don't believe him, because in a shrill voice he says, "After we eat I'll take you there and *show* you!

"They tried to force me to keep staying there," he goes on. "They told me it was my fault for hanging my clothes up to dry in the apartment.

"So I moved into the hotel and I was just sitting around, waiting. Now, making money makes me happy, but I'd rather be somewhere playing than sitting around here doing nothing, getting fat—I'm too young not to play. It's not just the money: I love the game. So I was gonna settle for less than they owe me, way less, so I could go play somewhere."

"But you're still here."

"Because I didn't have my money. My agent kept saying, 'Whatever you do, J., don't leave without your money or you'll never get it.' So I just sat around, trying to think of something to do. The hours got boring."

"So you've finally talked to them, and you're supposed to settle it tonight. How much?"

Eubanks giggles uncomfortably. He told me earlier that he's received two of the ten monthly payments on his contract, $15,000 each, but he's reluctant to say how much of the remaining $120,000 he's agreed to accept. "It's terrible. You would ask me, Why are you taking that? You'd never respect me. But I wanna go play somewhere."

I assure him that whatever the figure, it's sure to be more than most people earn in a couple of years, so what's the difference?

"Naw, I'm not gonna tell you. It's bad."

Finally Eubanks confesses that he and Marr have tentatively agreed to settle for fifty thousand dollars, on top of the thirty thousand he's already received.

"It's not shabby," he says, "but it's not what they owe me. Plus, they hurt my career. If I had played well all season, you don't know what might have happened next year."

"What are your plans," I ask, "if you settle the contract in the next couple of days?"

This doesn't brighten him up. I feel for him: he might be getting fifty thousand tomorrow, but the future is a big unknown. He's one of a thousand-and-one players on the fringes of professional basketball. As he'd said at one point, "I don't know where else I could make a hundred and fifty thousand dollars a year," and I knew he could say the same of fifty thousand. Less.

"If I settle tonight," Eubanks says, "I'll probably cut out of here tomorrow night or the next morning. Go back to Louisville first. Then I don't know what I'll do. I've had calls from the CBA, the Global League. An agent over here said he had something in Belgium. I don't know. It might be a chance for me to finish up school, then start back up in the summer. I really don't know. When I get back home and get tired of sitting around, I'd probably end up in Georgia, playing in the CBA. Last year Chris Corchiani got called up to the NBA from there. Hopefully something good will come out of all this."

"Do you think about playing in the NBA someday?"

"Everybody who plays basketball dreams of the NBA. But sometimes the reality is that it's not possible. Everybody can't play in the NBA; there's only so many spots. So I was thinking, If I can't make it in the NBA, make a name for myself over here."

He knows it's not going to happen now.

By the time we finish eating it's ten-thirty. J. J. had said he's supposed to talk to someone from the organization at eleven, so I ask if he'll drop me off on the Via D'Annunzio, down by the beach, where I can catch the bus back to Riccione.

He insists on showing me the apartment first. "You gotta see this, or you wouldn't believe it. You'll see why I wouldn't stay there."

Five minutes later, a few blocks away, I see. It's a nice enough apartment, roomy and well furnished—but just as J. J. said, large patches of the walls in almost every room are covered with disgusting green mold. "I'm convinced," I tell him. "Get me outta here."

Just then the phone rings, presumably someone from Marr looking for him. I wander back through the apartment while J. J. talks.

He looks cheerier when he's done. "It was my agent in the States. She might have something for me in Spain."

J. J.'s not at the hotel when I call in the morning. I take the train to Bologna, where I'm meeting Alberto for lunch and then watching Scavolini-Knorr in a Euroclub Championship game; I'll call J. J. later from there.

I tell Alberto that Eubanks's story doesn't make the Lega Pallacanestro Italiano look very good, but even the league's PR director won't make excuses for the Rimini *società*. "It's true, I'm sure. That's Rimini. Rimini went from the 'B' league to A-2 last year, then to A-1 this year, and shouldn't be there. Many people have problems with Rimini."

As it turns out, I don't get back to J. J. this day. When I call the hotel the next morning they tell me he's checked out.

Spain? Belgium? Home?

Fortunately, he gave me his mother's address in Louisville. Someday, I want to know how it all turned out.

"C'è Solo un Brunamonti"

Alberto joshes that I'm in love with Knorr Bologna point guard Roberto Brunamonti.

What can I say?

Here's what others say. Retired star Romeo Sacchetti, his eyes threatening to mist up: "I love Roberto like my brother. We play together many years on the national team, roommates when we travel. Roberto and Meneghin are the two Italian players I respect the most. Meneghin is the image of the strong player; on the court he is *pissed*, you understand?—with the referees, with the players. 'Berto is also strong, but he's lovely."

Mark Crow, an American who played nine years here and is now an agent at the International Basketball Center in the republic of San Marino: "A class act, a true sportsman. He's proof you don't have to be an asshole to be a competitor."

Rudy Hackett, a Syracuse University star in the seventies who played nine seasons in the *lega* and now coaches the Series "B" team in Pesaro: "A gentleman on and off the court. The type of guy that, if he passed by me during a game, I'd never give him a pop; he doesn't merit it. If he's gonna get by your screen, you let him get by—you just don't cheap-shot a class act. I take my hat off to him."

Laurel D'Antoni, Mike's wife: "He's so sweeeeeet . . ."

Enrico Campana, world-weary editor of *Super Basket* magazine: "Brunamonti's not a player, he's a *saint*."

And the Bologna fans, who put up the huge sign over the top of the bleachers at the Palasport: C'È SOLO UN BRUNAMONTI. *There's only one Brunamonti.*

I hadn't heard much of this when I first met him, which was after Alberto and I watched the Knorr-Marr game in Rimini. Brunamonti, returning after his back problems, had played thirteen minutes off the bench. He was hardly an impressive physical specimen: 6'2" or so, maybe 180 pounds, knobby-kneed, almost frail; not especially quick, not a leaper. Sure, he was thirty-three years old and getting over some injuries, but even though he played hard and clearly had some leadership qualities—the phrase "coach on the floor" came to mind—it was hard to imagine him an icon, even in this league.

I met him afterward. Alberto went into Knorr's locker room and told him the *americano* writer wanted to touch base with him, and Brunamonti emerged a few minutes later, his thinning black hair damp from his shower.

I was struck right away by his warm smile, his quiet, relaxed voice, his obvious humility.

He couldn't have been more accommodating when I asked about getting together sometime. "When you can," he said in struggling English. "You come to Bologna, we go eat in my restaurant and talk. You tell me when you want to come."

After we'd agreed to meet the following Wednesday, I said—out of habit, after dealing with so many inconsiderate NBA players—"You won't forget?"

Brunamonti nodded, smiling. "I'm old, but only in the basketball. The mind is okay."

He picks me up at the Bologna train station, warm and friendly, in a little gray Fiat Uno.

The restaurant, a mile away, is tucked at the end of a sort of alley—no sign outside, nothing, just BENSO on a glass door that might have taken you into a fleabag hotel. But it's nice inside: small, intimate, classy but casual. There are some framed basketball pictures on the walls (I don't see any of Roberto) along with other photos and artwork.

We sit at a table in the corner of the back room. On the wall beside me there's a picture of the '89–'90 Knorr team in uniform, here in the restaurant, holding up glasses of champagne: 1990 EUROPEAN CUP CHAMPIONS it says underneath. I recognize longtime NBA center Clemon Johnson, Bill Walton's backup on the '77–'78 Trail Blazers; Micheal Ray Richardson, his giddy grin standing out among a bunch of guys saying cheese; and Roberto in back, down at one end, unremarkable, just another one forcing a smile.

I start asking questions. Roberto struggles with his English, stopping frequently and muttering "How do I say . . . ," pronouncing "practice" *prack-teek* as if all *c*'s are the same, speaking almost exclusively in the present tense.

He comes from Spoleto, a small town near Rome where kids didn't play much *basket;* tennis was young Brunamonti's game. He was fourteen when some school friends talked him into playing some basketball one day.

He was instantly hooked. "When I start, I never before see *basket*, but I love it. Now, at thirty-three, I have the same, how I say? . . . *passion*. Now it's work, it's money, but I still love to play."

After two years in the junior division, the sixteen-year-old Brunamonti moved to the town of Rieti and entered A-1, playing for the meager pay of the late seventies. By twenty he was playing every summer for the national team. Like Meneghin and most Italian pros, who are earning money and playing ball nine or ten months a year before they're out of *superiore* school (national-team players are at it all year round), he didn't go to college.

Brunamonti played seven years and became a star before

Rieti, desperate for money, sold him to Bologna in 1983. In his second season Granarola Bologna won the championship, beating one of Dan Peterson's great Meneghin-D'Antoni teams in a three-game series in which the visiting team won each game. It was the highlight of Brunamonti's career.

"I had the responsibility of the team. I played against Mike D'Antoni, and it was a big test for me."

His career took off then. He'd won the European championship with the national team the previous summer, now he'd won the league, and as Roberto says, "something was changing" in Italian ball: more and bigger sponsors got involved, salaries started going up.

He's been an institution in Bologna ever since. He says the organization went through a period of confusion in the mid-eighties, constantly changing players without any real plan—" 'We'll take you, you, you' "—and other teams offered him big money, "but I always wanted to play in Bologna." Roberto puts his hand over his heart and says, with charming sincerity, "Sometimes you put on a uniform and no matter what happens you say, 'This is my uniform, my team.' "

He says he was at his best in '87 and '88. But back surgery after the '88 season caused him to miss the Seoul Olympics, which would have been his third, and though he was back with Knorr in the fall and rejoined the national team the next summer, he's the first to say he's never been the player he was before. In three of the five seasons since the operation he's been out for extended periods with back trouble. He's become a player who relies on experience, guile, and tenacity. He retired from the national team after the loss to Germany last summer that kept Italy out of the Barcelona Olympics ("Detlef Schrempf was too much for us"), and he knows he doesn't have too many years left in the league.

With a wife and two young kids, Roberto thinks about the future. He's in the fourth year of a five-year contract that pays him substantial but not stratospheric money (I've heard three hundred thousand dollars a year), and early in his career even the top players weren't earning much more than the average businessman, so he's hardly set for life. "I must work," he says.

Coaching, maybe? Seems like a natural for someone who strikes everyone even now as, in one coach's words, "a coach in a T-shirt."

"I don't know," he says doubtfully. "I expect from other players what I give to a coach. I don't know if it's possible."

Trust me, he's not patting himself on the back; he's not talking about talent. Brunamonti is so little impressed with his talent that I go away from this first interview convinced I've been misled by the people who tout him as one of the Italian greats. He's talking effort; even Roberto, apparently, gives himself credit for that.

Maybe, he says—as Dino Meneghin said of himself—he could coach kids.

Any other ideas?

He doesn't know what he could do outside basketball. "You're thirty-seven, thirty-eight, with no experience. They hire someone with experience, or someone twenty-two. So I hope to stay in basketball. But I don't expect nothing from the club."

"But you're the kind of guy a team wants to keep around. You've given them everything, the fans love you . . ." I'm reminded of the huge sign in the Palasport, up above all the others. "You've seen the sign the fans put up?"

He smiles. "I see it. I like it. But," he hastens to add, "I don't say, 'Put that there for me.' "

"No, but it shows how people feel about you. That's why the team might keep you around."

"I don't know. For the club to say, 'We'll give you a chance'—why? If they want to, okay, but it's not normal. It's possible they say, 'Finished, *ciao*.' "

"How long do you hope to play?"

"The future depends most on injuries." He smiles. "I hope

to play to forty-two, like Meneghin. I know this is not possible, but even if it ends tomorrow, I'm lucky. We're all lucky. Basketball is not a job."

"If I were president of this club," says Knorr coach Ettore Messina in his near-flawless English, "I would offer Roberto a job, as soon as he retires as a player, as head coach of the junior team. I would pay him a lot of money, anything, just to keep him. If he's the team manager, he must take care of stupid little things like lunches and trips; you waste him. It's better if he coaches the young team and sometimes comes to watch the senior team as kind of an advisor. That would be special."

An interesting pair, Messina and Brunamonti. They're both thirty-three years old, and while Messina is Italy's up-and-coming "young" coach, Roberto is a "broken-down warhorse" nearing the end of a long career and wondering what he'll do when it's over. Though they arrived in Bologna within a year of each other—Roberto in 1982, an established star at twenty-two, Messina as a precocious twenty-three-year-old assistant coach a year later—and have experienced many things together, good and not so good, they've never become especially friendly or spent time together away from *basket*. Roberto is just another player to Messina.

Then again, he's anything but just another player. *C'è solo un Brunamonti*.

"I respect him very much," Messina says. "He's like Dino Meneghin, he's never had a problem with a coach. He's always the first one to work. If there's a problem, he's always on the coach's side. If he thinks the coach is making a mistake he waits, then comes to you and says, 'I think you're making a mistake.' He never makes a scene, never talks about the coach to other players. You know everything is always under control in the locker room.

"Do you know about his family? He lost his parents when he was very young [in his late teens], and he's very, very attached to his wife and children. Sometimes he's not a person up-to-date with this world we're living in. Success, material things—he doesn't care. He cares about the money, obviously, because money is very important, but being at the top is not his call. And he's not the kind of player who would play in the third division just to make money. He's the kind of player who would retire with a big game against another big European team and everybody would give him a big hand."

When I remark that I've heard nothing but wonderful things about the guy, Messina deepens his characterization.

"The only thing I tell him is that sometimes he's like San Sebastian. You know"—he jabs his index fingers at his chest and stomach—"with all the arrows. Sometimes he sees everything as if the end of the story is sure to be like San Sebastian.

"He's like the typical Greek hero, Ulysses or Achilles or Ettore. The typical Greek hero is a sad hero, and Roberto is like this; he's not always in the light.

"For example, when he hasn't been playing, or playing well, because of an injury, he has a tendency to think the other players will not accept what he says. It's not true, obviously. We went through a little crisis three years ago, my second year as head coach, when Micheal Ray Richardson decided not to play in an Italy Cup game, a very important game, because he wanted to renegotiate his contract—typical of the American superstar here. We went out of the Italy Cup competition because Micheal Ray didn't play that game, and the Italian players could have killed him in a second. Roberto was very good about keeping the team together, but he was shy about it because he was out with an injury and he thought the team could not respect him. But the team respects you because you're Roberto Brunamonti, not because you scored twenty points the night before."

But while Messina recognizes that a humility that verges on self-abasement sometimes compromises his captain's leadership, he's quick to add this: "Of course, if he were not like this he would not be Roberto Brunamonti."

In the big picture, you wouldn't want him to be one whit different than he is.

In December and January, Roberto's wife Carla spends three weeks in the hospital with a mysterious blood problem that causes a high fever and a lot of pain. Shortly after, Messina tells me that Roberto, behind the scenes ("He's very shy and didn't want anyone to know"), organized a drive to raise money for a machine the hospital needs.

Brunamonti, when I inquire, shakes his head as if to dispel the notion.

"I do nothing. When I talk to the doctor, he say the hospi tal badly needs this very expensive machine. I take the idea from Walter Magnifico [of Scavolini], to have a lottery for the jerseys of famous players at halftime of our home games. The first time, eight jerseys, eight million lire [about six thousand dollars]. But I do nothing. I make a few phone calls, I invite the old players to the game. Nothing."

He seems truly surprised when I say that everyone I talk to speaks so highly of him, and his response is interesting to one who's so accustomed to hearing boors like Barkley and Canseco and McEnroe insist the public would feel differently about them if they knew the real person, who's so kind and considerate.

"*Signora* D'Antoni? I've talked to her maybe three times, just to say '*Ciao, come sta?*' Mark Crow, the same." As if these people and dozens of others are mistaken, as if they would never say nice things if they got to know him.

I had to watch him play only a couple of games to understand why the Bologna fans, who will never meet him, stretched the big sign along the wall in the Palasport. In the course of the season I see Knorr play more than any other team, and while it's fun to watch Danilovic and four young national-team players, it's Roberto I look forward to seeing. Not so much to seeing him play—just to seeing him. I like it when, as their captain, he leads the line of Knorr players out of the tunnel before the game, jogging to the foul line, where the group huddles and then breaks with the wave to the crowd, the little touch I like so much. I know most of the players think it's bullshit (Bill Wennington tells me, when I ask what's said in that huddle, "Oh, Binelli usually says 'Wave to the pussy' "), but Roberto looks as if he's conscious of a connection between all the human beings in the building. I like watching him put his unremarkable body through a long series of exercises on the sideline. I like it when the teams take the floor for the tip-off and he first of all shakes hands with the referees, then, with one of his rare, wonderful smiles, greets a Meneghin or Walter Magnifico—another veteran, an old friend he hasn't seen for a while—before going around and connecting with each opponent. (*Connecting:* not just nonchalantly slapping five but looking them in the eye, shaking hands, saying something.)

I like the peacemaking during scuffles, the respect for even the most inept referees, the way he seeks out the opposing coach to shake hands after every game.

His ballplaying is secondary. Sometimes he's good, sometimes not so good, and even at his best—distributing the ball flawlessly, driving to the hoop and dishing off, hitting the open outside shot—there's nothing snazzy about him; not these days, anyway. I like watching him lead: call the plays, call the defenses, flit around instructing and encouraging his teammates when there's a pause for free throws. I like seeing two young players letting a questionable ball head out of bounds, each hoping the ref will give it to his side—and then Roberto, brittle body and all, flying hell-bent past them and flinging it back over his head just before he goes over the railing and into the seats.

Best of all is the night in January when the Croatian club Cibona Zagreb comes to Bologna for the second half of the two teams' home-and-home Euroclub Championship competition. It's an electric night. Back in October, Knorr was worried about taking Danilovic, a Serb, to Zagreb for the first game. In the end, two bodyguards went with him.

Danilovic got death threats, the crowd harassed him, former teammates wouldn't speak to him. The tough kid was a basket case and played horribly as Knorr got routed. He didn't recover for a month; I saw him have games of 0-for-10 and 1-for-11 shooting.

Comes January and Danilovic is smoking, Knorr is playing great ball, and they've got Cibona at home with the Forever Boys screaming bloody murder. It's a blitz from the start, Knorr leading by twenty points at halftime. It gets worse in the second half, and late in the game the fans amuse themselves by taunting Asa Petrovic, Drazen's older brother, who played one season in Pesaro and is remembered for taunting opponents with "the airplane," in which he ran down the floor in jubilant moments with his arms spread out like wings, tilting one way and then the other like a plane doing stunts. Tonight, a front-row fan behind the Cibona bench is leaning over the rail screaming at Petrovic and airplaning. During a time-out with a few minutes left, thousands are on their feet doing it. Petrovic, preposterously, tries to make like he doesn't notice.

With three minutes left and Knorr's lead at forty points, Brunamonti torpedoes out of bounds, over the rail, and into the seats to sling a loose ball back into play.

The next time I see him, I ask him why he'd risk a broken neck in those circumstances.

"Because with us," he replies, absolutely serious, "Cibona many times wins."

"But you were forty points ahead."

"Yes, but forty-one is more," he says, as if I'm missing the obvious. "I think the respect of other persons comes when you're up by twenty-one and you say, 'I want to make it twenty-three.' You don't *say* that to them, you show them. Especially," he adds, "with the Cibona coach, the brother of Drazen Petrovic."

I ask, What about him?

"He was a good player, but when he win he always show you"—Roberto points a finger overhead, as if at a scoreboard. "Or he does this"—an ever-so-brief airplane. "To me, you don't do this. So to me, when you're winning by twenty points with him you say, 'Okay, I must make it *thirty*.' I hustle even the last minute.

"But when it's over, it's over. I saw many persons in the crowd doing this"—he briefly imitates the airplane again—"and yes, it's funny, but when we finish the game I go to Petrovic and shake hands."

"Do you shake hands with the opposing coach after every game?"

"Not always." The tiniest smile appears in his eyes. "But with him, yes."

"Why?"

"For me it's not, 'Look at this,' " Roberto says, gesturing toward an imaginary scoreboard. "Just beat him by forty points, get the ball when it's going out of bounds, then shake hands with respect. Inside, to me, *this* . . . is like this is for him"—and one last time he mimics Petrovic's airplane.

I've got no idea how Roberto came to be the way he is. Maybe he's repressed; maybe it's not all good. But this I know: if such a concept as "athlete-as-role-model" existed in Italy, he'd be the one.

But then, it's got nothing to do with sports. I wish I were more like him myself.

C'è solo un Brunamonti.

Thanksgiving at the D'Antonis'

I dimly remember Mike D'Antoni: an unremarkable white guard who passed through the NBA in the mid-seventies with several teams including, as I recall, Philadelphia and Milwaukee.

It turns out I remember him even more dimly than I thought. The *NBA Register* tells me D'Antoni never played for those teams, and I finally realize I've had him lumped together with Milwaukee Bucks coach Mike Dunleavy, an unremarkable white guard who did.

After averaging 3.3 points in 180 NBA and ABA games, mostly with the old Kansas City–Omaha Kings, D'Antoni came to Italy in 1977. Here, he *was* remarkable. Everyone assures me he's the greatest point guard the *lega*, if not all of Europe, has ever seen. "The heart of Milan," Roberto Brunamonti says. "The idol of many players in Italy." When Philips Milan management decided to purge the roster of its three late-thirtyish former superstars after the team fell from a championship in 1989 to tenth place in 1990, Meneghin and McAdoo were sold and D'Antoni was named head coach.

I write to him in mid-November, after Alberto tells me that D'Antoni and his wife Laurel always put on a Christmas get-together for American players from miles around. I'm shameless enough to ask if, for research purposes, I could drop in.

A week or so later (the minimum time it takes a letter to travel between any two points in Italy, even if they're only two hundred miles apart) I receive a fax saying the party is at Thanksgiving, not Christmas, and the D'Antonis would be happy to have me. Not only that, but if I don't mind cats I'm welcome to stay at their apartment, spend the weekend, watch the Philips-Panasonic game on Sunday, and have dinner with the team afterward at the Torchietto restaurant, where Milan teams have gone after home games for the past fifteen years. It's the equivalent of Pat Riley asking me to come spend a few days with him in the middle of the season.

So on Thanksgiving morning—just another morning in Italy, people off to work and to school, shops opening up—I make the four-hour train trip northwest to Milan, up near Switzerland. The fog shrouding the countryside recalls pre-Thanksgiving days a few years ago, when I'd go with my stepdaughter's grade-school classes on their trips to farms outside Portland to traipse through soggy pumpkin patches.

I make a new friend when the attractive woman sitting across from me, with whom I've been knocking knees and trading glances, asks me something about the train's stopping in Reggio nell'Emilia. *No capisco*, I reply with a shrug. Ah, she says. *Americano?*

She speaks pretty good English, with a light English accent. She's wearing jeans and reminds me of a round-faced, round-bottomed woman I once fancied, down to the round wire-rimmed glasses. Cristina is her name. She's single, lives in a house on a lake in the mountains beyond Milan. Divorced, I gather. A clothing designer of some kind. I think she fancies me a little, *americano* or not. Hmmmmmm. I imagine her nice old house on a lake in the mountains, a fire burning, maybe a bear rug or something . . .

Next I'm imagining her in my apartment, because she says she's been working right down in Pesaro and will be going back for another couple of weeks after spending this weekend at her lakeside place. I tell her I'm in Riccione and mention maybe getting together sometime.

As the train pulls into Milan we exchange addresses. I tell her she can call or fax me at Amici di Riccione (Friends of Riccione, a branch of the Palazzo de Turismo, where Marina arranged fax and phone privileges for me). I half believe she will, even if I don't contact her first. But even if I never see her again, it's nice to feel a little juiced. Not many women have appealed to me much since my divorce.

They say Mussolini considered the cavernous station in Milan one of his great triumphs. It reminds me of Termini in Rome: a little city itself, with newsstands, restaurants, shops, bars—you name it. Dozens of ticket windows on the lower level. A long, constantly moving line of taxis out front. I hop into one when my turn comes and, instead of telling the driver where I'm going, hand him the slip of paper I wrote the address on, hoping he'll note the name *Mike D'Antoni* and not screw me too badly.

The apartment manager lets me into the building and tells me that the D'Antonis' housekeeper will let me in upstairs. I'm waiting for the elevator when D'Antoni himself, in sweats and basketball shoes, comes in the front door of the building, just back from Philips's morning practice. I recognize him from the pictures I've seen in the magazines: straight black hair, mustache, and such a baby face that he hardly looks old enough to *have* a mustache. He greets me with a light West Virginia accent, shakes hands, and we ride up to the fourth floor.

A couple of minutes later Laurel arrives, an outgoing thirty-three-year-old former model from Seattle who's worked for Olimpia Milano for six years doing promotions, marketing, and whatever else needs doing.

The apartment has high ceilings, two large bedrooms, two baths, a big living room, and a den whose walls are covered with a few framed action pictures of D'Antoni and several frames crammed with snapshots of the coaches, players, wives, and girlfriends of the great eighties Milan teams at the Torchietto, at parties, everywhere. Bob McAdoo and his late wife Charlena (a great friend of Laurel's and co-originator of these Thanksgivings six years ago, who died of cancer last Christmas Eve), Dino Meneghin and Caterina, Joe Barry Carroll, Dan Peterson, dozens of people I don't recognize. "Great years," Laurel muses as she identifies people and places and occasions.

After lunch at Mike's squash club around the corner, Laurel goes back to the office and Mike and I drive out to the arena, where Philips will be having afternoon practice a little later. The two-year-old Forum is impressive: bowling alleys, squash courts, a hockey rink, offices, VIP rooms, convention areas, a restaurant. The arena, capacity twelve thousand, is the second-largest in the league to Rome's Palaeur, which was built for the 1960 Olympics and seats about one thousand more.

As a few early arrivals work out, we sit in the courtside seats and D'Antoni explains how he went from high-school prodigy to NBA washout to Italian legend.

He grew up in the little coal-mining town of Mullens, West Virginia, son of a renowned high-school coach and the kid brother of a local sensation (now a high-school coach in Myrtle Beach, S.C.). Young Mike was a sensation too.

"That was one thing I had on McAdoo," he recalls with amusement. "Some magazine rated me eighth among high-school seniors in '69. Much later [after former NBA scoring king and MVP McAdoo came to Milan in 1986] I found out Bob and I graduated the same year and I thought, 'Hmmmmmm, I don't remember McAdoo's name on that list.' I thought it would be great if he was below me, 'cause he's always talkin' himself up, so when I went home that summer I went through all these scrapbooks and finally found this old clipping, 'Top 75 High School Players in America.' I'm looking: 'Where's McAdoo? Where's McAdoo?' " He bursts out laughing, as if he still can't believe it. "He wasn't there! I brought that clipping back and showed it to him and he said, 'What do you expect, man? I was black, playin' down south—there was no way I was gonna be on there.' I said yeah, yeah . . . Boy, I laughed about that for a long time."

D'Antoni passed up the big schools for Marshall University a few miles down the road. "I was from a small town, not the most self-confident guy in the world. My brother had gone to Marshall. And Marshall had a good basketball program then. We were eighth in the nation my junior year. My one regret about going there is that I never had the competition to make me mentally tough, which I think hurt me in the NBA."

In the 1973 NBA draft the K.C.-Omaha Kings took him in the second round, twentieth overall. "I was so high," D'Antoni recalls; "it was just an unbelievable feeling. The NBA was my dream. I signed a two-year contract, no-cut. To me it was all the money in the world, about fifty thousand dollars a year, and to realize I had two years in the NBA *for sure* was an overwhelming feeling."

He didn't have the speed or leap to be a top NBA guard. Worse, he lost his confidence. "I let the coaches convince me I wasn't a shooter. I let them say I couldn't shoot, and it got to the point where they were right, I couldn't . . . instead of me sayin', 'No, they don't know what they're talkin' about,' and playin' my game and bein' tough mentally."

Released a few games into his third season, "I just went home and felt sorry for myself." Later that year he played fifty games with the ABA's Spirits of St. Louis. That summer, when the two leagues merged, he signed with San Antonio, but was waived after playing in two games in the fall of 1976.

In 1977 he came to Italy, to Milan, for twenty-five thousand dollars. "I was down about basketball, and then a big romance fell apart, and I just came over here to get away from everything and keep playing ball and have an educational experience. Just play a little ball, get my money, and go back to the States. I had no idea I'd make a career out of it, or make a name; I just wanted to have some fun.

"I did pretty well my first two years. Peterson came in as coach my second year and we got all the way to the finals. I had a lousy finals, so it kind of ended on a sour note, but people liked me and thought I was a pretty good player. I was one of the few American point guards, and I did a little fancy dribbling and passing and they liked that. And the way I played—I gave everything, every second. If a ball rolled off I was divin' for it, and they appreciated that.

"I just kind of caught on. I had an Italian background, I spoke the language, I was twenty-five or twenty-six years old, single, driving a Maserati; I had a kind of style. Not that I really had one—I was from West Virginia and shy as can be—but I was kind of a novelty."

But he wanted to try the NBA once more, and autumn 1979 found him in camp with the Chicago Bulls. "I thought I was doing pretty well too. But then one night I was lying in bed thinking, 'I'm scrambling to make the team, worrying about every ball, every shot. I could be making more money over there, and I won't be on the bubble all the time.' I thought, the hell with it, and got up and packed and left.

"Things fell into place over here. I had worked out all summer before Chicago's camp and I came over here in great shape. The team had done badly in preseason, but when I got here we started winning everything and I was averaging about twenty-seven points a game. That kind of launched me. We made it to the semifinals that year—where I messed up again.

"But I just got better. Part of it was Peterson: he told me I could shoot, he made me shoot. My shot got better, I started getting confident. And every practice, every game I worked hard.

"We lost another heartbreaker in the playoffs. But people liked us because we played so hard. Peterson came up with his famous line, '*Sputare sangue!*' 'Spit blood!' "

Peterson brought in the supposedly washed-up Meneghin

for the next season, 1981–82, and Billy Milano won the championship. It was the first of eight straight appearances in the league finals. Five championships, the European Cup in '85, the Italy Cup in '86, and the Grand Slam sweep in '87. Various of those clubs included John Gianelli, Earl Cureton, Antoine Carr, Russ Schoene, Wally Walker, Joe Barry Carroll, Ken Barlow, and Rickey Brown, and the '87 Grand Slam team featured McAdoo, but the only constants, beginning to end, were D'Antoni and Meneghin.

"Mike was the single greatest joy of my coaching career," Dan Peterson says. "He translated my every idea into on-the-court action. Had he not had injuries he would have stayed in the NBA, because he was very smart, a coach's kid, and although Mike plays up the fact that he wasn't a great athlete, he was a very good athlete. He could dunk with two hands at six-three, had tremendously quick reflexes, quick hands, quick feet."

Franco Casalini, Peterson's assistant in those years and now head coach in Rome, says, "Mike was in effect coaching the team. He called not only the plays, he called our defenses. Or if we called a defense in the huddle, we asked Mike, 'Do you want to do it?' Peterson was the first to use the point guard this way, and he had the right player."

Bob Morse: "Mike had a great feel for the game and what his team was trying to do. I remember games where he wouldn't shoot at all until the fourth quarter, then he'd bury a couple of three-pointers or hit some drives or make some assists. A hell of a guy to play against, because he was always in the right place at the right time."

Mark Crow recalls, "Mike would go oh-for-five on three-pointers, but at the end he would always make the shot to win the game. Or he'd steal the ball, or whatever. Always."

D'Antoni reluctantly admits to having made a fair share of game-winning shots (though he doesn't mind being pushed to admitting it). "A lot of it was Peterson. I don't know how many times, in the last four minutes, he called me over and said, 'I want you to make every important play, take every important shot.' That takes all the pressure off. Because even if I messed up—and I did mess up—he'd say, 'That's okay, just keep doin' it.' "

Like everyone else, Rudy Hackett describes D'Antoni the player as a tremendous competitor, but he surprises me by adding, "He wasn't always a likeable guy on the court because of his incredible intensity." I interviewed Hackett after having spent considerable time with the D'Antonis, and the remark surprises me because Mike is so low-key and considerate that I've assumed he was a gentlemanly Brunamonti-type on the court. But in time I'll hear the same from others, including *Laurel*, who says "He isn't the sweet boy he looks like" and tells me about the time Mike sucker-punched a Varese player after a game. ("The guy gave me a cheap shot in the last minute or so," Mike says in self-defense, "and I wasn't going to let it end like that." He does admit that he used to run certain opponents into Meneghin's brutal picks just to hear their teeth rattle.)

"Mike's personality on the court never bothered me," Hackett goes on, "because as a forward I never had to put up with him much, but other players on my teams were afraid of him. His talent, and just being who he was, made players afraid of him. He could yell at officials and get away with it, he could say things no one else could . . . because they were Milan, the big team, and he was Mike D'Antoni, and he had Dan Peterson behind him."

Peterson, Meneghin, McAdoo, Casalini, D'Antoni—all describe those years as a high point, or *the* high point, of their lives. Like the Celtics of various eras, like the Lakers of the eighties, they learned that winning was more fun than anything.

D'Antoni says, "One of the reasons we won is that everyone put the team first. Dino was great that way. I'm sure he bitched at home about not getting many shots, but out on the floor he'd just set the pick, give you the ball a hundred times, say 'You're the greatest'—never any problems. That's why Dino's won championships wherever he's been. I'd come home, by myself or later with Laurie, and I'd bitch like a maniac: 'McAdoo does this,' or 'This SOB does this,' or 'Coach can't do this shit.' But when we were on the floor, *fine*. 'Okay, Joe Barry is this way, *fine;* how can we win with him being this way? Antoine Carr is like this; what can we do?'

"Guys would always call me from the States; if the team was trying to sign an American, they'd tell him to call me. I'd tell 'em I couldn't be sure they'd adjust to Italy—you never know—but I could always tell 'em it would be fun playin' ball here.

"Once we started doing well, it was almost like college again for me: I'm runnin' the team, it all depends on me, it's almost like I'm Michael Jordan. It's fun going into a game knowing you can dominate. It's not like, 'Oh God, I better play good so I don't get embarrassed.' If I missed ten shots in a row, no big deal—just, 'I better make the eleventh one.'

"And Milan is such a great location," he goes on, one memory triggering another. "One winter Mike Silvester, C. J. Kupec, and I rented a house in the Alps, up in Switzerland. We usually had Monday and Tuesday off, and as soon as the game was over on Sunday we'd be gone to the Alps, skiing for two days. Peterson was always saying, 'Okay, guys, no skiing,' and we'd say, 'Okay, coach, no problem.' Then about Friday we'd say, 'Hey, coach, we got some pictures to show you'—guys skiing, havin' a great time."

But no matter how much they won, no matter how much fun they had, Italy wasn't home, and D'Antoni packed up and took everything back to the States at every season's end, thinking he wouldn't be coming back. Unfortunately, his career was winding down just before the salary boom (D'Antoni the player peaked at about $150,000, approximately one-third of his present pay), the restaurant he and his brother owned in Myrtle Beach never did much, and by the time Milan called with an offer for another season, Italy and basketball always looked pretty good.

If there was a downside to all the winning, it was the built-in expectation of more winning—especially in Milan, the basketball capital of Italy ever since Pallacanestro Olimpia Milano won four championships in a row, 1936–39, and fourteen of eighteen between 1950 and 1967. (The Boston Celtics still have a lot of work to do.)

"Once you win three championships in a row," D'Antoni says, "you *gotta* make that foul shot, 'cause they expect you to make it, or you expect yourself to make it. You're playing not to lose. And towards the end of your career, when you know you're slipping a little bit but you can't slip because second place isn't good enough, it gets a little hairy. I'm sure that's why Dino told you he was glad to get away from the pressure to win every game. It's tough."

Peterson knew the end was coming and quit after the '87 Grand Slam, which assured his being remembered, as he says, as the "undefeated heavyweight champion." After the last-hurrah championship under Casalini in '89, the bottom fell out with the ignominious tenth-place finish the next year. The upshot was McAdoo and Meneghin being sold and D'Antoni being asked to replace Casalini.

What could he say, a thirty-eight-year-old coach's son, a de facto coach himself, on his last legs as a player?

Sì, sì.

When we get back to the apartment after the Philips practice, Laurel and a friend are setting things up and doing a little cooking. People start arriving shortly, bringing meats and salads and vegetables and pies: Pace Mannion and his family from Cantu, Ron "Popeye" Jones and John Fox from Arese, Johnny Rogers and Danny Vranes from Varese (Vranes with a fantastic ham and his renowned cinnamon rolls), Hansi Gnad and Mark Davis from Desio, Bob Thornton from Pavia and, from Philips Milano, Marco Baldi and Antonio Davis (with his mother and two beautiful daughters, visiting from Texas); plus the odd model, jazz singer, flight attendant. Twenty-six people in all.

Laurel goes around with a video camera, having people

identify themselves and share memories of Thanksgivings past . . . though we'll discover the next day that after she got me and a couple of others, she set the camera on the floor without turning it off and captured forty-five minutes of a blank wall, then turned it off—thinking she was turning it on—when she resumed her interviewing.

When all the platters and bowls and bottles are finally out, buffet-style, on a long table in the living room, Laurel calls everyone into a big circle where we hold hands and, one by one, tell what we're thankful for this year. Everyone cracks up when Marco Baldi, a gentle hulk, says, "I'm thankful to be here with all of you even though I'm not American."

At the end, Pace Mannion, a devout Mormon, says grace, then we serve ourselves and sit or stand wherever there's a spot in the living room, kitchen, or den.

On the TV in the den, a bunch of us watch the end of Scavolini Pesaro's Euroclub game against a Spanish team, Joventut Badalona, which features Harold Pressley and Corny Thompson. For the third time this month, Scavolini's Carlton Myers hits the winning shot at the buzzer.

Next, the replay of tonight's Euroclub game between defending *lega* champion Benetton Treviso (Toni Kukoc, Terry Teagle) and a Belgian team. It runs past midnight.

By now the crowd is thinning out and the remaining players are in the living room watching Mike's "NBA Superstars" video for the second time. It's interesting to see these guys, pros themselves—former NBA players, some of them—marveling at the feats of Michael, Magic, Bird, and the rest. I imagine they're feeling something like I do when I read *Light in August*.

An hour later they're watching it for the third, maybe the fourth time, and I'm wishing they'd leave so we can go to bed.

It's 2 A.M. when the last ones go. Mike and Laurel look as wiped out as I am.

• • •

Laurel says Mike is the ultimate creature of habit. Last year on his fortieth birthday she had cards waiting for him everywhere she knew he'd go: newsstand, espresso bar, squash club lunch counter, etc. He made every stop.

Friday morning I go with Mike (as I will on Saturday, Sunday, and Monday) to the newsstand on the corner, where he buys the *International Herald Tribune*, *USA Today*, and one of Italy's sports dailies, *La Gazzetta dello Sport;* thence to the bar across the intersection, where he orders a cappuccino and a roll (as he will on each succeeding day) and scans the papers.

The press here is something else. Italy has three daily sports newspapers; in the U.S. a few years back people thought one, *The National*, was overkill. And though *basket* is a distant second to soccer in popularity here, there are two weekly hoop magazines, *Super Basket* and *Il Gigante del Basket*. A lot of coverage, especially considering that the teams play so few games. A lot of writers screaming for your attention.

The result is lots of nonsense. With so few games to report on, the space is filled with "analysis," speculation, innuendo, and advice. The short thirty-game schedule makes every game important—it's more like the NFL than the NBA—so that if you lose two in a row, by the time you play again you haven't won a game in three weeks. You're *in crisi!*

In Milan, where people are accustomed to great teams and there are four competing daily newspapers aside from the national sports dailies, things are magnified even more.

And things haven't been going well. After starting off 6–0, Philips has lost three out of four, and there are even rumblings that Mike, a god in Milan, might be in trouble. Never mind that Philips made it to the last game of the finals in his first season as a coach, then made it to the Euroclub Championship Final Four and topped the A-1 regular-season standings last year.

Panasonic Reggio di Calabria, coming to town on Sunday, is tied with Philips and two others at 7–3, a game behind

Knorr and Benetton. D'Antoni feels his team should win if Alexander Volkov, the former Soviet star who played for the Atlanta Hawks the past two years, doesn't hurt them too badly.

Then again, he's not happy after today's practice. He's concerned about Aleksandar Djordjevich (GEORGE-uh-vitch), his point guard and big scorer, who hasn't shown much leadership in the past few weeks. And he's having trouble getting his team to go hard all the time, which I've heard is always a challenge with Italian players. Meneghins and Brunamontis are freaks here.

Mike's a basketball junkie.

Friday evening, all three of us tired, we pick up some Chinese food and stay in. Laurel spends hours in the den, picking the music for Sunday's game and working out the halftime promotions, while in the living room I get a crash course in eighties Milan basketball. Mike pulls tape after tape down from a shelf and shows me parts of title games, Italy Cup games, European Cup games. Two or three times we watch the incredible aftermath of the deciding game of the last championship, in Livorno in '89, when the officials reversed a last-second call to give Philips the title and a near-riot ensued: Livorno maniacs surrounded the arena, and Philips stayed in the locker room for two hours before making a dash for a couple of paddy wagons.

Mike enjoys reliving the glory days. Midnight comes and goes. One o'clock. Laurel goes to bed. I'm fading on a couch. Mike, wide-eyed, is in his chair, three feet from the TV, fast-forwarding, reversing, replaying high points with the remote control, telling stories. It's 2 A.M. before he's bleary enough to call it a night.

On Sunday we're at the Forum hours before game time. Laurel, stylishly dressed and energetic, is buzzing around:

up in the booth making sure the music is ready; down on the floor organizing Lufthansa's halftime promotion; off in a corner giving instructions to the Forum ushers.

The arena is jazzed up with signs. PANTHER POWER says one at the end where the Philips cheering section sits. Another: BASKET CLUB MIKE D'ANTONI.

In the upper deck at the other end, the Reggio di Calabria rooters—who've come some eight hundred miles, from the southern tip of Italy, and are roaring ninety minutes before tip-off—have a huge Confederate flag draped over the railing and signs everywhere: TOTAL KAOS, FORZA VIOLA, CRAZY CORNER.

It's the first game I've seen where the starting lineups are introduced. The first Panasonic player doesn't even know what to do when he hears his name: he looks around, bewildered, until someone shoves him out toward the foul line.

It's a back-and-forth game. Mike's the calm type on the sidelines, pacing in front of the bench with his arms folded across his chest, except for the occasional eruption, as when a missed Panasonic free throw falls into, then out of, the hands of Davide Pessina, Philips's maddeningly passive "power" forward.

Philips leads by two at halftime.

The attendance is announced as 6,732. No wonder the team's got financial problems. (No wonder the league does. Knorr draws 6,212 today, but the average attendance at the other six A-1 games this weekend is about 2,800.)

In the second half, Mike's worst fears are realized. Djordjevich is tentative; Pessina keeps playing soft; Antonello Riva, the all-time leading Italian scorer (fourth in league history behind Oscar Schmidt, Bob Morse, and Chuck Jura), throws up shots but does little else, and not many shots fall; and worst of all, Ricardo Pittis, an NBA prospect at twenty, but cocky, overpaid, and unmotivated at twenty-four, keeps playing such boneheaded ball that Mike keeps him on the bench for most of the second half. The only bright spot is the young American *pivot*, Antonio Davis, who finishes with

18 points, 23 rebounds, and 5 blocked shots.

Panasonic beats Philips, 95–90.

Fifteen minutes later the two head coaches appear and sit at a table at the front of the press room, answering questions from reporters who sit at little elementary-school–style desks. Mike is calm and pleasant, even smiles a few times, though he knows that Philips—and the coach—will take some heat in the press after their fourth loss in the past five games.

Mike has described his coaching style as one of constant encouragement and positive reinforcement, but back in his office he vents some frustration and says he chewed the team out after the game, especially Pittis and Djordjevich. "Maybe I should have done it before this. Maybe I've let this stuff go on too long."

Finally we collect Laurel and head home, where a few people will join us for a while before we meet the team at the Torchietto for dinner. In the car Mike vents some more. "Sasha [Djordjevich, who gets the same tag as his old Partizan Belgrade teammate Danilovic and Panasonic's Volkov] was making excuses when I chewed him out, telling me he wants to play all forty minutes and it ruins his rhythm when I take him out. I told him that if he'd keep pushing the ball up like I want him to, he won't be *able* to play forty minutes. Besides, he's not playing well enough for me to keep him in. And I didn't know *what* to say to Ricky Pittis. I just told him, 'Ricky, you're not doin' *shit*.' "

Laurel, the supportive wife (and not yet the basketball expert she's working toward becoming), asks open-ended questions, giving him the chance to get things out: "How about Flavio [Portaluppi]? How about Antonello [Riva]? How was the defense?"

Mike's not pleased with anyone except Davis and a couple of subs who at least played hard.

At the apartment we're joined by the general manager, Enzo Lefebre, and his fiancee; the younger assistant coach, Marco Crespi, and his wife; and a friend of them all, the sportscaster Flavio Tranquillo. We eat snacks and drink wine and talk—except Mike, who sits in his chair in front of the TV, watching a tape of the game and letting off more steam.

At the restaurant a little later, our group sits at a table in the front room; the players, well into their dinner when we arrive, are in back, which is probably for the best.

With some wine, pasta, steak, bread, salad, and sympathetic conversation, Mike starts getting the game out of his system.

But it will take a while yet. When, during our dessert, the players troop out of the back and stop to say *ciao* on their way out, Mike grips his steak knife and growls at them, pretending—I think—that it's all he can do not to start bloodletting.

It's midnight by the time we get home. Laurel turns in. Mike and I watch the game tape again, and afterward, since I know he won't be going to bed anytime soon, I ask to see more from the old days. For one thing, it might get his mind off his current troubles.

So he goes to the cabinet, and soon we're living in the past again. Here's D'Antoni in his thirties—slim, pale, baby-faced number 8—calling plays, hitting threes, diving after balls. McAdoo, poker-faced, hitting from all over with that peculiar rainbow shot, and saving the last game of that last championship by chasing down a Livorno fast break and tapping the ball out of bounds, allowing Milan to set up on defense. Signor Dino, *il monumento*, rarely shooting, not even rebounding very much, just *there:* passing, screening, knocking opponents down, always in the middle of things. Stubby Roberto Premier, hurling himself after balls and drilling important shots so that Mike finally says, "I never understood why Peterson liked him so much, but watching these films I can see why." And "Big Pete" himself, all 5'6" of him, emoting on the sidelines.

We watch parts of Mike's duels with Brunamonti in the classic '84 series when Granarola Bologna knocked off Simac Milano for the championship. The young, quick, springy Roberto goes up and dunks in traffic, as people have told me, and I can see he was a hell of a player. D'Antoni goes crazy when the refs rule that one of his hoops didn't beat the buzzer, ranting and raging and kicking over courtside signs.

I see the famous incident in Pesaro when, as the teams left the floor at halftime, a coin hit Dino in the head; he missed the second half (largely out of spite, according to Mike) and Milan was given the game a couple of days later, enabling them to win the series and move on to that last championship.

We're up until almost 4 A.M. I've got to catch the train home in a few hours.

"So," I ask before we pack it in, "did you end up feeling pretty good about your career?"

"Real good. But I will always feel bad about not making the NBA. I made it, made it there for two and a half years, but I didn't *really* make it. I mostly blame myself for not being mentally tough enough at that point, but I also feel like I really didn't get a good shot. You know, I thought I could stick."

"How good do you think you could have been?" (When I ask McAdoo, a few months later, what the difference was between D'Antoni and an NBA point guard, he seems surprised. "Nothing. It's just a matter of being in the right place at the right time.")

"I think I could have been a third guard on a lot of teams, played maybe ten years. Somebody like Rick Adelman played a long time—I think I could have been as good as that. I thought I could find a niche and contribute to a team. So I feel bad about that."

He pauses, and seems to be thinking about all the big games we've watched the past few nights, about Dino and McAdoo and Peterson and dozens of others, and the rented chalet in Switzerland and the travels all over Europe and the championships and being remembered as the greatest point guard in Europe, and the fact that he's now a monument of sorts himself in Milan, making a half million dollars a year as a head coach and still only forty-one years old.

"But not that bad," he adds.

Sugar

The *lega* had never seen anything like Micheal Ray Richardson. Oh, Bob McAdoo had been knocking 'em dead for two years with his big-time shooting when Micheal Ray arrived in 1988, but Micheal—"Sugar" Ray, to be sure, with a game so sweet—was a truly rare talent; even the NBA hadn't seen many like him.

I've never forgotten the first time I noticed him. I was in the Fish Grotto bar in Portland in December of 1978, half watching the Blazers and the New York Knicks on TV, when this Knicks rookie I'd never seen, Micheal Ray Richardson, grabbed a rebound, turned, and glided down the floor, effortlessly quick and completely in control, head up, the ball as surely an extension of him as it was of Oscar Robertson, gliding, pushing it deeper into the retreating Blazer defense, then positively exploding, shunning the dish-off and simply soaring over two defenders at the basket and whacking it down. This was before Magic Johnson: guards didn't do that.

But Richardson was 6'5" and strong—and fast, and a leaper. And he had a feel for the game, he had instinct. And he had style. He looked like a basketball version of the young Willie Mays.

He became an All-Star: playmaker, 20-point scorer, All-

Defense. But Maysian talents don't get shuttled around unless there are big problems, and Richardson went from New York to Golden State to New Jersey. He got hung up on cocaine and was repeatedly suspended. One strike, two strikes, three strikes and he was thrown out of the NBA.

He was so talented he'd been able to play in the League even when he was strung out, and he was so naturally mercurial that people usually thought any erratic behavior was just Micheal.

No doubt some of it was.

"When I went to Detroit," Darryl Dawkins says, "Isiah Thomas told me Sugar was the only guy who gave him *serious* trouble. When I was with the Nets, Sugar would strip the ball from Isiah, and outrun him *with the ball*, and then tell him [Darryl does a high-pitched squeal, imitating Richardson's stammer on the first word], 'Y-y-y-y-you little motherfucker, you can't guard me!' Then he'd come back and shoot a jump shot right in Isiah's face and say, 'Take that, y-y-y-y-you bitch!' And then he'd penetrate and dish to me and I'd get a dunk and Sugar would run right up in Laimbeer's face and say, 'We're kickin' your motherfuckin' ass!' Sugar was always hyper like that.

"We played New York one time and Sugar dished to Buck Williams and Buck dunked in Pat Ewing's face, and then he came back and dished to me and I dunked in his face, and then Sugar came back and faked like he was gonna dish it off and he rolled it up on the glass and it went in, and he turned around and [Darryl clamps one hand hard on the other wrist] clapped Pat by the arm and said, 'We kickin' your motherfuckin' ass!' And Pat Ewing got mad and . . . but he couldn't get his hand *loose* from Sugar. Sugar was strong. Pat *Ewing* could not get loose. And everybody's going, 'Pat, take it easy, man, this motherfucker's crazy, you *know* Sugar's crazy.'

"Sugar was just a hyper guy. But he could play basketball."

Basketball was the easy part. It was life that kept throwing Micheal. Drugs. Divorces. Drummed out of the NBA after his third suspension for drug abuse, he surfaced in Bologna in 1988. He was thirty-three years old, past his prime, his body abused, but he had more talent than Italians had ever seen. The fans loved him. Knorr won the Italy Cup in '89 and '90, and in '90 took the Cup of Cups, the European competition between the winners of the various leagues' versions of the Italy Cup. There's a great picture of Micheal and Roberto Brunamonti holding a Cup aloft after one of the victories.

A photo of the Cup of Cups team doing a champagne toast hangs in Roberto's restaurant, with Micheal grinning as if he's already had a few glasses. The other *straniero* in the shot is Clemon Johnson, who, I'm often told, "got fat in Bologna, with Sugar feeding him so much."

Basketball wasn't the problem.

Ettore Messina was a twenty-eight-year-old assistant to head coach Bob Hill when Micheal arrived in 1988. When Hill left Knorr for the Indiana Pacers the next season, Messina took over.

"The first day Micheal showed up for training camp," Messina says now, "I told my assistant coach, 'I cannot handle this guy.' " He feels Hill gave Richardson special treatment. "It was the NBA mentality, where the superstar has the power to get the coach fired. But I cannot accept that. I said to myself, 'If you must go, you must go in a way that you can respect yourself.' So I told Micheal what he must do, which was doing the hard jobs and not only scoring points. After a few days I benched him during a game because he was playing lazy. After the game I told him in front of the other players, 'Micheal, I've got a master's degree in business. I can coach junior teams in Italy for the rest of my life, because I'm very well respected for this job. I don't live to be a head coach in A-1. So either it's my way or, hey, no problem—they will fire me, and there will be another one, and you will be in the same situation. You will probably need to fire the second one, and then the third. So it's up to you.' I was not bluffing. I was telling him the truth. Micheal understood, and from that point on he had a terrific season. We won the Italy Cup and Cup of Cups, I became a famous coach, blah blah blah."

Enter drugs.

Messina says he knows Michael Micheal was clean during his first two seasons because Knorr had to test him every week and send monthly reports to FIBA, the international basketball federation. After that, apparently, Micheal was on his own. It wouldn't have been hard to work around the league's random testing system: one player from each team is tested after every game.

No one knows when Micheal started using cocaine again. Roberto Brunamonti says Micheal's play was up and down that third year and his moods changed frequently and unpredictably—but, Roberto adds, Micheal had always been flighty, so you didn't necessarily suspect drugs.

Messina says that was the year Micheal angered his teammates by skipping an Italy Cup game. It was the year Micheal was suspended for five games for fighting. Erratic behavior.

"And he had the first serious injury of his career," Messina says. "I think he started to see, 'Hey, I'm not invulnerable, I'm not Superman.' This put pressure on him, because Micheal can make a living only out of basketball. He doesn't have anything else. And he has big financial problems—two divorced wives, plus he's got holes in his hands, as we say in Italy. What he gets, he spends."

Messina didn't want him back the next season. "At the end of the year I told him, 'Micheal Ray, I don't think you're in the kind of shape we need you to be in. If it's up to me, I don't know if you'll be here next year.'

"I wanted to get Pace Mannion to replace him, but our president extended Micheal's contract. I said, 'Okay, fine, I'll stick with Micheal Ray.' I like Micheal Ray, even though I had my doubts about how much he could help us."

What actually happened when Micheal came back to Italy in late summer of 1991 depends on whom you ask.

According to Messina, Micheal needed to have a medical checkup, including a drug screen, before the team departed for ten days of preseason training in the mountains. "The first two days, Micheal called in with excuses. Then, right before we go to the mountains, he gets tested. Ten days pass, we come back from the mountains and go to a tournament, and then we get the news that Micheal tested positive for drugs even before we went to the mountains. Then Micheal goes back to America, saying he's getting divorced from his wife—like he does during every training camp—and when he comes back the club tests him again, and he's positive again."

Knorr fired him.

But it wasn't as simple as saying, *Ciao*, Micheal Ray.

Micheal got together with agent "Lucky" Luciano Capicchioni of the International Basketball Center in San Marino. Capicchioni, no doubt with an eye to picking up a lucrative client, overlooked Micheal's track record and went about proving . . . well, he didn't prove anything (or disprove Knorr's charges), but he hired some lawyers and threatened a lawsuit if Knorr didn't pay off Micheal's new seven-hundred-thousand-dollar contract. Micheal's side claimed that there hadn't been two witnesses present for either test, that the tests weren't analyzed in a proper lab, that the results were tampered with, etc. On top of that, Micheal claimed he'd flunked the second test due to some medication he'd been given while having some dental work done during that trip back to the States.

It sounded like chest-pounding and bullshit. Surely Micheal didn't want to open up a lawsuit that, no matter how it turned out, would have brought his drug problems into the open yet again. A suit would have been unpleasant for everyone.

What Micheal's side wanted from Knorr, in exchange for not suing for the seven hundred thousand dollars, was a public admission that OK, maybe the tests hadn't been administered properly, and maybe the dentist back in the States *had* given Micheal some painkiller that showed up as illicit

Teammates Dino Meneghin and Mike D'Antoni led Tracer Milan to the Grand Slam in 1987 and dominated Italian basketball through much of the eighties. (G. Palladino)

League PR Director Alberto Bortolotti and Executive Secretary Daniela Pazzelli helped me get settled and made me feel like a welcome friend my entire time in Italy.

Greg "Cadillac" Anderson and Tellis Frank, two members of the ever-changing cast of *stranieri,* check out stats in the *International Herald Tribune* and think about getting back to the NBA.

After fourteen seasons in the NBA, Darryl Dawkins found a second basketball life and happiness in Italy. Still known for his monster slam-dunks, he's also loved for his generosity and sense of humor.

(Robbie Dawkins)

Up-and-coming coach Ettore Messina spoke perfect English and quoted the sages while leading his Knorr Bologna team to the *scudetto* (the league championship).

(Gabriele Guerra)

Knorr's Roberto Brunamonti, a fourteen-year veteran of the national team, is highly respected throughout Italy—as a player, but even more so as a man.

(Roberto Serra)

Alberto Bortolotti (seated, third on the right) introduced me to some traveling Knorr Bologna fans before a game in Rimini.

What Toni Kukoc lacked in off-the-court charisma, he made up for with his fine passing and keen basketball sense. He is now a member of the Chicago Bulls, and time will tell if he can become a winner in the NBA.

(Gabriele Guerra)

Many think that Serbian star Predrag "Sasha" Danilovic (5), here stalking Benetton's Terry Teagle, has the *grandi coglioni* to make it in the NBA.

(Roberto Serra)

Carlton Myers is perhaps the most talented of the young Italian players, but nobody knows whether he'll be able to translate that talent into success.

(Anne-Marie Capicchioni)

Micheal Ray Richardson came to Italy in his prime and wowed the Italian fans, but sadly his problems seem to have followed him across the Atlantic.

(Roberto Serra)

At forty-three, Dino Meneghin (11), now playing for Stefanel Trieste, is still making his teammates better and has left no doubt that he is truly a *campione*.

(Arturo Presotto)

"The Great Oscar Schmidt" of Brazil, the Italian league's perennial scoring champion, is still making his living by shooting every chance he gets.

(Gabriele Guerra)

Superagent (and former *lega* superstar) Mark Crow now plays matchmaker for dozens of players and teams across Europe.

Kenny "Sky" Walker made a short stopover in Fabriano and dazzled the crowd with his NBA athleticism, but when the team's fortunes didn't change he was soon released.

(Andrea Fabi)

During his short appearance in Italy, Chris Corchiani led Benetton Treviso to the *Coppa Italia*, but he and his teammates fell short in the league finals.

(*Il Giganti* Magazine)

By April, Lou Colabello, the American-born team manager of Telemarket Forli, and I were having our Monday morning gab sessions—about players, teams, and his precarious fate—on the beach.

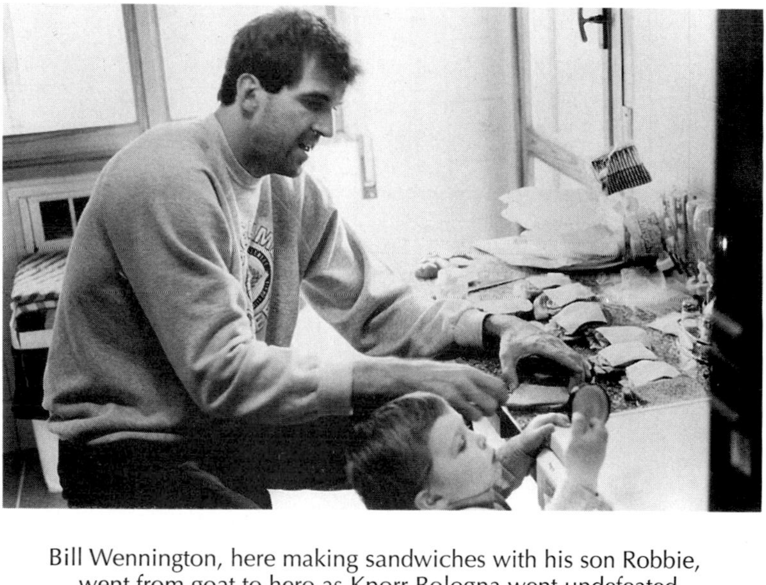

Bill Wennington, here making sandwiches with his son Robbie, went from goat to hero as Knorr Bologna went undefeated throughout the playoffs.

Brunamonti (seated) and Messina outside Benso, Roberto's restaurant, the night Knorr won the *scudetto*. (Gianluigi Zanni)

Mike and Laurel D'Antoni after the big win in Treviso. Their friendship, along with that of Ettore Messina, Lou Colabello, Mark Crow, and Alberto Bortolotti, made me feel like a member of the Italian basketball family.

drugs, and so on. Micheal just wanted to find somewhere else to play.

Knorr went along. What did they care, as long as Micheal was gone and they were free of his contract?

Capicchioni found Micheal a job for that '91–'92 season with Toni Kukoc's former club, Jugoplastika, in Yugoslavia.

This season he's got him back in Italy, with Baker (a rum company) Livorno. Earning around a half million dollars, Micheal is a lucrative client for Capicchioni and IBC.

And even as he closes in on thirty-eight—and looks forty-eight—he's too much for even the top players over here, and he simply toys with everyone else.

I'm thinking, Maybe Micheal will *want* to talk. Surely he knows his name is mud in the States; maybe he'll jump at the chance to tell his side.

Capicchioni calls ahead and lets him know I'm okay.

Micheal's new Italian bride answers the phone when I call. When Micheal comes on he's warm and friendly, seemingly eager to make a good impression. He's easy about getting together over in Livorno, any time I want to make the considerable trip.

At two in the morning a few days later there's a storm blowing off the sea and whipping me with the cold rain as I wait for the last bus to Rimini station, where it's an hour's wait for the train to Livorno (via Bologna and Pisa). When the train comes it's jam-packed—at three-thirty in the morning, packed! Dead on my feet, I squeeze into the space at the end of the car, jammed in with a couple of dozen others, miserable and asking myself why I'm going through this.

But that's easy: *Micheal Ray!*

There's a stop in Bologna; it's cold, my bones ache, I can't keep my eyes open. *Micheal Ray!* I suffer through the couple of hours to Pisa, where I wait some more, keeping myself awake with espressos in the near-empty station bar at dawn, my senses gone haywire like when I used to work the graveyard shift. *Micheal Ray! Sugar! One of the greatest guards who ever came into the League!*

I feel bad for Micheal, somehow. Maybe it's the way he sounded on the phone, with the stammer and the eager-to-please tone. He sounded like a nice guy, a guy who maybe just didn't have too much upstairs and never got much guidance. His being a nice guy makes his ruined NBA career and his other problems even sadder to me.

No, I don't mind coming so far and being so miserable to see Micheal. That is, I wouldn't mind coming so far *if Micheal were home*.

I start calling at 9:00 sharp, the appointed time, from the Livorno station. No answer. I dial Micheal's mother-in-law's number in Bologna; no answer. Over and over. I'm exhausted, it's cold in the station, there's loud construction work going on. I remind myself, *Micheal Ray!* But now it's more like, *Micheal Ray #$%&**@!!*

But maybe it's my fault. Something must have come up and, as I don't have a phone and didn't think to give Micheal a message number, he didn't know how to reach me.

After two hours of fruitless calls and a lot of swearing to myself I locate Alberto in Bologna, who within an hour gets Micheal's cellular phone number for me. I sigh relief. Micheal probably just forgot me, but he's probably nearby.

Well, not exactly. While I've come from the east coast to the west, Micheal is in *Trieste*—up in the northeast corner of Italy, bordering the former Yugoslavia! "Our owner lives up here," he explains. "I came up here to sign a contract for next year."

Well, *bravo!* But how about me?

"W-w-w-w-w-wait, w-w-w-w-w-wait," Micheal says, cleverly sensing I'm put out. I still feel bad for him about the stammer, but now it makes him sound guilty instead of eager to please. "L-l-l-l-l-look, can you w-w-w-w-w-wait? I'm drivin' back in a half hour, I'll be there by four. I got practice at six, but we can spend that time together."

Well, I don't want to make this trip again.

I go out for lunch. Walk the streets of little Livorno. Get caught out in the rain. Shiver in the train station some more.

Four o'clock, he's still not home. I call him on his cellular again. Micheal says he's up in the mountains somewhere, caught in a snowstorm. I guess it's possible, but Micheal's stammering badly, he's not apologetic, he's nothing like the warm, welcoming guy I talked to the other day. I don't get it.

But I've had it, I'm catching the next train home. "I'll call you some other time, Micheal."

"W-w-w-w-w-wait." Guilt seems to be getting to him. "You live near Bologna? I've got Monday off, we're goin' to Bologna after the game Sunday to stay with my wife's mother. Call me there Tuesday morning at nine or so, and we can get together for a couple of hours before I go back to Livorno."

"Gotcha. Tuesday morning. Your mother-in-law's." Simple.

If only Micheal were in Bologna on Tuesday morning.

I get up early and take the 7 A.M. train so I'll be there in time to call Micheal at 9:00. I arrive at 8:30, buy the *Herald Tribune* and *USA Today*, kill time until straight-up 9:00, then dial his mother-in-law's number.

No answer.

I dial his number in Livorno, knowing *this* time he'll answer, and he does. "Oh," he says, recognizing my voice. "Uhhhhhh . . ."

"Did you forget we were gonna meet today? In Bologna?"

"Uhhhhhh, weeeeee . . ." he stammers, and then the rest rushes out, "didngotoBologna. Uhhhhhh . . ." and he hesitates forever, thinking hard, before finally offering, "my little girl wasn't feelin' well."

I thought up better lies when I was in the third grade—like, "The dog ate my homework." And I probably pulled them off more convincingly.

I don't get it. I'm even more baffled when, on top of this, Micheal says he'll be staying in Bologna after Baker plays Knorr on Saturday night, and if I call him on Sunday morning, we should be able to get together that afternoon.

Weird dude. Maybe I'll call, maybe not. I'm losing interest in Micheal Ray.

Messina's not surprised I got stood up again. "Micheal always does that. If he doesn't want to do something, he just won't be there; then he'll make up some bullshit excuse."

The Baker-Knorr game marks the return to the Palasport of the most sensational player Bologna ever had.

"Shoo-guh! Shoo-guh! Shoo-guh!" The fans react the moment the Baker club jogs out of the tunnel for warm-ups. Micheal, with the obligatory diamond in his left ear and a lopsided grin on his face, waves in all directions. He recognizes some people behind the basket and gives them a thumbs-up. Darryl Dawkins, who's come up from Forli to watch his old pal from the Nets—stylin' in a brown suit, shiny black loafers, and a tan overcoat, with heavy gold on his wrists and fingers—walks down to courtside and the two embrace briefly and chat for a minute.

Oh, the talent. Micheal will be thirty-eight next month, but you can still see the talent. During layup lines, just for fun, he throws bounce passes way out in front of his teammates, but with such spin and such precision that when the ball hits the floor it comes back toward the receiver and, invariably, right into his hands. Just to make warm-ups more interesting.

He gets a big ovation when the lineups are announced and he comes out looking rambunctious. On defense he's all over Danilovic, who's getting his first dose of NBA strength and athleticism; Sasha's first shot hits the side of the backboard. On offense Micheal glides downcourt with the ball, calling to mind Scottie Pippen as he effortlessly swallows up ground, gliding yet threatening to burst into overdrive—but this time he just pulls up, as if overdrive is too much work, and flicks in a soft three-pointer. The next time he drives to his left, draws three defenders, and then slings some kind of near–physically impossible backhand pass out to the right.

He repeatedly backs defenders toward the basket, then wheels into the lane to draw fouls. He's even controlling the boards, soaring right over seven-footers Wennington and Binelli to snap down rebounds. Impressive. He reminds you how incredibly good NBA players are.

And he reminds you what a sad case he is. He coulda been somebody.

Baker Livorno pulls ahead of first-place Knorr. Micheal backs Danilovic into the lane, turns, and pops an NBA fade-away jumper right in his face.

As Darryl said, Micheal's hyperactive, laughing and chattering and capering so much you wonder if he's hallucinating. In the second half he's in a manic little scene with Carera, Knorr's brawny reserve center: elbows fly, then they're nose to nose, jawing for about three seconds before Micheal abruptly spins away and bursts out laughing; he does a quick turn around the key, looking like a guy on one of those speedy old movie clips, and then he's right back in Carera's face—but grinning now, and cuffing Carera lightly, affectionately on the side of the head. Nutty.

He lofts in another three-pointer.

He keeps embarrassing Knorr's big men by outjumping them for offensive rebounds. He grabs another one, starts to dribble out, but suddenly snaps a left-hand bounce pass to a teammate cutting down the lane. Talent.

But fatigue starts to show. Nearly thirty-eight years old, Micheal plays every minute, does everything, and with eight minutes to go he's walking the ball up the floor. Finally he's too tired to do anything but put up long jump shots—more like set shots, actually, at this point. By any name, they're not going in. Knorr fights back and finally ties the score with :06 remaining. With the Forever Boys hanging over the railings howling, Micheal takes the inbound and gets across half-court in plenty of time, but he simply doesn't have the energy to go to the hoop for the winning basket or a foul. He hoists another bomb—*clang!* Overtime.

Knorr takes a one-point lead down to the end of OT.

Micheal comes down with a few seconds left, last chance, win or lose. But this time he dishes off to number 18, a kid named Lauro Bon, who lets go a twenty-footer that's perfect. Knorr doesn't have time to get another shot. Upset!

Micheal's beside himself, like Jim Valvano after N.C. State's NCAA championship in 1983, racing around the court, leaping in the air. He runs to the courtside railing stabbing a we're-number-one finger in the air, then whirls around and runs to hug Lauro Bon.

The Bologna crowd watches, stunned. The Knorr players, wandering off the floor, look stunned.

Micheal bounds around some more, celebrating with his teammates. He got tired and tailed off at the end of the game, but hey, he's almost thirty-eight, and he came in here with a crummy team and played the entire forty-five minutes, handling the ball all the way, scoring 32 points and collecting 15 rebounds. And his crummy team beat mighty Knorr, the team that threw him away. No wonder he's ecstatic.

But it gets even better for Micheal. As he and his teammates finally start toward the tunnel, the fans, who've been screaming for Knorr all night, break into a huge ovation, chanting "Shoo-guh! Shoo-guh! Shoo-guh!" For an instant Micheal looks surprised, then he pauses just long enough to wave in all directions and blow some kisses and jab that index finger in the air again before disappearing as if swallowed up in the roar and the affection of the thousands who loved him for three great years.

Many of them still believe their Sugar got a bum deal from Knorr, got run out of town on bogus charges because Messina didn't like him or Cazzola, the owner, didn't want to pay him, or whatever. All they know is that the club accused Sugar of using drugs, then backed off when he threatened to sue them.

Here's what they don't know.

Regardless of whether Micheal was medicated by a dentist

in Arizona back in August of 1991, regardless of whether the two drug screens were administered properly, and regardless of what he says publicly, Micheal admitted to Messina that he *was* using drugs.

"He came to me after testing positive and said, 'Yes, I took it, I made a mistake, please help me.' So I know what happened."

And yet, Messina says, when Micheal came to Bologna with Jugoplastika for a Euroclub Championship game last season, a few months after Knorr let him go, he carried on for the fans as if Knorr, and Messina, had done him dirt.

"He played the role of the betrayed. He doesn't shake my hand, he wears a nasty face. He scores a basket and runs by our bench and yells something at me—for the benefit of everyone else—then, when he comes by our bench to take the ball out of bounds one time, he turns to me and goes like this [a wink and a smile]. So I understood that he was playing this role.

"And earlier this season we played in Livorno, and after the game Micheal comes to me in the locker room, with all the players, and he embraces me, shakes my hand, blah blah blah. So no problem. He knows what happened, I know what happened."

Only the fans don't.

Per Micheal's instructions, I call him at his mother-in-law's place on Sunday morning. (From Riccione. I'm not the smartest guy in the world, but I'm learning.)

Micheal says he'll be in Bologna all day and doesn't have much to do. I wouldn't say he's friendly, but it seems like he'll be compliant if I'm nice. That's all I want.

When he asks what time I want to meet, I leave it up to him. "I can get to Bologna anytime. Just tell me what's convenient for you."

Inexplicably he turns impatient: "How long is this gonna take?"

I'm impatient too—I've been blown off by this idiot all over Italy, and now he's worried about keeping it short when we do meet—but I have to be polite: Micheal is the star. "Look, I'll accommodate you. I'll meet you whenever you can meet, for as long as you'll give me. Just tell me." But I can't help adding testily, "If you don't want to do it at all, we can just skip it."

It's just what Micheal wanted to hear. He considers for a short moment, then says, "W-w-w-w-well then, m-m-m-m-maybe I'll just pass on it."

Fine. I hardly care anymore.

A few weeks later, Capicchioni tells me Micheal lost interest in doing an interview because I never said anything about paying him.

Which, however, still doesn't explain his jerking me around.

For one irritating moment, it's like I'm back covering the NBA.

"Killer Myers"

Everyone here laments the lack of new Italian stars. Greats like Renato Villalta and Pierluigi Marzorati have recently retired; Meneghin, Brunamonti, and Magnifico are near the end.

The great hope is a kid named Carlton Myers, who lives with his mother just up the beach from me in Rimini and plays just down the beach for Scavolini Pesaro.

No, he's not pure Italian. His mother is, but his father, who's apparently no longer in the picture, was a black sax player from the island of St. Vincent in the West Indies, and Myers lived in London until the age of ten. But he is an Italian citizen, he came up through the Rimini *società*, he'll play for the national team. And many people believe he'll be the first Italian in the NBA.

Thursday evening, December 10, I take the twenty-minute train ride down to Pesaro to watch him in a Euroclub Championship game against Maccabi Tel Aviv. I've already seen him a couple of times, but I'm meeting with him tomorrow, and maybe he'll do something tonight that will be worth talking about.

It wouldn't be a first. In November alone he hit three last-second, game-winning shots. Last week, a few days after he beat the Spanish team on Thanksgiving night in the game we watched in Mike D'Antoni's den, his picture was on the cover of *Super Basket*—a circle around his face, giant letters saying WANTED and a headline talking about LA SINDROME DEL KILLER MYERS spreading through Europe.

Even before his recent triumphs, there was lots of talk about him. I heard about him in *Street and Smith's Pro Basketball* preseason issue: "A sure player to be taken in the 1993 NBA draft is 6'7" Carlton Myers, an athletic, strong, 21-year-old who is the son of an American GI and an Italian woman." (Myers is actually 6'2", and they're all wrong about his father, but who's quibbling, except maybe his father and NBA scouts?)

I figure Myers must be feeling pretty good about himself, and sure enough, from the moment Scavolini takes the floor his every move says, "People, you're looking at 'the Man,' 'the Killer.' " When the team comes out and huddles at the foul line, then waves to the crowd, Myers brings up the rear; as I'll note at every Scavolini game I see, he doesn't join his teammates in the huddle, doesn't acknowledge the fans.

His affected cool positively screams *Look! Check out the Killer!* During warm-ups, out near midcourt by himself, he does this self-conscious, super-slow-motion behind-the-back and between-the-legs dribbling; it's obvious that he's doing it slow so that he won't bounce it off his foot, and *exaggeratedly* slow so that you'll realize he *means* to be doing it slow, the implication being that he *could* make like Isiah Thomas anytime he wants. During layup lines he flips up pointless underhand slop, looking more at the crowd than at the basket, and occasionally stops at the railing to chat with an acquaintance.

When they start shooting he's just as casual: idling around, occasionally taking a little hop off one foot and heaving a long one-hander from his shoulder, nothing resembling a shot he'd take in a game. Now a left-handed hook from three-point land. Who needs practice? I imagine he thinks this is how the big NBA stars do it.

I remember Larry Bird, two hours before a game, alone on the court with a ball boy, shooting; Drazen Petrovic when he arrived in Portland, out there alone before and after every practice, one perfectly formed jump shot after another.

While it's clear, once the action starts, that he's got extraordinary speed and leaping ability, it's just as obvious that Myers is lacking in fundamentals. Going to his right with the ball, he can jet past a defender, but he can barely bounce the ball with his left hand. Defense? As the famous coach Sandro Gamba tells me later, "Carlton needs to read the book from the first page. On defense his team plays four-against-five."

Much of this is correctable, of course, and Myers certainly has the talent. More problematic is his lack of instinct, court awareness, basketball sense. It's a common problem in Italy, where *basket* isn't taught to kids in school and even many of the pros didn't start playing until their early teens.

Myers didn't start until he was fourteen. Then, in junior ball and with Marr Rimini, first in Series "B" and last season in A-2, he managed to dominate with his individual skills and rarely concerned himself with the other four guys on his side. He's fast and explosive, he can flash past his man—going right—or stop on a dime and float up, up, up for a jumper, as he did on all three game-winners, but his game is almost totally solo. It's handy when his team needs someone to create a shot in a few seconds, as at the end of those three games last month, but the rest of the time his teammates too often stand around looking frustrated while Myers tries to beat his man. At this point he lacks the vision, the sense of the whole game, to make his move and then hit a teammate going to the hoop.

Previous coaches bear some responsibility in this. Telemarket Forli head coach Piero Pasini, who was in Rimini the past two years and on the one hand remarks, "Carlton speaks only to the basket," also tells of isolating Myers and his defender in a "B" game and watching him score 21 points in three minutes. Contrast that to Dean Smith checking

Michael Jordan at North Carolina: Jordan never averaged 21 per *game*, but went away knowing not only how to play with others but how to share the glory.

Despite his heroics in a few recent games, Myers is hardly money in the bank. Tonight he blows past his hapless defender, soars, and slams a dunk over the *pivot*—then, encouraged, dribbles into three defenders the next time and gets his shot smacked into the seats. He hits one of his effortless jump shots—getting clear, rising, hanging there endlessly like Jordan before finally letting it go—then, next time, forces up an off-balance rock that almost cracks the backboard. He pushes the ball up, gives it to a teammate on the wing, bolts to the hoop and takes a return pass—and blows the layup. His quickness lets him steal the ball once in a while, but mostly he's lost on defense. He's a mixed blessing.

But he's young. He's got time to harness the wildness. Maybe he can learn, as Pasini says, to play *with* other good players.

And as Ettore Messina says, "He's surely got the balls to do something when it's important in the game."

The problem for Myers—and so for the whole *basket* world, in particular incoming national-team coach Messina—is that at twenty-one he's already earning four hundred thousand dollars a year and driving an eighty-thousand-dollar car and wearing diamonds in his ear. His picture is on the cover of national magazines. His game has huge flaws, but where will he find the motivation to improve?

"The young players here make money and are treated like superstars since they were sixteen," says Dino Meneghin, "so they think that basketball is work: 'They pay me this, I do this.' Only a few have heart."

"Dino Meneghin," Rudy Hackett says, "is the role model that Italian players should follow, but they don't. They don't want to put themselves through that mental and physical stress. The people you're asking to do that, they feel they've already made it. These days a kid can come off a junior team and make thirty thousand dollars right off the bat, seventeen years old, and he can't run up and down the court and put the ball in the basket."

Many people believe the lack of motivation in Italian players is inherent in Italian life. "You notice that Italian teams often win the game they're supposed to lose and then lose the game they're supposed to win," Ettore Messina says. "It's the mentality. In our lives, with the sun, the beach, the good food . . . many times, what you can do today you can probably do tomorrow. So you say, 'Okay, let's do it tomorrow.' It's very difficult to say, 'No, we must do it today.'

"I grew up playing on the playground in the snow, like you probably did in America. But it's changed in Italy in the last ten years, because people have had more money. Kids in Italy never play playground ball. The only basketball they play is from five to seven every day with a coach, a system, an organization—not because they really have fun. It's like a job for them, even the junior players. That's the biggest problem we have."

"Basketball over here is not a street sport," Hackett says. "You don't have kids growing up with that spirit to compete. In America, sports is confrontation. It's competition: you against me. They don't have that here. When kids go out to the playground they don't go out to face a challenge, they go out to run around and joke and have a good time. They don't play competitively; they don't know what it is to go out and try to be better than someone else on the basketball court. And if you don't have that, if you're never confronted not only with an opponent but with yourself, how can you improve? But kids here don't put themselves under that kind of pressure."

"We need more talent," Mike D'Antoni sums up. "One of the league's biggest problems is that there are too many guys who can't play. There's no fear factor in the system. There's no Italian with even a little talent who's afraid of losing his job. One team might let him go, but someone will buy him.

So there's no call to improve, to work extra, to go home and maybe think about how you can do a better job. Because you're gonna make your money for the next ten or fifteen years, as long as you stay healthy."

Making the NBA would seem to be Myers's only real motivation to improve. Many people here, blinded by his remarkable quickness and spring, believe he can make it if he wants.

Personally, I can't envision Myers in the NBA. First, he's a spindly 6'2" shooting guard who isn't a great shooter and clearly isn't obsessed with becoming one. Even Rudy Hackett, who can picture Myers in the League, adds the little qualifier that Myers will probably have to learn to play point guard to make it, which to me is as inconceivable as asking a pitcher breaking into the major leagues to play third base and hit home runs instead. A guy with such striking tunnel vision and such a lust to score, suddenly becoming a distributor?

Then there's the toughness issue. In the Euroclub game against Maccabi I saw Carlton catch a little bump on the chin that wouldn't even qualify as a love-tap in the NBA, but for the next fifteen minutes, even when the ball was in play, he made a show of tenderly touching his chin and lips over and over, looking at his fingers each time as if he expected to see blood (or, more accurately, as if he wanted the crowd to believe he'd been hit so hard that he expected to see blood). He might as well have held up a sign declaring, HERO! PLAYING IN PAIN! He's got no idea that in the NBA, if you show 'em they've hurt you a little they'll whack you twice as hard the next time.

Nonetheless, Brad Greenberg of the Trail Blazers assures me Myers will be drafted next summer. Even if he's not, Myers's agent, Antonio "Toto" Ricciotti of International Management Group, talks of sending him to some NBA summer camp for the experience.

Larry Middleton, an excellent guard in Italy who finds Myers "full of himself" and remarks, "I brought him down a little—I think I scored thirty-five on him," thinks Myers would be overwhelmed among hungry American rookies and free agents. "Physically they would destroy him. I haven't seen him respond very well to being hit. He's a great finesse player, but contact is a big part of the game in the United States now. In the States, who plays with finesse anymore?"

Others are cynical about the idea of Myers's going to an NBA camp at all. "Bullshit," says Mike D'Antoni, though he's a friend of Ricciotti, the agent. "That's an agent talking. Myers can't play in the NBA."

As the season progresses, I keep hearing and seeing things about Myers that turn me off.

The man who drives Marr's team bus says that one day Carlton, driving his Mercedes in Rimini, spotted the bus, cut in front of it, and stopped in the middle of the street and sat there. Finally the driver got out of the bus, pissed—at which point Carlton flipped him and his former teammates the finger and sped off.

I see him saunter out when Scavolini takes the court, not deigning to huddle with his teammates at the foul line or acknowledge the crowd.

I see the absurd pregame routine, which always reminds me of Oscar Robertson saying, "I never take a shot in practice that I wouldn't take in a game"—because Myers doesn't take a shot he *would* take in a game; it's all thirty-five-foot hook shots and dipsy-doos.

Myers's teammates aren't enchanted either. "A nice person," point guard Haywoode Workman tells me, "but a very selfish player. When he gets the ball he wants to shoot, that's all. He wants the fame. A couple of games, I stopped passing him the ball.

"He's only twenty-one and he's got the world—the Italian world. But he doesn't know how to be humble enough to get more. He only thinks about himself. Against Fabriano, [coach Alberto] Bucci took me and Pete [Myers, Scavolini's other *straniero*] out at the end and left Carlton in with two subs and two junior players. And Carlton shoots the ball every time! I'm on the bench yelling, 'Carlton, give the kids some shots!'—they never get to play, they only practice. But no way. He wants to get nineteen points, keep his average up."

It turns into a rough season for Myers. No more game-winning shots. In fact, so much erratic play and forced action, so many turnovers and unconscionable shots that, in two consecutive games against Knorr in February, coach Bucci harangues him during late time-outs and then keeps the erstwhile Killer on the bench. In the second game, Bucci has to put him back in with a minute left when someone fouls out, and as Myers takes the court Bucci is screaming after him and jabbing his index finger at his temple as if to say, Play smart!

Myers complains in the *Gazzetta dello Sport* that Bucci doesn't get him enough shots. The fact is, Myers has been shooting poorly, and the day after he puts himself on the spot with his comments in the *Gazzetta* he goes 2-for-14.

Scavolini, a perennially strong team that played Benetton for the championship last season—with Darren Daye instead of Myers—hovers a little over .500, the most unpredictable club in the league. They beat powerful Knorr three straight times, including Euroclub games, but lose to various doormats. Myers is a big reason for their fits and starts.

Messina, who in December is chosen to take over the national team next summer, tells me, "Carlton is surely blessed, and he could be very important to the national team. Or he could be my biggest problem. But," he adds, "I'll have three or four players who can do what he can do, so if he doesn't play with the team, I won't use him."

Certainly, Myers's judgment and sense of team play don't improve over the season. Even his former coach, Pasini, who loves him, says, "If he passes the ball and his teammate doesn't score, he won't pass to him again," and sums up this way: "The duel with the basket is still too important to Carlton."

Myers is indisputably the most gifted of young Italian players—many say the most gifted ever. The NBA isn't out of the realm of possibility, and it's easy to picture him dominating in Italy for years. If he improves his shooting, learns to beat his man going left as well as right and, most important, to deliver the ball to open teammates after he attracts two or three defenders, he could control games at the offensive end. He could lead the league in scoring *and* assists.

He could play a big part in bringing the national team back to the Olympics in 1996.

Could. Could. Could.

Italy's *basket* world is watching and waiting. It's never had one like the Killer.

I Say a Little Prayer

I spend the week before Christmas with the D'Antonis. Mike and Laurel are gracious hosts again, though Mike is consumed by his team's struggles. Philips has lost twice more since I was here at Thanksgiving, and after that 6–0 start now stands just 7–6.

The papers, melodramatic as ever, are saying that Mike is *rischiare la panchina*—"risking the bench," which apparently means his job might be in jeopardy—and that if he were anyone but Mike D'Antoni, a Milan monument, he'd be gone already.

It gets worse. On Sunday, December 20, Philips loses to Knorr Bologna—a tough overtime loss to the top team in the league, but a loss just the same. In a couple of days we're heading up to Treviso for Philips's Wednesday game against last year's champions, Benetton, with Toni Kukoc and Terry Teagle.

Mike's getting desperate. He barely touches his food at the Torchietto after the Knorr game, and though it's well past midnight by the time we leave he asks the broadcaster Flavio Tranquillo, a confidant, to come back to the apartment to talk about *stranieri* who might be a suitable replacement for Djordjevich, the point guard who has been disappointing both in his play and in his leadership. Since Mike is naturally thinking about Americans, I'm not sure what he wants with Flavio; I know Flavio is an expert on the NBA, but the only players who'll be available to Mike are *obscure* Americans.

At home Mike brings out a list of the current CBA rosters and Rick Barry's annual book of player analyses and starts tossing out names. It's instantly obvious why he wanted Flavio. Ricky Blanton, a former LSU player who's in the CBA? He can play number three or number four in Italy, Flavio says. (Mike's thinking of making Portaluppi, a reserve, the starting point guard, and filling Djordjevich's roster spot with a big guy.) Blanton, Flavio says, can do this for you, can't do that. Irving Thomas? Flavio's got the word on Thomas. Ron Grandison. This guy, that guy, guys I've never heard of, Flavio knows 'em. This one rebounds but can't shoot. That one shoots but can't rebound. One plays good *D*, nothing else. Another is smart but slow. This guy's a head case, that's why he's not in the NBA. Amazing.

"Flavio," I ask, "how do you know all these guys?"

"It's a sickness," he joshes, pleased. "No, really, I just try to follow the CBA. I see a few games when I go to the States, I have a few tapes sent to me."

"*CBA* tapes?"

"I told you, I'm sick."

Mike finally lets him go around 2 A.M., then tries calling a couple of agents in the States to find out who's available. Can't reach anyone, but it's just as well, he says, because agents are more interested in getting one of their players a job—and getting themselves a commission—than in helping Mike D'Antoni find just the right player for Philips Milano. He needs to talk to one of his NBA player-personnel connections, the Milwaukee Bucks' Lee Rose or the Trail Blazers' Brad Greenberg. He tries Rose, can't get him.

By the time we finally call it a night he's saying, "You know, we really didn't play all that bad today, considering. We're not that far away."

He's right. There are no dominating teams here, not even

Knorr, and with one more good player Philips is competitive with anyone. Stand pat, though, and they'll go on struggling and wind up around .500.

The lega has scheduled a full slate of games for Wednesday, December 23, so that the Christmas weekend is cleared for everyone—a noticeably humanistic touch to an American accustomed to hearing NBA players gripe about having to travel or play a game or at least work out on Christmas Day.

Tuesday morning, Laurel and I take off in the D'Antoni's Saab for Treviso, a town of eighty-five thousand about two hundred miles due east, twelve miles north of Venice. We're invited to lunch out at La Ghirada, the Benetton sports complex, with Benetton general manager Maurizio Gherardini. Mike and the team are practicing in Milan this morning and coming over later on the Philips bus.

After checking in at the Hotel Al Fogher, we drive out to La Ghirada. It's impressive, created out of the vast fortune of the three brothers Benetton: apartments for the players on the Benetton junior basketball, volleyball, and soccer teams; outdoor basketball and volleyball courts; a soccer field; a merchandise store; a restaurant where we enjoy a splendid lunch. This is the other end of the spectrum from the clubs that play in ancient gyms and don't pay their players.

Wednesday afternoon, December 23, while Mike and the team eat their pregame meal and relax at the hotel, Laurel and I take the short train ride down to otherworldly Venice. Come out of the station, walk down the steps, and there's the water—the Grand Canal. Not a car to be seen, not a *street*, just gondolas and light boats and big flat-bottomed water-buses trafficking up and down the canal. We hire a private boat—a "taxi"—and head for St. Mark's Square, a bracing wind in our faces as the driver speeds us along under the bridges, past gondolas parked at doorsteps, past centuries-old palaces and apartments and museums, pointing out where Casanova and Mozart and Marco Polo lived and where Lord Byron died. We see the vendors around St. Mark's and the famous pigeons in the square, stroll through the narrow alleys, have pasta and wine in a little family restaurant and Drambuie and espresso in Hemingway-famous Harry's Bar. Before heading back we seek out the Bridge of Sighs, where women used to pray for their husbands imprisoned in the jail, and Laurel offers a little prayer for her man and Philips Milano.

Maybe the prayer helps. Maybe it's just that Mike benches Djordjevich in the second half of tonight's game and takes a chance with a new, smaller and quicker lineup to counter Benetton's superior size and talent. Either way, Philips mounts a tremendous comeback, with Ricardo Pittis repeatedly burning Kukoc down the stretch, and when Teagle misses at the buzzer the skid is over. Mike bolts from the floor as if the gods might change their minds if he sticks around to celebrate.

Laurel and I follow the team bus back to Milan and pick up Mike at the offices. We get back to the apartment at 2 A.M.—the twenty-fourth, Christmas Eve. Looking as if the weight of the world's been lifted from his shoulders, Mike changes into sweats and relaxes on the couch, cooing to his cat, Medea, while Laurel whips up some tuna pasta.

It feels like it's okay to show Mike the new *Il Gigante* I bought at the train station in Venice, the piece where his old pal Dino is telling what he would give various people for Christmas: "For Mike D'Antoni, five boxes of Valium, because the last few times I've seen him on TV he looks very agitated."

"Ho-ho, funny guy," Mike says, stroking Medea and showing a bit of a smile, which is more than I've seen since my last visit.

But it's not as if he's won the championship. Though it's past three when we finish eating, and the D'Antonis are leaving in the morning for a couple of days in Monte Carlo, Mike settles on the couch with the CBA rosters and Rick Barry's book.

"We've gotta make the change. We're not that far away from bein' as good as anybody. Believe me, I feel bad for Sasha [Djordjevich]—I know from my NBA days what it's like to be strugglin'—but you see how he's playin'. We *gotta* do somethin'."

We kick around a few names, but after five or ten minutes, punchy, I say good-night.

Three minutes later, drifting off in my guest-room bed, I hear Mike down the hall calling Bob McAdoo in the States. On Christmas Eve last year McAdoo's wife Charlena, a great friend of the D'Antonis, died of cancer.

The next morning, after joining Mike for cappuccino as always, it's time for me to go. My bag is packed and waiting by the door, but I walk down to the guest room as if to check once more for anything I might have forgotten. I'm actually going to get Mike and Laurel's Christmas presents, which have been hidden under the bed since I arrived—a couple of Van Morrison CDs and Rosita Nicoletti's superb first book of photographs, *La Mia Riccione (My Riccione)*. I wanted to leave them in the living room or somewhere just before departing, unknown to the D'Antonis, so they wouldn't buy me something out of a sense of obligation.

It doesn't work. I make it back to the living room and slip the packages under the tree, but I haven't even straightened up when Laurel, as if she's been on to me all along, walks in with a long, narrow, gift-wrapped box in her hand.

"You're not so clever," she says. "I knew you'd do something. Now you take this."

All I can do is hug her and try, for a few seconds, to express my inexpressible gratitude for their friendship and generosity, before she tells me to hush and just make sure I stay in touch, let them know if they can help me in any way, and come again before too long.

• • •

Back in Riccione at mid-afternoon—glad to be home after almost a week away, and sleep-deprived—the first thing I do is call Alberto and tell him I'm going to decline his kind offer to come to Bologna tomorrow and celebrate *Natale* with him and Annarosa, his wife, and three-year-old Francesca and some of their relatives. Simply having been invited felt so good that whether I actually make it seems almost beside the point—though I should have expected it of Bortolo, who has taken me out with his friends, gone to games with me, had me over to the apartment for lunch, and who has in so many other ways far exceeded his professional duties to me. I regularly get choked up just thinking about his kindness.

Before leaving for Milan last week I was also invited to spend Christmas with my friend Elio and his family. Elio is the guy who ended up fixing my computer, at a shop right here in Riccione, after I couldn't get the job done in Rome on my ill-fated trip at Halloween. He's about thirty, a longhair with a scraggly beard whose few remaining teeth are black and crooked and clearly won't remain much longer. He spent two or three years in L.A. a while back, loves all things American, and was happy to meet someone he could speak English with. He's got tattoos and likes heavy metal music. He smokes cigarettes so nasty that in his car I have to hang my head out the window and at my apartment I ask him to smoke out on the balcony (and I'm *not* a Please-Don't-Smoke type), yet we've hit it off somehow. He often drops by around noon and takes me to eat lunch at the fast–Italian-food restaurant his wife, Roseanna, and her mother and brother operate. We hang out at their little apartment outside Riccione, where I play with little Stefano and Janis while Elio tries to get me interested in his myriad computer programs. Sometimes he drops over with the kids on a weekend, and after a quick whiskey over at the Savioli (soft drinks for Stefano and Janis) we take them down the street to the *sala giochi*—"room of games," literally, a video-game arcade like a million in the States.

I try calling him on Christmas Eve to let him know I'm

wiped out and intend to lie low for a couple of days, but no answer.

I awaken on Christmas morning (close to noon) to marvel yet again that I'm in Italy, with a contract to write a book, and that I can conceivably turn this into a writing career and a permanent breakaway from the drone's life. I can't help recalling all the Christmases during which I put in eight hours in one mental ward or another, as if it were any other day or night. Who would have even imagined this a year ago, when after working 11 P.M.–7 A.M. I spent the day alone in my apartment in Portland, crying in my beer over the fact that a year before *that*—a few days before I had my climactic fit and moved out—I was opening presents with my wife and stepdaughter, and my wife was laughing uncontrollably over Jay Leno's book of crazy newspaper headlines, and we had a great and happy meal, totally unaware that I'd be gone five days later and that we would never spend another holiday together, nor any other day or night.

Who would have dreamed, last Christmas, that I'd be in heaven when this one rolled around?

But I am.

Except that I'm alone.

Except that I'm *not*. Alberto said they'll have a place for me if I change my mind and decide to come. Elio and his family and relatives invited me. The first thing I saw when I got out of bed and walked out to the living room was the D'Antonis' gift sitting on the table. (It's an Armani tie; I guess Laurel doesn't realize I never wear a tie except at the occasional wedding or funeral. Maybe she envisions publishing parties and TV appearances in my future.) When I open my door, heading out for a walk, I find a box of chocolates from the Nicolettis.

Alone? No. Choked up again, is what I am.

Lou Colabello Sweats

With the second half of the regular season beginning on December 29, Telemarket Forli needs a win. They've lost their last five games and stand at 5–10, tied with Panna Firenze (Florence) for next-to-last in A-2—bad, because the two bottom teams at the end drop to Series "B" next season. Dropping from A-1 to A-2, as at least two teams—and usually several—do every year, is bad enough—you lose big sponsors, you probably won't get on TV, you get "footnote coverage" in the newspapers and magazines—but falling to Series "B" is disastrous.

Lou Colabello, Telemarket's team manager, is especially edgy. An hour before the game, gazing out at the empty court, he says softly, "If we don't win one soon, we'll all be out of a job. I've never been in a position where ten guys held my job in their hands."

His anxiety builds as tip-off approaches. "I've worked all my life to get a job like this, and now these ten guys have it in their hands."

I don't get it. "What are you talking about? A team loses a few games, they don't fire the team manager."

"Money, baby. If we drop to Series 'B' next year, which we're in serious danger of, they won't keep a team manager.

They've got a GM, they figure he can do what I do. I'll be back to scramblin'."

The last few days, Lou's been on the phone to the States. Giorgio Corbelli, the owner, has decided to dump Rob Lock, and Lou, the American, has been appointed to call agents, scouts, NBA execs, anyone who can tell him who's available and might be a fit. So far he's gotten a few disconnected numbers, some no-answers, and a lot of "Mr. West is out of town for the week" and "I'll have someone get back to you . . . you're in *Italy*, you say?"

So Lock will play tonight. His parents, visiting from California, are sitting in the second row near midcourt. Lou says they're leaving in a couple of days; he hopes they're gone before the ax falls on their boy.

Poor Lock. He's a good player, a 6'10" *pivot* who averaged 20 points a game the last three years in Pavia. No doubt he expected to be the big man here after Forli bought him last summer, but then Philips let Darryl Dawkins go and the starstruck Corbelli snapped him up. Lock became a forward in name but remained the back-to-the-basket inside player he's been all his life. He and Darryl get in each other's way. It doesn't work.

Of course, Telemarket could cut Darryl instead. He's not as mobile as Lock, not as versatile. He doesn't score as many points. Sure, he's the big bruiser, but Lock even gets a few more rebounds. But Darryl's got the big contract. Cut him and you've got to settle with him, plus pay a new player. You owe Lock too, but not nearly so much.

I'm surprised Corbelli worries about it. He's supposedly got millions, and he's so eager to win that he's promised his players big bonuses for even a little streak.

But no one understands Corbelli. Mark Crow says, "This league is just like the NBA or NFL or Major League Baseball: the clubs that work well are the ones with a president who is very strong financially but intelligent enough to hire basketball people and delegate responsibility. Corbelli doesn't do that. He owns basketball players and thinks he knows basketball. He doesn't know basketball."

Thus the reversals every time I talk to Lou. *Lock's fine, Darryl's got to do more*, I heard early in the season. Then it was, *Darryl's Superman*, *Lock has disappeared*. Back and forth. It all comes from Corbelli, who really has no clue.

People know something's going on. As Telemarket and Teorematour Milano warm up and Lou Colabello frets at courtside, Robbie Dawkins tells me that Darryl has entertained the possibility of being released. "He knows it could happen; he doesn't feel he's above it. He wouldn't feel bad. He says he'd just go home, enjoy our new house in New Jersey, and wait for someone to sign him for next year."

Corbelli figured Darryl as a gate attraction, but it's clear the people of Forli won't come out for a losing team. There can't be more than one thousand in the house tonight. Even the rooting section is thin.

Darryl, setting off Telemarket's green-and-white with a red wrist band, comes out fired up, directing his teammates on defense, patting them on the butt, and encouraging them during dead balls. ("A *lot* of them were fired up," Lou says later. "Corbelli was here.")

But Teorematour, tied for second in A-2, leads by two at halftime. Lou's stewing: "I can't believe my job is in the hands of these ten guys."

Telemarket comes back in the second half. Darryl takes entry passes and dunks when he can; when he can't, he sends it back out, and tonight Claudio Bonaccorsi hits from the perimeter. Lock, the endangered one, rebounds and scores inside, runs the floor and jams at the end of fast breaks, bringing his exultant parents out of their seats a half-dozen times.

As if the fans aren't happy enough over Telemarket pulling ahead, Darryl thrills them with one of his inimitable displays of athleticism, skying high, *high* for a rebound (though no one's within fifteen feet) with his elbows out and his legs spread, one huge mitt inhaling the ball the way a mortal's hand snatches a tennis ball. Ooooooo! Aaaaaa! *Never* been anyone like Darryl in Italy!

Telemarket pulls away and wins, 92–81, with a giddy Lou Colabello screaming down the stretch. The ebullient Telemarket players huddle briefly at the foul line and break with a wave to the loyal thousand. Rob Lock's parents come out of the stands to have their picture taken with the one and only Darryl Dawkins. The fans stick around to cheer when the scoring totals are announced. (Lock shoots 12-for-15, scores 29 points, grabs 15 rebounds. Darryl scores 22 on 10-for-11 shooting, bumping his percentage to .843, with 9 rebounds—and *10* turnovers.)

Lou moves giddily around the floor, shaking hands with wives, friends, reporters, kids, and utter strangers before finally heading for the winners' locker room.

Two days after the game in Forli, New Year's Eve afternoon finds me eating lunch with Elio at the Savioli, which is buzzing with tourists and the extra help that the owners, Fausto and Geo, have brought in to handle them. Elio says people come to Riccione for New Year's because it's considered good luck in Italy to observe the *primo gennaio* dawn, and true sunrise is when there's light at the eastern shore. Before daybreak tomorrow, he assures me, they'll be out on the beach, waiting.

I mark midnight and the New Year by shooting off fireworks with Elio and Roseanna and the kids at their place outside town. When Elio brings me back to my apartment around 2 A.M., we stop for a quick Jack Daniel's at the roaring Savioli, then I walk around for another hour. The streets are packed. Restaurants and bars and hotels that closed in October have opened up for these few days, after which they'll be shut down until mid-April.

I oversleep in the morning. I wanted to be down at the beach at dawn to see if, as Elio claimed, there'd be a crowd, but the celebrating in the street kept me awake until nearly five. It's tough enough to drag myself out of bed at eight, but I want to see if there's any tag-end activity.

It's gray and cold out, but without the wind that's usually whipping in it's actually pleasant if you're bundled up. It's very quiet; very little movement, virtually no one around.

Anyone who might have been on the beach earlier is gone, but the sand is littered with the remains of shot-off fireworks and occasional wine bottles. The parking circle down near the Center is strewn with broken glass. A couple of cars are parked facing out to sea, filled with burnt-out revelers dozing among pillows and blankets and bottles and beer cans. One car starts up and moves uncertainly past me; the kid at the wheel rolls down his window and says something that doesn't sound pleasant, but a giggly girl in back swigging out of a long-necked bottle trills "*Buon anno!*" and I smile and the driver smiles and they drive off.

There's life in the Center; the cafes and bars are open every morning. I pass on through and take the Viale Dante back toward home. Church bells ring in the distance, a few couples are out walking, groups of kids who haven't been to bed yet are singing as they careen down the sidewalk.

A new year. I'm about as far as I can be from Portland, Oregon, and my old life, and it's all to the good. People here seem happier than what I'm used to, and the attitude rubs off. I've eased off flogging myself for losing my marriage. I'm filled with warm feelings from Thanksgiving and the Christmas season; I've got friends. I've got a book to write.

I've got a new life.

A few days after their big win, Telemarket gets ripped by Darnell Valentine's Burghy Modena club.

Two days later, Rob Lock is told he's finished. He had a good game against Burghy, and for the season he's averaging 19.7 points and 10 rebounds per game to Darryl's 17.2 and 9.5, but Corbelli's set on making a change and he's not about to let Darryl go. Darryl is more intimidating defensively, and coach Pasini likes his influence on the other players: Darryl works hard in practice, encourages the others, etc. Most important to Corbelli, he's *Darryl*, the awesome "Baby Gorilla," the *famoso* NBA superstar.

At lunch in Forli, Lou Colabello tells me they gave Lock the news this morning. The club made a deal for him to go play with a team in Spain and remain Telemarket's property in Italy, just in case Corbelli decides to release Darryl at the end of the season and bring Lock back next year.

Bizarre. Corbelli doesn't know what he wants.

More bizarre yet, Telemarket hasn't signed a replacement for Lock, so though Lock has been told he's not wanted any longer, he's got to stay and keep practicing with the team in case they can't get someone over here in time to play on Sunday.

Lou's been on the phone at all hours, but no luck. "These agents," he says, "talk up their players like they're All-Pros. 'This guy jumps outta the gym, goes to the basket like Michael Jordan, shoots like Larry Bird, passes like Magic Johnson.' So you're asking yourself, *Why is he in the CBA?*"

He's been talking to the Atlanta Hawks about Andre Spencer; Atlanta signed Spencer to a ten-day contract a few days ago, and Corbelli is offering them ten thousand dollars to release him early so that Spencer can be here by Friday, which is the league's deadline for a player to be eligible for Sunday. Telemarket offered Spencer fifty thousand dollars for the remainder of the regular season, an additional twenty thousand if he gets them into postseason play, and two hundred thousand for next season.

They're also considering Ron Grandison, but Grandison is considering an offer from Australia.

Telemarket remains *in crisi;* Series "B" next year is a distinct possibility. Lou Colabello sweats. He can't believe ten basketball players have his job in their hands.

Buon anno, Lou.

A Toast to the *Stranieri*

The Phonola Caserta situation isn't a happy one. They're treading water near the bottom of A-1 despite the presence of Greg "Cadillac" Anderson, the *lega*'s big NBA free-agent catch this season. A top-ten rebounder with the Denver Nuggets last season, in his prime at twenty-eight, Cadillac signed a three-year deal for about $2 million per to make Caserta fans forget Charles Shackleford.

Phonola's game of musical *stranieri* is all too typical. After two forgettable seasons with the New Jersey Nets, Shackleford came to Caserta two years ago and promptly averaged 19 points and a league-leading 16 rebounds per game, carrying the team to a surprise championship in 1991.

When he turned around and signed a fat contract with the Philadelphia 76ers, Phonola brought in thirty-six-year-old Mychal Thompson for $1 million last season. Anthony Avent replaced the other championship *straniero*, power forward Tellis Frank, who signed a non-guaranteed contract with the Minnesota Timberwolves. Phonola staggered; at mid-season Avent was released and Frank, cut by Minnesota, returned. (Now, less than a year later, Avent is an NBA starter with Milwaukee, and Frank, according to the newspapers, is in danger of losing his job in Caserta.) Phonola finished at .500 and got knocked out of the playoffs early.

Last July, Thompson, who had averaged 16 points and 10 rebounds, was home in Portland getting ready to come back when he got word that Caserta wasn't picking up the second year of his contract. They were shelling out for the younger, stronger Cadillac Anderson instead. Big bucks, big expectations in Caserta. *Cadillac was Top Ten in the NBA; he'll double what Shackleford did! Cadillac inside, Gentile and Esposito outside, look out!*

It's not working. Phonola's losing, and the word is they're not happy with Cadillac, though he leads A-1 with a 12.8 rebound average. Apparently they feel $2 million should deliver more than 14.5 points per game.

It's amazing how these teams keep assuming that an NBA player will double his scoring average over here. Anderson, like Rick Mahorn, was an NBA role player: a banger, a deluxe rebounder. He was never a shooter, never a big scorer. He wasn't going to come to Italy and discover a lot of moves he never knew he had.

In Cadillac's case, it's not that he couldn't score 20 points a game here. He always had more of an offensive game than Mahorn.

"You can't just blame Cadillac for the problems down there," D'Antoni told me a few weeks ago. "He's got enough talent that he should dominate in this league. But you've got to have guards to get him the ball, and they've got a couple of complete idiots playing guard down there, [Nando] Gentile and [Enzo] Esposito. Good Italian talent, but they've got no idea about running a team. I know Cadillac's having a hard time. I haven't talked to him, but I've watched him play twice and I *know* that's how he's feeling.

"That's why a lot of American big men struggle over here. They get on a team where the outside guys can't pass the ball. They don't get the ball when they need it, and they start coming out a little further to get it; they start to go outside their limitations, start forcing things, and then they *really* look bad."

I've already heard that Phonola won't bring Cadillac back next season, "guaranteed" contract or no.

Some don't last even a year. Or even half a year. You don't know what happened, you just see the names and dates and stats in the record books and you know they were here.

The great Marques Johnson: thirty-three years old, he played thirteen games for Fantoni Udine in 1989–90, averaging 23 points and 7 rebounds. Did Marques start the season, then get cut as the club foundered near mid-season? Did he get hurt? Or did he come over as a mid-season replacement himself, hoping to revive his career after the back injuries, and play those thirteen games . . . and not get an offer for the next season? Or did he get an offer and decide he didn't want to come back? Did he have enough experiences like I had in Rome on Halloween weekend that he swore, "Never again"?

Norm Nixon, one of the great NBA guards of the late seventies and early eighties until injuries took him down, played seven games for Scavolini Pesaro in 1988–89 and then was never seen again. What happened to Norm?

Albert King played in fourteen Philips Milano games the same year, scoring 116 points and sinking all 16 of his free throws.

Kent Benson, eight games for Vismara Cantu in '88–'89, never heard from again. (Some of these sponsors, like Vismara, have also dematerialized.)

Wally Walker, eleven games in Milano in '84–'85 (with an assist in getting Mike and the future signora D'Antoni together).

The one and only Marvin Barnes, after wearing out his welcome in every organization on the first six continents, scored 107 *punti* and snagged 77 *rimbalzi* in seven games with Hurlingham Trieste back in '80–'81.

Billy Thompson, Wes Matthews, Gene Banks, Ron Lee, Larry Krystkowiak, Al Wood, David Wood, Leon Wood,

Robert Reid, Lorenzo Romar, Tito Horford, Winston Bennett, Mike Smrek—all, at some time or other, listened to someone's Italy pitch, thought it over, and decided to come; studied maps of Italy, got passports, said good-byes, and got on the plane and made the long trip; stayed in Italian hotels and hoped people would be helpful, saw familiar TV shows with Italian voices coming out, struggled to order food; wore odd uniforms and played in front of insane fans in cramped gyms, with and against sallow guys from northern Italy and swarthy guys from the south, all of whom were shorter and slower and less talented than the *americani* were used to.

But none of them were here long enough to know tagliatelle from tortellini.

With Phonola Caserta visiting Bologna to take on Knorr, I've arranged to spend some time with Cadillac at the Holiday Inn a few hours before the game. Arriving at the hotel, I find the players shuffling into the restaurant for their pregame meal, and general manager Giancarlo Sarti kindly invites me to join them.

Cadillac's sitting at the end of a long table, wearing a green felt hat and a wild, flowered short-sleeve shirt, and when he stands up to shake hands—*big*, 6'10" and 245—I see he's wearing knee-length blue-jean shorts despite the fact it's snowing outside and drafty in the hotel.

Tellis Frank, sensibly dressed in jeans and a cozy zip-up sweatshirt, sits across from Cadillac, a couple of empty seats separating them from the Italians—my first firsthand clue that all is not well with Phonola. It's a marked contrast to Philips Milano's camaraderie, or Knorr's.

The giveaway comes when, pulling up a chair to the end of the table, I ask how their basketball lives are going, and Tellis simply shrugs and says, "It's a business, that's all it is"—softly, reflectively, as if the word is pregnant with new meanings for him.

(The two recurring phrases in our conversation are Tellis

saying, wearily, "It's a business," and Cadillac saying "It's *different*," meaning Italy, his resignation making it clear that the differences are to be borne only for the sake of $2 million this year.)

Cadillac Anderson is the first prominent NBA player to come to Italy during his prime years. A twenty-eight-year-old free agent who's among the League's top rebounders might expect some serious suitors, but Anderson says Denver wanted to re-sign him at the same pay as before and no one else had made a solid offer when he heard from Phonola.

Mahorn and Terry Teagle got here the same way, though they were slightly past their best days. Because NBA teams don't start preseason camp until October, they can hold off on signing any but the real star free agents. But Italian camps open in early August; teams that don't have *stranieri* lined up will make serious offers in July, and a Mahorn or Teagle or Anderson takes the sure thing.

"They put a great deal on the table over here," Cadillac says, speaking slowly to counteract a pronounced stammer. "Three years, with a couple of options where if I wanna go back to the NBA, I can. You can't beat that."

"More money than Denver offered?"

Cadillac chuckles over his pasta. "Way more." Plus a nice place to live, the use of a Lancia, etc. It's a chance to sock away some big money.

Which, along with having his wife and two little girls in Caserta with him, seems to help Cadillac take things in stride. He's more relaxed and less cynical than Tellis, who's not only alone here—his wife doesn't like Italy and is in the States with their two small children—but whose job might be in jeopardy.

Do they feel they're catching unfair blame for the team's poor performance?

"I haven't gotten it from the team," Tellis says, "and I don't read Italian, so I don't know what's in the papers. When you're from America your skin is already thick, so as long as you get your money, that's really the bottom line."

Cadillac, twirling spaghetti around his fork, says, "I just try to do the job that I can control: rebound, play defense. Everything else, I let it take care of itself."

But pressed for detail, Cadillac elaborates. "I was led on. I was told that they had two of the best guards in the world, that if you're open inside they get you the ball like, *boom*. But that's not the outcome. You got zone defenses here, and if the guy don't hit you on time you got a problem.

"But you can't let that bother you. I just go out and do the job I'm known to do, and that's rebound and block a few shots. They can't control that."

"Nothin' you can do," Tellis sighs. "It's their world over here—you just try to adjust. It's a short period in your life, and you gotta live after it's over, so you just put away the money."

Cadillac says he would play in the NBA for less money than he makes here. "You like to be in your own country. One thing I've learned here is that things can't always be as expected."

He says his two daughters are over here with him and his six-year-old son is back in the States "for the education," living with his grandparents. "We were told they had good American schools here, but when he enrolled he was more advanced than the other kids, so he was sittin' around bein' bored. Besides that, the school was on the army base in Naples. It might take an hour to get there in traffic, so we were gettin' up at five-thirty in the morning to have him there at eight. We'd get back at nine, ten o'clock, be home a while, and then head back to pick him up at three.

"I took this chance to get ahead in life, you know, to secure myself—basketball is a business—but the main thing is my family. So if it means takin' a pay cut of one hundred thousand, two hundred thousand, I'd go back to the States. As long as my family gonna be together and everybody gonna be happy, that's all I care about."

He's thinking about going back next season. On the court, off the court, it's just not working out over here.

"It's *different*," Cadillac repeats with a sigh. "Can't put it no better than that."

Spencer Haywood, Reggie Theus, Michael Cooper, Derrek Dickey, Dave Corzine, Swen Nater, Sidney Wicks, Mark Olberding, Mark Acres, Mike McGee, Bill Laimbeer, Tom McMillen, Harvey Catchings, Otto Moore.

George Gervin, John Roche, Artis Gilmore, Jim Chones, Jim Ard, Antoine Carr, Joe C. Meriweather, Olden Polynice, Wilbur Holland, Earl Jones, Johnny Neumann.

They came, they stayed a year, they were gone.

A few were on their way up, most on the way down. Some didn't like it in Italy; some weren't liked.

Most often, they didn't meet the teams' expectations on the court. Sometimes the expectations were unrealistic, other times the players were NBA veterans who had lost not only their skills but, knowing they were finished in the League, their motivation. "Over here," one executive tells me, "when you buy a player from the States, you're pretty much buying a piece of paper."

Another says, "We've got sixty-four foreigners in Series 'A'." I'd say half are inadequate, not to mention all those who come and go in the course of the season."

Thus the constant traffic in *stranieri*.

You're doing well to last a full season, even if, whether by your choice or the club's, you don't come back for a second. Hats off to Adrian Dantley, Glen Gondrezick, Pat Cummings, Ron Behagen, Frank Brickowski, Dan Roundfield, Fred Roberts, John Mengelt, Neal Walk, Larry Drew, Reggie King, Dave Feitl, Alex English, Joe Barry Carroll, and the rest.

Leaving the Holiday Inn dining room, Cadillac spots a copy of the *Herald Tribune* on a deserted table. He picks it up, goes to the sports page and, with Tellis reading avidly over his shoulder, starts poring over the NBA scores.

"O'Neal got twenty-three and twenty-three [points and rebounds]," Cadillac murmurs. Tellis notes, "Phoenix beat Houston by twenty-three," and a moment later, "The Clippers beat Boston *again*."

They go on scouring the standings, remarking on players, coaches, life in the League. They've been there, and they might be back, even Tellis. Look at Anthony Avent. Look at Vinny Del Negro. *Super Basket* magazine recently printed a list of about thirty guys in the NBA who've played in Italy.

"Look at Ewing," Cadillac is saying, pointing at the Knicks line score.

"Wheeeew! Look at Phoenix!" Tellis exclaims.

Finally they head up to their rooms to rest for a couple of hours before the bus ride over to the Palasport. I hang out in the lobby for a few minutes, have an espresso at the bar, and call Alberto, who tells me the *Gazzetta* insists Tellis Frank will soon be replaced. Then I meet with Sarti, the GM.

Sarti describes Tellis as a nice guy and an intelligent player. "He had a great year when we won the championship. Last year he was gone half the year [with the Minnesota Timberwolves]. This year he started out well, but now he's up and down. I don't know what's wrong. Maybe he's homesick." But Sarti denies Tellis is on his way out.

He admits he's not altogether happy with Cadillac. "There's always an adjustment period at first when a player comes here, but . . ." Sarti makes a pained expression, as if to say *We gave him way too much money; he's had plenty of time to settle in and he's still not doing squat*. "He's got two great guards to get the ball inside," Sarti says—Gentile and Esposito, the "couple of complete idiots"—"and he's still not doing so much.

"We wanted Cadillac because he was one of the top rebounders in the NBA last year. We expected him to do at least what Shackleford did two years ago, seventeen per game, but he's only getting about thirteen."

But he's leading the league, I point out.

"But not by much."

As far as scoring goes, Sarti says Cadillac will beat his defender but isn't prepared for other opponents closing in and slapping at the ball. And that once he does make a quick move to the basket, he'll lay up something soft. "A guy like that playing over here, we expect him to slam it down."

Will Cadillac be back next season?

"I don't know. He's expensive for us. If we do well our owner might say, 'He's expensive, but we'll keep him anyway.' If not, maybe 'He's expensive, we'll let him go.' "

A lot of it is luck: where you play, whom you meet. But even in the best of circumstances, it's not easy. Let's toast some of the *americani* who've managed to skirt the hazards and stick around the *lega* for two or more seasons: Jammin' James Bailey (one of the players who set off the big-money era that has crippled the league), Jim McMillian (two years in Bologna, '80 and '81, recalled as one of the great Americans who've played here), Jeff Lamp, Jim Brewer, Abdul Jeelani, Tom Owens, Charles Pittman, Charlie Sitton, Darwin Cook, Darren Tillis, John Gianelli (a championship in Milan), Steve Hawes, Steve Hayes, Frank Johnson, Reggie Johnson, Jan Van Breda Kolff, Cliff and Roscoe Pondexter, Marc Iavaroni, Art Kenney, Clyde Mayes, Scott May, Harthorne Wingo, Sam Williams, Rich Laurel, Michael Young, Larry Wright, Tom LaGarde, Walt Szczerbiak.

And cheers to the honor roll, the perennials, the guys who not only played well but fell into favorable situations and got along with people and adapted to change and learned the language and—many of them—married Italians and started families, true career Italian-League players: Mitchell Anderson (six years, '86–'91, all in Florence), Mike Bantom (seven years), Roosevelt Bouie (eleven), Joe "Jelly Bean" Bryant (seven), Dan Caldwell (six), Mark Crow (nine, six in a row in Fabriano), Leon Douglas (eight), Bruce Flowers (six), Rod Griffin (eleven), Rudy Hackett (eight), Cedrick Hordges (eight), Otis Howard (eight), Kim Hughes (nine), fourth-leading all-time scorer Chuck Jura (eleven), C. J. Kupec (nine), Dave Lawrence (seven), the great Bob McAdoo (six), the great Bob Morse (eleven), Kevin Restani (six), Wayne Sappleton (eight), Willie Sojourner (seven), Dale Solomon (nine), Corny Thompson (six, now in France), Ernest Wansley (eight), and Tony Zeno (six).

A few players are currently in the midst of what have been or seem likely to become extended careers: Joe Binion, Dallas Comegys, Darren Daye, Dean Garrett, Dan Gay, Clemon Johnson, Pace Mannion, Chris McNealy, Larry Middleton, Mike Mitchell, Micheal Ray Richardson, Elvis Rolle, Ron Rowan, Russ Schoene.

And others playing here now: Bill Wennington, Pete Myers, Haywoode Workman, Antonio Davis, Adrian Caldwell, Albert "A. J." English, Larry Spriggs, Jay Murphy, Cozell McQueen, Johnny Rogers, Bob Thornton, Bobby Lee Hurt, Popeye Jones, Anthony Frederick, John Ebeling, Darnell Valentine, Todd Mitchell.

No telling how long it will last for any of this last bunch. Or for Cadillac or Tellis, who, for different reasons, might be gone next season.

It's a business, man, that's all it is . . .

Oscar

You could hang around the Italian League for a long time and never know he's got a last name. Or you might think "Oscar" *is* his last name. There he is in Fernet Branca Pavia's box scores, "Oscar," between "Thornton" (Bob) and "Pratesi" (Gabriele). In the weekly stats the league puts out he's on top of A-2 scoring at 38.3 per game, "Oscar," ahead of "Rowan," "Mitchell M.," and "Mitchell T."

The official league record book acknowledges "Schmidt," but still, "Oscar Schmidt" atop the all-time scoring list is followed by "Morse Bob," "Jura Chuck," and "Riva Antonello." In the index of all the *stranieri* who've ever played here, "Oscar Schmidt" falls between "Orr Louis" and "Owens Tom."

Everyone calls him Oscar. I've never heard the last name uttered.

Oscar wouldn't have it any other way. "It's because in Brazil we always call somebody by the first name, never by the second or third name. So when they put me up on the board as 'Schmidt' when I first played in Italy, I said, 'No, no, I want *Oscar*.' "

Whatever the name, there's never been any confusion about his basketball identity: *Shooter*.

"Oscar's not a basketball player," Messina chortles affectionately, "he's a shooter. Do you see the look in his face when he gets the ball? It's like when you're with a woman and you're right at the moment"—he closes his eyes, clenches his fists, trembles—"for Oscar it's like this."

For years before seeing him in the Tournament of the Americas in Portland last summer, I knew him as the Great Oscar Schmidt. I had never seen him, but I'd heard about him plenty: "The Brazilian national team upset so-and-so behind thirty-nine points from the great Oscar Schmidt." "The great Oscar Schmidt buried umpteen straight bombs as Brazil buried so-and-so."

He became *big* news in 1987: "With the great Oscar Schmidt scoring forty-six points, Brazil shocked the U.S.A. in the Pan American Games."

He achieved international fame playing for his country a couple of months every summer, but since 1982 Oscar has lived for most of each year in Italy. Eight seasons in Caserta, now three in Pavia. He's the *lega*'s all-time leading scorer by far (though entering this season he was only number one hundred in games played), and as he approaches age thirty-five he's still averaging 38 points per game.

"I've seen some great shooters," Rudy Hackett says, "but I've never seen anyone else shoot the ball the way Oscar can shoot it. *Incredible*. Makes 'em from any distance, makes 'em with people hanging on him. First second of the game, last second, it's the same for him."

Dan Peterson: "I have never seen a three-point shooter like he was at age twenty-six. I would have paid to see him shoot against Larry Bird for about twenty-five thousand dollars."

Rob Lock, who played with him in Pavia the past two years, swears he saw Oscar sink forty-four consecutive three-pointers after practice one day. Someone else swears that only last week the lights went out while Oscar was shooting after practice and he made thirty-three in a row with the trainer standing under the basket with a cigarette lighter.

Dino Meneghin, like everyone, smiles when Oscar's name comes up. "Oscar's a nice guy, like a kid. A typical Brazilian—always smiling, nice to everybody. On the court, a specialist, a shooter. Unbelievable sometimes, when he fall in a trance; he can do anything he wants. Talking with him sometimes is fun; he say, 'Sometimes the basket is like a swimming pool, I can score with my eyes closed.' And when it looks small he keeps shooting because it has to get bigger.

"The problem is," says Dino—Dino, for whom every action on the basketball court is evaluated on its contribution to winning—"sometimes he shoot too much and his teammates get pissed off. He always score twenty or thirty points, but you must look to his percentage, because sometimes it's not so good."

This is the other side of life with Oscar.

"Oscar's one of the nicest, sweetest guys you'll meet," Mike D'Antoni says. "And he's been good for basketball to a certain extent, because even people who don't know basketball know *him:* 'Oh, Oscar. Oh, Oscar.' But I don't like him as a player. His biggest thing is to keep his point average up there, and he doesn't guard anybody. I don't think you can win with Oscar."

I meet Oscar at the Hotel della Citta in Forli the night before the Fernet Branca Pavia–Telemarket game. He comes downstairs wearing white sweats and basketball shoes. He's about 6'8", slender, with brown brush-cut hair and a friendly, lined, thirty-five-year-old face. As we sit talking in soft chairs off the lobby he smiles easily, laughs often. There's something of a big, happy kid about him, even though he's a family man with two children who's played professional and international basketball for the better part of twenty years.

"The shooting is just natural," he says with a shrug, speaking of his unique talent as if it's something apart from himself. It is, in a sense: this is Oscar, a regular guy sitting here chatting, and then there's this thing he can do when he's inside a basketball gym. A very narrow thing, he seems to realize, and a thing he won't be able to do (for pay) much longer. Then he'll just be regular Oscar. This narrow thing he's being permitted to do so freakishly well for a few years doesn't make him any better than anyone else. It just happened to him.

He started playing for a junior team at fourteen. Tall for his age, he played inside. At sixteen he joined a club team in Sao Paolo and started to realize he had a pretty good long-range shooting eye.

"When I find out I can shoot, I start to practice sometimes eight, nine hours a day. Often with my wife . . . we were boyfriend and girlfriend then, and we would go out and she pass me the ball and I shoot, shoot, shoot, many hours a day." He chuckles, thinking back. "That was very funny for us, that she comes with me every day."

When he was nineteen the national-team coach moved him outside, and he started becoming The Great Oscar Schmidt. He came to Italy in 1982, twenty-four years old, and in eight years in Caserta he averaged 32 points per game, shooting well over .500, over .450 on three-pointers, almost .900 from the foul line.

I tell him what Messina said about how, for Oscar, shooting is like being with a woman at "the moment."

He bursts out laughing. "Yes! Yes! Yes! I never heard this before, but it's perfect!"

He laughs when I relate the stories they told at the D'Antonis' on Thanksgiving, with affection, about Oscar's lust for scoring. Johnny Rogers, for instance, telling about a game when Oscar looked peeved after a teammate flung the ball up from midcourt as the first half expired; *Oscar* wanted to hoist the last prayer, maybe get a cheap three.

"You *can* compare the feeling to 'the moment' with a woman," Oscar says. "Latin players love to shoot. In America they play playground, they want to go inside and dunk, but in Brazil, Mexico, Spain, Italy, players want to shoot.

Maybe because we are not so athletic like the black players.

"But this year I do much more the other things. Shooting for me is normal, but this year I have more assists, blocked shots. I don't know how, but I'm improving, *trying* to improve. I always did good rebounding, but nobody cared, they only look at how I shoot.

"I am not," he concedes, "a good defensive player. I have problems to guard quick players. I prefer to guard somebody near the basket. I try to do the best I can. This year I'm doing more; I think I'm doing my best tournament [having my best season]."

But Oscar's nearly thirty-five, and he says it's time to start taking summers off, at least.

"For so many years, I never have a break. One year, only, I have two months of vacation." He smiles, kidlike again. "I go to Orlando. Two months. Orlando, this is my paradise. I stay in a residence [hotel] with my family and go everywhere: to the parks, to Daytona Beach. The best vacation of my life. That was two years ago. I didn't play for the national team, I ask for one summer just for me: 'Just let me rest for one year.'

"I love to play for my national team, but it is time to retire from that. There's never a substitute, they'll ask me to play, but let's make the young players play. My generation played together for ten years, so now it's better to get the younger players ready for the World Cup in two years and the Olympics in four years."

As for his career in Italy, Oscar plans to keep on until no one wants him.

"When you do just one thing in your life, it's hard to say, 'I stop now and do another thing.' I never prepare for another profession, so I won't stop until I can't run anymore. I cannot think about stop now."

Shooter for hire, making his fortune while he's still got

that magical but fleeting ability, before he becomes just regular Oscar.

He's been married for twelve years to the woman who rebounded thousands of shots for him back when they were "boyfriend and girlfriend." It's easy to believe that Oscar is a devoted husband, as everyone tells me, and an easygoing father to "little Felipe," age six, and two-year-old Stephanie. He seems an uncomplicated, contented, good-natured fellow, and I can picture the young Oscar: the happy middle-class son of a navy pharmacist in a place called Nathal, near the beach in sunny, happy Brazil, where people use first names only. Life was good even before he discovered his gift, and since then it's been one amazing ride.

I ask, does his wife like living in Italy?

"She loves to be with me, wherever I go," Oscar replies cheerfully. "We are a family, a real family. We are in love from seventeen years old, and we have two kids, and I have my basketball, so I cannot ask anything more. I'm very happy."

He's loose and even friendly during warm-ups on Sunday. Instead of pretending not to hear, as an NBA idol would do, when the Pavia rooting section starts chanting "Oh-scar! Oh-scar!" during layup drills, he gradually breaks into a grin and finally looks up and waves to them. A few minutes later, doing stretching exercises on the sideline, he smiles and winks at someone at courtside. Spotting me behind the basket he smiles, points an index finger, gives me a thumbs-up. I like it, though I know that if I'd seen a Portland Trail Blazer joshing before a game I probably would have busted him for being insufficiently "focussed."

Oscar's record indicates he focusses when a game starts. Maybe the NBA "game face" is overrated.

Rob Lock starts for Telemarket. Atlanta held on to Andre Spencer. Ron Grandison wound up in Lliria, Spain.

Lou Colabello, rings under his eyes after a week of staying up all night calling all over the States about players, is nervous.

Oscar certainly starts the game with his eye on the basket, launching (and badly missing) a three as soon as he touches the ball, even with Darryl flying at him.

Defensively he's less inspired. His man scores easily on Telemarket's first two possessions, and Oscar's coach screams as if it's all too familiar.

Five minutes into the game Oscar cans a three, but the scoreboard has barely rung it up before his man breezes in for two more at the other end. Right in front of me the Pavia coach stomps from one end of the bench to the other, screaming at the floor. What can he do?

Coming down alone with three defenders waiting, Oscar pulls up and misses a three. A minute later he *airballs* one. Oscar!

Of all things, he drops in a little hook over Darryl in the lane. After his man scores a three-pointer at the other end, Oscar misses a short jumper, grabs the rebound and misses an off-balance putback. It's clear he's out there with complete license.

He does dish a couple of assists. At the top of the key he looks to shoot, and defenders fly at him, but this time Oscar deftly flicks a pass to a teammate cutting to the basket. Then he feeds off on a fast break when everyone in the house expects him to pull up and pop.

When he snaps in a three-pointer opening the second half, I'm thinking it's the start of something. I'm hoping it is, because a streak shooter is something to watch when he's on. You can see Oscar knows what that's like. He shoots with supreme confidence and utter abandon; he takes a pass and turns and just flicks his wrist and the ball is gone, in and out of his hands so quickly I'm reminded of Bird's famous touch-passes—only, Oscar is *shooting*, twenty-five feet from the basket.

Unfortunately, few are going in. Telemarket clings to a

slim lead. They need the game badly. The crowd's the loudest two thousand people I've ever heard (every crowd over here seems the loudest I've ever heard), whistling and screaming at players and leaning over the railings, bellowing at the refs.

With five minutes left and Pavia trailing by seven, Oscar forces a runner that falls three feet short of the rim. He clutches his head with both hands, anguished, and the crowd hoots. Sometimes it seems he puts up any old shot simply because if he passes off he might not get the ball back—that is, he might not get to shoot at all this time down the floor.

But whatever his imperfections, it's obvious in the final 1:20 why Oscar has been so feared for so long, around the world, and why there's always a place in basketball for a deadly shooter.

Pavia trails by seven, it looks grim, but Oscar busts a three. Maybe it's not over quite yet.

Telemarket eats some time but eventually shoots and misses, and Pavia scrambles down the floor and gets the ball to Oscar, just inside the circle, who in one motion catches, turns, and lets fly—two points, easy. He's in the trance. Telemarket's lead is two.

But Telemarket uses up some time and then gets a couple of free throws. Breathing room.

Hah. Pavia helter-skelters down the floor, and Oscar's hung up in traffic but suddenly pops free and races out beyond the arc. His teammate whips him the pass and Telemarket can't get there quick enough: once more the all-in-one-motion catch-and-release, *flick*—three points. Forty seconds, three bombs, eight points.

Telemarket holds on; Oscar doesn't get the one last chance to win the game. But Telemarket was scared. This is what Rob Lock meant when he said that you've always got a chance to win when Oscar's on your side.

Thirty-eight for Oscar, his average. But except for the spurt at the end, the most unremarkable 38 I've ever seen. Lots of bad judgment, lots of misses.

In Oscar's defense, it works out mathematically. "Year by year I shoot more three-pointers," he told me, "because if you make forty percent, it's like making sixty percent on two-pointers." Tonight he's 6-for-16 on threes for 18 points, which converts to 9 two-pointers. *Nine*-for-16, along with Oscar's 6-for-14 on actual two-pointers, comes out to 15-for-30, .500, excellent work by any standard. Free throws, 8-for-9.

Makes sense on paper, but you wonder. You don't see a Pavia *team;* it's Oscar's show. You wonder how his teammates feel when he takes 30 of Pavia's 69 shots.

But that's Oscar. As Lock said, "Oscar makes his living shooting, and that's what he's gonna do."

Not Looking for Love (in All the Right Places)

On the increasingly rare occasions when I fall to brooding, I wish there was more *basket* to occupy me than a game every weekend and, sometimes, a Euroclub Championship qualifying game in Bologna or Pesaro during the week. But most of the time the proportion of hoops to real life seems perfect. Once or twice a week I'm a jockhead reporter; the rest of the time I'm a very fortunate guy living in Italy and getting along better than I ever dreamed, frankly, thanks to people on all sides looking out for me. *Thriving* isn't too strong a word.

I'm missing romance, maybe, but I know I'm not likely to find it in Italy, not unless the perfect American or Englishwoman is here and somehow falls into my path. Yes, Lou Colabello and Mark Crow and Rudy Hackett are married to Italians and seem to do fine, but for me the language barrier is prohibitive. Even with people whose English is very good, such as Alberto or the number-one secretary at the *lega*, Daniela, I'm constantly defining words or illuminating shades of meaning or explaining cultural references. To someone who learned too late that true communication is everything in a relationship, and that often you're not achieving it even when you like to think you are, it seems all but impossible that I could manage it with a foreigner.

And I'm not looking for love anyway. I'm *recovering* from it.

Besides, as Proust reminded me as I lay in the tub reading one recent night, in many ways it's best to be alone in new surroundings. You move when you want, stop and study things when you want. You see and later recall things entirely through your own filter, uninfluenced by the perceptions or even the mere presence of someone else. You see much more: on a train, say, you're taking in the passing countryside instead of talking with a companion. You're forced to cope with waiters and shopkeepers yourself.

I just want to travel light while I'm here, in every way. I don't need any emotional entanglements, and I don't want to be hung up on one person when there are so many to experience. The list expands by the week.

At least—at last—I can tell Lou Colabello I got laid. Not that I was worried about it, but Lou—the typical married man who, for whatever reason, thinks about it constantly—invariably asks me whether I've scored when we meet for coffee and gossip in Rimini on Monday mornings, and usually when we talk on the phone in between.

On the Wednesday after I saw Oscar in Forli, there was a fax waiting for me at Amici di Riccione. Cristina, whom I hadn't contacted nor heard from since meeting her on the train to Milan at Thanksgiving, would be finishing her work down in Pesaro on Friday and wondered if we could get together in the meantime.

Why not? I've got nothing to do, and she was very nice, and I had a fond memory of a round bottom that had reminded me of a round-bottomed nurse I once fancied.

I called, and Cristina said she'd come up that evening if I wanted to have dinner and maybe go to a club.

She didn't make it until nine, but we made up for lost time. We ate, yes, but never bothered with a club. We walked back over to my apartment and the lights were out in ten minutes.

She was better than gelato, and I think she'd say nice things about me too.

It was perfect. I liked having her stay all night, but I was glad she had to get back to Pesaro early Thursday morning.

But I was glad she could come over again that night.

And though it was wonderful once more, I was glad she had to leave again Friday morning. Better yet, as we waited for her train she confessed she's got a boyfriend living across the lake from her up north, so though she'd like to get together again I think I can legitimately decline if she calls, depending on how I feel at the time. I know it's not going to be a romance, and sex without love, for the first time in my life, hardly seems worth the bother.

Partly a symptom of age, I'm sure, but partly a matter of being in a new place with endless new stimuli. I'm rereading Proust on these cold nights, and the great one reminds me that we're truly alive only when we're in unfamiliar surroundings, when we can't sleepwalk through our days, when every walk provides new sensations and every interaction stirs new feelings and thoughts.

Being here isn't brand-new anymore—even in the first moments of awakening each morning I know where I am—but neither do I know the language, the customs, or even my acquaintances well enough to do anything by rote, even when I'm in Riccione. I still wake up each morning knowing I'll have had some new experiences and sensations by nightfall.

I still wake up filled with wonder at my great good luck.

The weather turned surprisingly cold as early as Thanksgiving. It's warmer down south, but I spend virtually all my time in the north, where it's much like Portland in the winter: overcast and dank much of the time, temperatures in the thirties or forties, bearable with the right coat but far from balmy. Here at the coast it's a little colder than elsewhere, with the constant wind—I rarely walk on the beach these days—and we get storms blowing off the sea that flood the canal a few blocks away and threaten to blow my windows out. During lulls I'll step out on the balcony, check out the huge gray foamy waves rearing up a couple of blocks away, and see how many more branches from the big trees are lying in the street since the last time I looked.

But I'm always cozy in my apartment. My windows will withstand the storms, especially since I realized I can close those big shutters outside. I've got heat that I don't even pay for; everything's covered by the six hundred thousand lire I give Rosita each month, which by now isn't worth much more than four hundred dollars. I've got a great shower—a necessity to me, but not found everywhere in other countries—and a big old-fashioned bathtub, where I loll for hours on these long solitary nights.

I stay up as late as I want—sometimes, when I'm desperate to hear English, until two in the morning, when *CNN International* comes on TeleMonteCarlo for a few hours. Sometimes I'll wake up in the middle of the night and think to go out and turn on the tube, and I'll bring a pillow and blanket and lie there on the living-room couch, drowsily watching the news and sports and Hollywood gossip. It all seems so far away. Clinton's in now. The Marines have gone into Somalia. The Suns are routing the NBA.

In *big* news, Di has finally ditched Charlie. Maybe there's hope for me yet.

In Italy the Mafia keeps blowing up judges. Corrupt politicians are killing themselves as investigators finger them. Blacks from Senegal—I'm told—sit shivering on sidewalks in Riccione and all over Italy trying to sell their pitiful wares out of battered briefcases even in the bitterest cold; here, one poor guy is huddled out in front of Angellini's supermarket as soon as it opens at 7:30 and stays until it closes at 12:45, then another guy takes over from 3:45 until 7:00.

Right across the water in the former Yugoslavia, people are getting sniped, starved, frozen, tortured, and raped. No one knows what to do.

It reminds me, not that I need reminding, how much I've got to be thankful for.

Every morning I get up, walk out on the balcony (if the elements allow), check the ocean, check the activity on the street. Sit around. Read. Think about how fantastic it is to be able to live this way. Take a shower. Go out and have a coffee, either at Aldo's bar next to the canal or at the Blue Bar or the Green Bar in the Center—though I'm lately enchanted by the blue-eyed barwoman at another place in the Center, and have been dropping in there. (I'm hooked on the potent little espressos. "I drank two of them one time," Darryl Dawkins said. "Figured them little suckers couldn't do nothin'. Well, I felt like my heart was about to jump outta my chest. I sat down and wrote nine letters, stayed up 'til three in the mornin'.")

People wave to me on the street now: shopkeepers out doing their windows, people I encounter day after day. Nearly every morning I'll see Rosita or Luca or Mariagrazia Nicoletti on their way to or from the Hotel Gambrinus; Signor, "the most important man in Riccione," is at the Palazzo de Turismo and various meetings all day, but the rest are spending the off-season working with architects and carpenters and painters on renovations.

Eventually, every morning, I make it to Amici di Riccione to make phone calls or just sit around with Cinzia (CHEENTS-ee-uh), the cute, buxom, vivacious twenty-four-year-old who manages the office and brightens my days immensely.

"*Ciao*, Cinzia!" I call as I come up the stairs, ever since I scared her once by coming around the corner unannounced.

"*Ciao*, Jeem!"

"*Come sta?*"

She's invariably beaming as I come around the corner. "Oh, you learn to speak?" And she starts rattling in Italian, teasing me, forcing me to say, "No, no, only *poco*." Very little.

We talk, we laugh. Cinzia speaks barely enough English to communicate, and we get stumped a lot so that even the dictionary is no help, yet we have long, wonderful conversations.

We always talk for a while when I get there—I come back behind the counter, pull up a chair, stretch out my legs—then I pull out my little directory and turn to *my* phone while Cinzia goes back to filing or addressing envelopes, humming along with her little tape player: an Italian singer she likes, or Frank Sinatra, or the *Big Chill* soundtrack.

I call Alberto almost every day. Usually I need some information, a pass to a game, something, but I'll call him even if I don't. Loretta or Tiziana or the redoubtable Daniela will answer the phone and invariably lay down a few quips before letting me know whether or not "the VIP," as we call him, the "*capo di tutti capi*" (boss of bosses), can take my call.

Most days I call Lou Colabello—again, just to chew the fat.

I'm always calling around—arranging my weekend trips, doing interviews, whatever. D'Antoni, Dan Peterson, this or that player, this or that club's PR man.

Racking up hundreds of *scatti* (long-distance units) on the meter on the wall, I worry about what I'll do if they cut me off at some point; I could hardly afford to pay for even my necessary phone calls. Cinzia (who's supposed to keep track of my *scatti* but, bless her heart, "forgets" to add the totals to her running list about half the time) says don't worry about it, but I worry. Every so often I ask her to ask Signor Nicoletti, the next time she sees him, if I'm too expensive. Apparently he always says there's no problem, and whenever I see him he gives me the same high-spirited high-five and "*Ciao*, Jeemy!" and, though he never learns a single word of English, somehow asks if there's anything I need, anything at all.

"*Ciao*, Cinzia!" I always say on my way out.

"*Ciao*, Jeem!"

"*Buona giornata*. I'll see you *domani*."

"I wait you," Cinzia says, beaming her big blinding smile. "*Buona giornata*, Jeem."

I treasure all of it, knowing that next winter I'll be far away and, in fact, might never see Cinzia again after I leave this spring. Some nights I fall asleep with a smile on my face, picturing Cinzia's smile and the way she says, "I wait you."

Sometimes I lie there thinking about how Signor Nicoletti, though he always looks so tired and so preoccupied with all his meetings, instantly brightens when he sees me and whacks my hand with that high-five (the last thing you'd expect, he looks so distinguished and correct) and, when I greet him with "*Ciao*, Signor!" insists I call him Italo, though I can only think of him as Signor or "the most important man in Riccione," as his kids teasingly call him, or the "*patrono*," as Cinzia says. I get sentimental thinking about all the Nicolettis, and Rita (Fabbri) and her daughters, who've made me feel like family. We all eat dinner together not every Thursday but every week or two, whenever it works out, and these are some of my happiest times. Laughs, kisses, high-fives, lots of wine, and, afterward, liqueurs. I still exchange long looks with Mariagrazia, who melts me with her big brown eyes; she's had this boyfriend for many years, but she makes eyes at me anyway.

After Amici di Riccione each morning I usually stop at Angellini's supermarket (eat cheaply in the afternoon, then go to the Savioli at night), where, heartbreakingly, the morning-shift Senegalese guy wrapped in coat, hat, gloves, and blanket sits on the cold pavement out front with his open case of lighters and key rings and string-bracelets and cigarettes, too dejected to hawk or even to meet your eyes—sitting there gazing at an endless traffic of feet and legs. I feel bad about not buying a lighter every day.

People recognize me in Angellini's. They know I'm more than a tourist: I'm here every day in the dead of off-season. The giggly girl at the prepared-food counter in back knows I'll want some chicken salad, maybe some fish, probably some fried potatoes. Sometimes she packs a free sample of a marinated meat, a seafood salad, a soft cheese, or one of Italy's myriad pastas, urging me to experiment.

Such a quaint life here in Riccione in the winter. I've

heard what it's like in summer, with 440 hotels full and the beach body-to-body and the streets teeming until five every morning, but now, with only the thirty-one thousand Riccionese and me here, it's just a little village. We are one.

At least, that's how the people here make me feel.

Every few days I stop at the *tabachi* across from Angellini's; sometimes they've got American magazines, and sometimes I'll even whiff, say, the equivalent of ten dollars on a *Playboy*. The perky, petite lady who obviously avails herself of the tanning booths around the corner knows me, and her daughter does too. They speak no English but they couldn't be friendlier.

Everyone's friendly. It's a different way of life.

I think *I'm* getting soft.

Afternoons in Riccione I . . . well, I play it by ear and do whatever feels right. Eat lunch, read, take naps, write letters, plan my trips, transcribe interviews. Once in a while the weather permits a comfortable walk on the beach.

Evenings can get long. Sometimes Elio picks me up and we go eat at his wife's family's restaurant, then go out for a coffee and a shot, then go over to their apartment and play with Stefano and Janis, maybe rent a movie. Usually, though, I go to the Savioli.

I'm undoubtedly their most regular customer this winter; since eating there my second or third day in town, I've rarely bothered going anywhere else. The food is excellent, the bar is stocked with everything, and they know me. Maurizio the bartender speaks some English, and while the rest are strictly soccer fans, he enjoys talking *basket;* he's a lifelong Virtus Bologna fan, like any *basket* follower in Emilia-Romagna. I feel tight too with Silvano, the world's greatest waiter, who whisks around balancing a dozen dishes at once and all but carrying the drinks on his head when it's busy, and who smiles and nods at everything I say though he doesn't know a word of English. The two partners, Fausto and Geo (who also own the huge roadside water slide on the way to Rimini and various other enterprises), didn't seem to know what to make of me for a while, but they loosened up as they saw me becoming friends with Maurizio and Silvano. I knew I was okay when Geo stopped ignoring me and Fausto started coming by my table and asking how the pasta was. ("*Buono*, Signor Fausto," I replied the first couple of times, until he said, "*No*. No 'Signor' Fausto. *Fausto*.")

After dinner on these cold winter nights, in the middle of long *basket*-less weeks, I lie in the big tub reading Proust for hours.

Of course, as he goes on and on about love and illusion it's easy for me to lapse back into my ruminations about Jenelle, and about myself in relation to her. *Bad*.

Just when I need a change, the weekend comes and it's time to "work": go somewhere, watch a game, interview someone. (See new sights, meet new people, try new restaurants.) Maybe it's Rome or Milan for three or four days, maybe only a day trip on Sunday for a game in Rimini or Pesaro or Forli or Bologna, but either way *basket* brings me back to the here and now no later than 5 P.M. every Friday afternoon, when, if I'm still at home, I watch Franco Lauro's weekly highlight program.

Saturday afternoons, there's the weekly TV game.

Sunday, somewhere, I go to the arena and ask for the home team's PR man. They all know about the *scrittore americano:* Alberto sent a fax around the league the week I arrived, to the effect that I could be very important to the *lega* and everyone had better treat me right. He calls the club whose game I'm attending each week to arrange my pass, and on Sunday they're not only expecting me, they're clamoring to attend to my every need and desire. (Me! It's almost *embarrassing*.)

If I'm in Rome or Milan or another relatively distant point, or if I've got someone to see on Monday (which most teams have off), I'll stay overnight after the game, but otherwise I like to get home on Sunday night. One of the things I most look forward to is meeting Lou Colabello up in Rimini on Monday mornings for cappuccino and a brioche and two or three hours of chat. Usually he's lamenting another Telemarket bellyflop; I sympathize for a while, knowing he's worried about having a job next season. Then we move on to news and gossip and Lou asking me if I've gotten laid. He lusts after Daniela, Loretta, and Tiziana at the league office ("How can Bortolotti stand it?") and virtually any female coming into the cafe who's not one-armed, humpbacked, cross-eyed, or spike-haired.

This week I drive him crazy by telling about Cristina. He asks questions until, sick of talking about it, I start asking him about Darryl and Lock, but he's quickly back on Cristina. She did *what?* And I'm not sure I want to see her again? Am I *nuts?*

I'm not nuts. What I am is alive, blissfully alive, with many things besides sex to amuse and fulfill me.

Movers and Shakers in the Long-Body Bazaar

"Lucky" Luciano Capicchioni's player agency, the International Basketball Center, is located on a mountaintop a half-hour's drive west of Riccione, in the tiny republic of San Marino.

Mark Crow, who along with the boss *is* IBC, is a 6'8" Phil Jackson ringer who graduated from Duke in 1977 and played part of a year with the New Jersey Nets, then came to Italy and played nine seasons (punctuated by one in Portugal and one in Spain). Along the way he became friends with Capicchioni, who invited him to come to work after his playing days were over. Mark, with an Italian wife and two kids by the time he retired in 1989 and no great desire to go back to the States, took him up on it.

The D'Antonis told me about him at Christmas, and apparently told him about me, and we met for lunch near his house in Rimini (such a small world, Italy!) and immediately hit it off. He's funny, loose, easy; likes his vino, and a shot of good whiskey at the end of a good meal. A few days later we went to a Euroclub game in Bologna together, after which he and an Italian friend took me out to a dark, casual restaurant specializing in all kinds of raw meat, where Mark ate with gusto and encouraged me with, "Come on, it'll make you virile! Virile!" A few days later I rode up to the office with him to meet Capicchioni and just hang out.

Mark comes to work in loafers, jeans, and a casual shirt—and a well-worn sports jacket, when he's got to be dressy. His office is as casual as he is. The wall behind the desk is dominated by a huge poster of Michael Jordan soaring, ready to slam one down. A bookcase is jammed with stacks of every hoop magazine from Europe and the States, rows of *NBA Guides*, Rick Barry's books, and basketball books I've never seen or heard of. There's a TV and VCR against one wall, under a couple of shelves that are two-deep and three-high with labeled cassettes of basketball games: pro, college, CBA, Europe, anything Mark can get from the PonTel film service back in the States, his father, coaches, or self-promoting players. Most are labeled with the relevant unknown player's name: Jeffrey Connelly, Eric Yankoway, Micah Bingeman, Dan Leahy, Rickey Edmond. Mark's got tapes of everything from a guy shooting baskets in an empty gym to a city-league game with a dreamy flute-music sound track ("Really bad," Mark says).

In one corner, a stack of newspapers rises waist-high from the floor: *USA Today*, *Herald Tribune*, the Italian sports dailies. In another, facing the desk for easy reference, rests a crucial furnishing in the agent's office: a blackboard with rows of last names scrawled on it, names of basketball players who are currently available—either unemployed or marking time in the CBA—and could conceivably play in Europe. A few I recognize, like Sitton (Charlie), Corchiani (Chris), and Higgins (Sean), but most are anonymities from the cast of thousands on the fringes of professional basketball.

Like John Bailey. The phone rings, a call from the States. "Hi, John," Mark says brusquely. After listening for a minute or two, he starts asking questions and scribbling down Bailey's answers. Brusque, impersonal, strictly business: "How tall are you? You play number four [power forward]? Any three at all? Where did you play last season? What did you average in points and rebounds? What are you doing now?

Anybody else trying to find you a job? How much money do you need to make? Okay, John. I don't have anything for you right now, but I'll let you know if something comes up."

Impersonal, but this is business. Mark's not unkind, but he's never met John Bailey and will probably never have occasion to meet him. Bailey is simply a quantity, a guy approaching thirty who played college ball at Carson-Newman and has been a pro in Venezuela, Argentina, Portugal, and Switzerland. Out of work this season, he's playing in three rec leagues back in Ypsilanti, Michigan, hoping a job opens up somewhere.

Another call from the States. Mark sounds like he did with John Bailey. "I'd like to be able to call you and say I've got a job for you, Dwight. There's nothing right now, but I'll let you know if something comes up." When he hangs up, Mark goes to the blackboard and prints MOODY.

Mark has never met Dwight Moody, but he's heard from him every so often for the past couple of years. Moody, a former Memphis State player in his late twenties, has played in Holland, Mexico, and the Philippines and spent the past two years in the CBA. He was playing in the Global Basketball Association this season until the league folded a month ago. Moody is about 6'6", Mark says, and plays 1, 2, and 3. (That is, point guard, shooting guard, and small forward. All job-hunting players advertise as—or their agents advertise them as—multipurpose. *What position do I play? What do you need?* It recalls Woody Allen's joke about bisexuality: it doubles your chances of having a date on Saturday night.)

After the two calls, it's a quiet afternoon. Mark says there's a lot of dead time for him. He and Capicchioni are busy in the summer, trying to get IBC players into jobs, but once the season starts he usually comes to the office only after lunch. Today he thumbs through a few magazines, scans the newspapers, watches part of a recent NBA game. He writes a letter to a 6'9", 230-pound, twenty-two-year-old in Czechoslovakia he's been following for a couple of years: "Not an NBA prospect, but good enough to play at certain levels in Europe. By twenty-six or so he might be good enough for Italy or Spain."

"Lucky" Luciano Capicchioni, the postmaster general of San Marino, coached touring teams for years and started his "sideline" business in the late seventies.

"Nice mustache Lucky's got, eh?" smirks a competitor in what Dan Peterson calls "the shark-infested waters" of agentry. "And did you notice how he never looks you in the eye?"

But the several agents I've met are all catty about each other, and most have shifty eyes, as far as that goes. Lucky does have a weak little villain's mustache, and he's self-interested like everyone in the agent game, but he's all right. People I trust, including Ettore Messina and Bob Morse, say he's got a good reputation, as agents' reputations go.

Employing Mark, some say, gives Lucky a credibility that others lack. With his ex-player's knowledge of the game and long-term friendships with coaches and executives around the league, Mark gives Lucky an edge over slick-talking lawyers and deal makers in cashmere sweaters who carried the water bucket for the high-school team—if they weren't out selling dope, precociously (and consciencelessly) entrepreneurial.

"That's why I brought Mark in," Lucky says. "He played basketball, he knows basketball. I handle the business end, so he has time to really evaluate players in the U.S., to follow the teams here and know what they really need, to talk to the coaches. So when we give a team a player, we're fairly exact."

Mark's job, essentially, is scouting talent and keeping track of player movement around the globe.

"Lucky runs the day-to-day operations of the company and does most of the contracts. I'm his eyes and ears. I read the papers and talk on the phone a lot, keep up with who's cut from the NBA, who's available. A guy who's cut, I make it my business to know what his characteristics are. I watch NBA films all the time, I read, I look at stats. I'm not the world-class expert, but I know enough about the NBA, the CBA, the GBA, the European leagues, who's getting out of college every year, who's cut, who enters in. If I see someone's free who I think can help our agency, I'll suggest it. If he's got a representative in the States, we might contact him and cut a deal to try to place his player over here."

IBC has been doing a lot of middleman work—helping Italian teams sign Americans, most of whom already have agents in the States, as mid-season replacements—for which it receives part of the agent's fee (usually negligible) and the goodwill of the team, the player, and the American agent. IBC itself represents several young American players, none as yet in the NBA.

At this point, the agency's strength is its stable of top Eastern European players: Toni Kukoc, Sasha Danilovic, Arvidas Sabonis (with Real Madrid in Spain), plus Serbian center Radisav Curcic, who is with the Dallas Mavericks. That's millions of dollars worth of contracts. Capicchioni is in the middle of the endless negotiations between Kukoc, Benetton, and the Chicago Bulls.

If IBC places any of its players in Italy—as opposed to Spain, France, Greece, or any of the other myriad scenes of professional basketball—so much the better for Mark. As Capicchioni's "area manager" for Italy, he gets a percentage on every contract IBC negotiates with Italian teams; for instance, he gets a sliver of IBC's percentage of Kukoc's huge contract with Benetton even though he had nothing to do with the discovery, wooing, or signing of Kukoc. He also gets a cut of IBC's cut of the contract of any player he brings to IBC, no matter what country the guy winds up in.

Capicchioni also has area managers in Spain, France, Greece, Switzerland, Germany/Belgium/Holland, Israel, and Argentina—coaches or journalists or ex-players who track young talent as well as recommend players to clubs in those countries that need *stranieri*.

• • •

The next Monday, Lucky has left on vacation, Mark is in charge, and things are happening.

Last night the coach in Desio (A-2) called: Hansi Gnad got hurt yesterday and they're looking for a player. This morning Mark faxed him a list of players (no IBC clients) he thinks are available. (John Bailey and Dwight Moody weren't included.)

Down in Fabriano, where Mark was a 23-point, 8-rebound, per game fixture for six years in the eighties, Jay Murphy got hurt yesterday, and Mark called his former coach, Massimo Mangano, suggesting former Knicks forward Kenny Walker as a replacement. Walker is represented by Bob Woolf Associates in Boston, with whom Mark stays in touch.

There's nothing much in it for IBC if Mark assists in getting a short-term replacement-player contract for one of someone else's players: a *share* of the agent's percentage of a small contract. But you're helping out the agent and getting a player a job: it's good karma, a chit accrued, you never know. It's business (though Mark assures me he and Lucky don't help out with the idea of *stealing* the player, like some he could name). Even this purist jock knows he's in business now. Anything he can do makes IBC a bigger player, and makes *him* bigger.

That's why, being human, he's got to be just as tempted as anyone to build up a player to get him a job, or to try to wedge an IBC player into a job he's not quite suited for. He's an *agent* (even though Messina recently mused, when I mentioned Mark, "He seems like a nice guy, you know? He doesn't seem like an agent").

Mark claims IBC is different from other agencies. "Companies that are based in the U.S.A. will get a call saying, 'Give me your best power forward,' and they'll send a number-three player [small forward] just to get this guy a job, even if he's a weak rebounder who shoots twenty-five times a game and this team specifically needs rebounding or defense. Or they just don't know the teams over here, they don't *know* who would fit.

"But it's important to get the right player for a team. If you put him in a bad situation where he's playing poorly and waiting for the ax to fall, he's unhappy with you and the team is unhappy. When you work with these teams all the time like we do, you don't want that."

It's a week before I see Mark again, Monday again. He's been busy.

"Last Monday I sent the Desio coach a list of players I knew were available to replace Hansi Gnad," he reminds me. "Tuesday I talked to the GM and suggested LeRon Ellis, but that was as far as it went; someone told me Phil Zevenbergen was probably going there, and I didn't follow it up anymore.

"On Monday I also called Mangano, my old coach in Fabriano, and suggested Kenny Walker as a replacement for Jay Murphy."

Why Walker?

"I had been in touch with Bob Woolf Associates and I knew they were trying to get Walker a job in Europe. I mentioned his name and Mangano was very interested, so I went ahead with that. We took care of the contract pitter-patter, how much Fabriano could pay and how much the player wanted. In a case like this it's not so much a matter of what the player wants as how much the team can pay. If it's a player of great market value and it's not enough, you just refuse the deal, but Walker had played in Spain last year and ruptured his Achilles, and it was important for him to get a job and prove he can still play."

Walker signed a four-game guarantee for about five thousand dollars per game plus car and apartment, pretty standard for a short-term replacement. Teamsystem Fabriano has an option on his services for two additional games. Beyond that, they'll see how things are going. If they win six straight, Walker probably stays the rest of the season, with bonuses.

"The money was no problem," Mark says, "so it was just a matter of getting him on a plane. He got here on Thursday and had to pass a physical on his leg, and there was all the documentation to take care of. But it all got done."

"Sky" Walker was in the starting lineup yesterday and finished with 23 minutes played, 14 points, and 7 rebounds as last-place Teamsystem lost to Micheal Ray Richardson's so-so Baker Livorno club.

The LeRon Ellis move hadn't gone as smoothly.

"After I mentioned LeRon to Desio on Tuesday, I stopped following that, because I heard Zevenbergen was coming in Wednesday. He comes in, practices, and they decide he's not in good enough shape. Wednesday evening I get a call from Sergio Scariolo, the coach, and he's interested in LeRon Ellis.

"LeRon had just joined the CBA the previous Saturday. Before that he was in Spain on a five-month contract, and when it expired they released him. Actually he was having a pretty good year: almost 15 points a game, almost 9 rebounds, the leading shot-blocker in the league. It wasn't like he was stinkin' it up; they just decided they wanted something else.

"So late Wednesday night, two-thirty in the morning [5:30 P.M. Pacific time], I'm on the phone with Reginald Turner, LeRon's agent in Los Angeles. They're very interested. Finally I think it's all taken care of. There are a few things to be done on Thursday, but as far as I know, we get it done. All we had to do was get five thousand dollars to the CBA—your eligibility card comes from your last club, and you have to give them five thousand dollars.

"It's impossible to get them five thousand dollars from Italy in twenty-four hours, and this all has to get done in order for him to play on Saturday. [Desio was playing in the weekly Saturday TV game.] So using a friend of mine at the bank in San Marino, where the Desio president has an account, Desio sends a fax authorizing five thousand dollars into my account in the U.S. I send a fax authorizing five thousand into the account of Reginald Turner. Reginald Turner, receiving these faxes, sends a fax to his bank telling them to send a wire transfer to an account in Colorado, where the CBA office is. The CBA then writes its letter of clearance for Ellis's card and sends it to ABA-USA [the federation that represents the U.S. within FIBA, the governing body of international basketball].

"Thursday night I go to a Euroclub game in Bologna, go out to dinner, drive back to Rimini, and call the States. I find out everything got done except the last step, which is ABA-USA faxing the CBA's letter of clearance to the Italian federation. A secretary in the ABA-USA office had too many things to do at the end of the day, quote-unquote, to send this one fax message. It's too late. LeRon can't play on Saturday.

"It's a problem. One, Hyundai Desio is on TV; they want to put a competitive team out there. Two, they're in first place by a game and a loss could make a big difference. Plus LeRon, who signed for six games, loses a sixth of his contract."

But what can you do? It's part of life, when you specialize in moving basketball players around the world on short notice.

Ellis signed for the same five thousand dollars per game as Kenny Walker. Hyundai Desio has an option for two more games.

IBC's piece of the two deals? A few hundred, maybe. "On deals like this," Mark says, "I probably spend more on phone bills than I'll make. But that's part of the business. You help out the agents in the States because you'd like to work with them in the future. Same thing with the clubs and coaches here—you want to have a good relationship. You never know."

Now what?

"Well, Venice is thinking about replacing a big man, either Cozell McQueen or Mark Hughes, and we've got . . . well, we *had* a guy who's very good, Ronnie Grandison, who recently signed in Spain; we work with his agent in Chicago. The same agent also represents Winston Bennett, who we've suggested to the club. And Sean Higgins, although he's not a power player, he can certainly give you points, and that's what they're looking for. He's tall enough, even though he plays like a small forward."

"Did Scaini Venezia [Venice] call you?"

"No; I read four or five newspapers this morning, and in at least three the coach had berated his Americans, McQueen and Hughes, who scored a combined seven points yesterday in Rome. When you see that a guy gets hurt, you make a phone call; when you read in three different papers that a coach wants to release one of his foreign players, you make a phone call. It's not like you're a vulture on a fence post; you're just doing your job."

Mark thinks other clubs are going to make changes too, as the season winds down. Teams are starting to worry about not making the playoffs, about not even making the playout, about dropping to A-2 next season.

"Torino has lost their last two at home, so they're one that's probably thinking, 'If we make a move now, maybe it's not too late,' whereas if they wait a little longer it might be."

It never stops. The basketball world is a monster that's got to be fed. In the States we rarely think beyond the NBA, which employs the three hundred-odd best players, but there are some *thousand* other Americans playing every season in professional leagues in England, Israel, Belgium, Switzerland, Sweden, Spain, Greece, Mexico, Germany, Turkey, Portugal, France, Finland, the Philippines, and the Netherlands, to name a few. IBC and dozens of other agencies, large and small, here and in the U.S. and all over, buy and sell and maneuver so that every night, everywhere there's a ball game, there are enough ballplayers. Or enough of what will pass for ballplayers.

Even John Bailey, playing in three rec leagues back in Ypsilanti, might get another call one of these days.

"Sky" Walker Comes to Fabriano

I hear the coming of Kenny "Sky" Walker is *big* in Fabriano, so on Sunday, January 24, I take the train a couple of hours down the coast and then inland, westward, to this little paper-mill town nestled in the Apennines. "A nice town," says Mark Crow, who played here for six years, "but you can only look at the one main street so many times."

The Palasport (yet another) seats about five thousand. Usually only a thousand or two attend Teamsystem games, but I'm told they expect a big crowd today for Sky Walker's first home game. (It's "Sky," or "Skywalker," to everyone in Fabriano. They might not even know his first name. They certainly don't care.) They had eight hundred in the gym the first couple of times Walker *practiced.*

Skywalker. All-American at Kentucky. NBA lottery pick in 1986, slam-dunk king in '89.

Of course, the Kenny Walker of 1993 is a guy who drifted out of the NBA, went to Spain last season, and halfway through, just about a year ago, ruptured an Achilles tendon. He didn't play another game until last Sunday. Not only is his future problematical, his present is very much in doubt.

The arena does fill up, to a degree. Attendance approaches three thousand. Defending champion Benetton is here, but they're struggling at 11–8 and neither Toni Kukoc (flu) nor Terry Teagle (foot problem) made the trip. The Fabrianese have come out to see big-time Kenny Walker.

Teamsystem has an upper-deck cheering section of its own—only twenty or thirty kids, nothing like Kleenex's Untouchables, Knorr's Forever Boys Virtus, or Scavolini's Inferno Biancorosso (Red-and-White Hell), but they keep up their share of noise with drums, horns, cheers, and snappy clapping.

From the moment the teams appear, all eyes are on the lanky, impassive Skywalker. Little kids press against the railing around the court, screaming, "Walker! Skywalker! Sky!"

Everyone roars when Walker, during layup lines, sails in and puts down a straight-on, no-frills dunk, just testing his legs. *Skywalker! An NBA dunk king, doing his thing for us out here in little Fabriano!*

But Walker isn't here to show off. The next few times, he just lays the ball in and jogs to the end of the line on the other side, rolling his shoulders and jangling his hands to get loose.

When he thinks no one's watching anymore, he dusts one off from his glory days. Twenty feet out, he bounces the ball high toward the basket, chases after it, soars, snatches it in midair, and whaps it down backward. Unfortunately, he's miscalculated and brings the ball down *on* the rim instead of through it; it rolls off, and Sky stumbles as he lands.

But hey, he's rusty. The Fabrianese are elated to have a player who can even imagine such feats. (Lottery pick! Dunk king!)

The crowd is as lusty as any I've seen. They boo and insult the Benetton players and finally ruin their warm-ups by streaming down a few hundred rolls of toilet paper.

When the game starts, the reedy 6'8" Walker, an NBA small forward, is matched inside against Stefano Rusconi, the beefy, ill-bred, fifteen-million-dollar *pivot* who always annoys me with his glowering and stomping and his baleful I'll-mess-you-up-man finger-pointing.

On the first possession, Rusconi powers in and misses a gimme, but taps it in. He's got forty pounds on Walker, but at the other end Sky gets the ball and soars over him for a short jumper. Sky's certainly got the old spring.

Rusconi powers in again, sends Walker sprawling, and lays it in. Walker, on the floor, looks at the ref incredulously—and helplessly. He can't speak Italian.

A moment later Walker receives a pass on the baseline, eight feet out, and clears himself to shoot by simply skying straight up, high over everyone. Unfortunately, he still shoots as if the rim's a moving target; the ball hits the side of the backboard. The crowd groans. Walker puts his head down and hustles back to play defense.

Coach Mangano told me Walker is good for only fifteen or twenty minutes, but Sky is on the floor for the first eleven and a half before he gets a breather. Benetton leads by fourteen; it can't get much worse.

Two minutes later he's back and immediately makes my day by rising to swat Rusconi's turnaround *over* the Benetton bench and into the seats. (Rusconi twitches. Watch your back, Kenny.)

Teamsystem hangs in, ten to fifteen points down. Walker cans a couple of his less-than-graceful jumpers in close, bricks them when he ventures out to twelve feet.

"Skywalker! Sky!" the kids scream when he goes to the foul line. Walker is stiff and disjointed there, like he always was. He bends his knees exaggeratedly, sights the rim, cocks, and then stiff-arms the ball up, his feet lifting off the floor at the end, very strange-looking. Not a jump shot, like Hal Greer used when he was shooting ninety percent from the line in the sixties; it's as if Walker *intends* to stay on the floor in his follow-through, he knows that's proper, but there's a flaw in his technique so that the pull of the ball leaving his hand lifts him up at the end; he can't help it. . . .

But he's hustling like he always did, and he pleases me again near halftime when he simply yanks the ball away from big Rusconi and, as Rusconi stands there with hands on hips, glowering at the ref, and the crowd roars in anticipation—*the Skywalker! Skyyyyyy! Gonna jam!*—he covers the wide-open floor in three or four long dribbles and swoops in for a dunk. Nothing fancy, but who cares? The people are high-fivin' in Fabriano! First jam for *their* NBA dunk king!

At the half it's 47–38, Benetton. It didn't look good at first, but with Kukoc and Teagle back in Treviso this game isn't out of reach for the home team. (Not with *Sky Walker*, it isn't!)

In the second half it gets worse before it gets better, but with twelve minutes remaining Teamsystem cuts it to 57–54 on a great drive by former Laker Larry Spriggs.

With six minutes to go Rusconi goes up to dunk, but Walker elevates to snuff him. And no foul! As Teamsystem grabs the ball and takes off, Rusconi snarls something at the ref, who whirls and slaps a technical on him—to which Rusconi responds by spitting on the floor. What a showman. I recall Caserta GM Giancarlo Sarti saying, "Rusconi's talented; he's just stupid."

It's tied with :25 left, the crowd in a tizzy, when Spriggs fakes his man beautifully, goes around him for a wide-open layup . . . and the ball curls around and around the rim before finally dropping off. Last possession, Benetton can win, everybody's on their feet. Benetton comes down, passes it around, fumbles it, gets rattled, doesn't know what to do . . . and doesn't get a shot off before the buzzer. OT.

Back and forth, back and forth. Benetton leads by a point with :08 left in overtime and has a chance to ice it with a 1-and-1 at the line. But the second is no good, and Teamsystem, two points behind, flies downcourt, chaotic, fumbling the ball but not quite losing it; someone gets it to Skywalker—who you *know* won't hit a pressured shot—and he nearly travels but somehow shovels it in to Spriggs cutting down the lane, and Spriggs lays it in to tie the game *and gets hacked!* Tied! Two seconds left!

Benetton calls time-out, but Spriggs, 10-for-10 on free

throws, strides confidently to the foul line afterward and drops in the winning point. Benetton can only inbound and fling a length-of-the-court prayer.

They're going crazy in Fabriano. Teamsystem over the defending champs! The crowd stays, whistling and singing, the upper-deck cheering section waving sparklers. They do the communal call-and-response with the PA announcer giving the scoring totals: "Guerrini, *quindici (Hey!)* . . . Spriggs, *ventuno (Hey!)* . . . Walker, *tredici (Hey!)*."

The cheering for Sky Walker goes on and on. He played thirty-nine minutes, it turns out, scored 13 points on 5-for-14 shooting (and 3-for-7 from the line), grabbed 8 rebounds, blocked 4 shots. Looked a lot like he always did: hustled, got up in the air, not much of a shooter.

But he gives the people athleticism they rarely see, and they love him. They're exhilarated. Teamsystem Fabriano moves up to 7–13. Caserta's only a game ahead, then there are three teams at 9–11. Teamsystem's in playoff range. Get on a little roll with Sky and anything's possible.

The fans stay on, now chanting "Lah-*ree!* Lah-*ree!* Lah-*ree!*" Spriggs doesn't return to the floor, but they go crazy when coach Mangano comes out for a radio interview. Fifteen minutes after the game, two-thirds of the crowd is still here, the kids up top hooting and twirling sparklers and throwing streamers down, people down below just hanging around socializing as Italians do on Sundays in cafes, marketplaces, and town squares. It's a pleasant day for little Fabriano.

Dino Revisited

BILL WENNINGTON: I remember seeing him at the 1984 Olympics in Los Angeles. I was playing for Canada, nineteen or twenty at the time, and I remember thinking, "This guy's a *man*." [Meneghin was thirty-four.] He was *big*. He was *strong*. He's not as big now as he was then.

And he had this beard. Not a big, fluffy, woolly beard; it was short-trimmed, but it was so thick and dark and he was so . . . I guess *burly* is the word. I was just a young kid in college, and I remember being sent into the game at the same time as he was, looking at him as we stood there waiting to go in and thinking, "Hmmmmmm."

DANNY VRANES: I saw him when I came over here on a Pan Am team tour back in '79, when I was in college. He was a *man*. A lot bigger than he is now, and very physical—he'd whack anyone who came down the lane.

MARK CROW: I've never had the pleasure of his company for dinner, or just sitting around. Everyone says I'd enjoy it; his teammates and everyone love him. But I've only known him on the basketball court, and he's dirty as hell there. Having played against him many times, I can say he's the dirtiest of 'em all.

The first time I played over here was on a tour against Italy's national team, an outdoor game. In the first half there was a loose ball near half-court, both of us going for it. I didn't know who Dino Meneghin was. He was big and beefy at the time, but he got the worst of the contact. It wasn't a dirty hit, just one of those things where our two bodies met and the strong part of mine hit the weak part of his. He went down, I didn't. I think he was stunned a little.

So in the second half we're pressing them, he's in the post, and I'm overplaying him on the side, and he takes an elbow and just smacks me right in the mouth. One time I cut through the lane and he just picked me up and threw me on the ground. He was a great player, but he was a dirty son of a bitch too.

The Italian refs let him do whatever he wanted. He would mug you, hold your arms, pull your shorts, kick you in the nuts, bite you, scratch you. You had to know where he was, because he could hurt you. Great guy to have dinner with, I'm sure, but an SOB on the court.

MIKE D'ANTONI: Dino? Dirtiest player I've ever seen. He does things that'll get you in trouble if you do 'em to somebody on the street.

ETTORE MESSINA: I believe Dino plays clean against clean players. If another player is dirty, maybe he's different.

MARK CROW: Bullshit. He'll do anything to win, anytime. Maybe he'd be sorry if he hurt you—I'm not saying he intentionally tries to maim and kill—but he's a strong man, and he's dirty enough that if he could chop your arm off when you were scoring, he would.

LARRY MIDDLETON: He'll hit you with everything he's got. I played with him the last two years, and I've seen him do things I'd think were unimaginable. Take a few guys *out*.

And if you take a guy out at a certain time, it can change the whole rhythm of a game.

RUDY HACKETT: Dino used dirty tactics sometimes, but he was not a dirty player. He was big and strong and used whatever advantage he could get away with. He would cheap-shot you a lot with his elbows and his forearms. He used dirty tactics to get an advantage in the game. But a dirty player does it to hurt you, and Dino never tries to hurt anybody, I'll swear to that. The thing that bothered American players was that he complained about things and the refs listened to him. If we did to him what he did to us, we'd be sittin' down, but he was still in the game.

DARRYL DAWKINS: Dino gets away with more pushin', holdin', foulin', and grabbin' than *any* human in the world. But he paid his dues—he stayed around this league twenty-seven years, so they're gonna let him get away with somethin'.

MARK CROW: Anything to win. It didn't have to be above-board. The playoff game Philips lost in Pesaro in '88 but was *given* to them, two to zero, because Meneghin got hit by a coin and didn't play the second half . . .

MIKE D'ANTONI: To tell you the truth, we were an old, tired team when that happened. And I think Dino was just fed up with all the abuse he'd taken over the years, and the abuse we all took on the road.

FRANCO CASALINI (Philips's head coach in that last championship season, 1989): I think when you play so many years and have all these troubles on the road, it's tough to resist this pressure. When we played in Rome in 1983 and Dino got hit and we lost, it was up to the federation to say, "Okay, Milano won." They didn't. So when it happens another time—and believe me, Dino was a little shocked after getting hit in Pesaro, he couldn't have played one hundred percent in the second half—I understand it's tough to decide a playoff that way, but . . . After that it never happens anymore. People don't throw things at such important games now. [*Wrong*, Franco.]

DAN PETERSON: No, I don't approve of Milan winning, two to zero, on a coin hitting Dino. [Peterson had retired after the 1987 Grand Slam.] Of course, that was the semifinal. The final was even more controversial: the final basket being allowed six minutes after the game was over. Hey, when you've won twenty-three championships like Milan has, do you have to win the twenty-fourth that way? I think otherwise. We were playing in the finals in Rome in 1983 when Dino was hit with a coin. We could have protested and won—we had the coin and Dino had the cut—but we pocketed the coin and played on. We lost that final, but I'd prefer that to any clouded win.

But I don't blame Dino for not playing the second half in Pesaro. I think the club had a lot to do with that.

ETTORE MESSINA: I don't know Dino very well, but I respect him very much. I had a little hard time in my second year as head coach. I was only thirty, thirty-one. We did very well, but we had a few sloppy games and that's not okay here. People were giving me a bad time. Even after we beat Stefanel at home, people were yelling. I'm leaving the court and this guy in the stands is yelling, "Hey coach, what a fucking game, what a shit game we just saw! What a bad way to coach the team!" I turned, and I was about to answer him . . . but Dino is behind me, puts his hand on my shoulder, and says, "Don't worry. Never listen to the people. Keep going for yourself. Just forget it. You don't need to waste your time with this." And I felt very good. He went on to his locker room, and later I understood how nice it was of him—Stefanel having played very poorly, losing by thirty—to have the great sense, the great feeling, to take care of somebody else. I went to him and thanked him afterward, and every time we meet now we talk a little. I respect him, yes, very much.

LARRY MIDDLETON: Dino's a great individual, a great man, because he helps you on and off the floor. If you be feeling kind of out of it one day, here he comes with his jokin' manner, and he charges your spirit. He's the type of person who can walk into a room and make the whole room high. His charisma . . . I think that's one thing they miss in basketball here in Italy, and that's why they always talk about him: his charisma on the court. He's dynamic. He's a warrior, and they don't have many warriors here.

At the same time, he's very gentle. On the court he's an animal, but off the court he's a friend to everybody.

We still talk a lot this year even though we're not teammates anymore. He called me the night I scored thirty-four against Panasonic on TV. "*Bravo*, Middleton! What are you doing scoring so many points there?"

Sometimes I call him just to get a laugh—he's always good for a laugh. Dino is *wild*, man.

ROBERTO BRUNAMONTI: Dino has played with three generations of Italian players. Now he has forty-three years, but his heart is like twenty-one. He's like Pilutti or Fucka [young Stefanel players]—he laugh, he joke. Inside he's young.

OSCAR SCHMIDT: I know Dino, yes! A *very* good person! He's great. A heart like this [spreads his arms grandly]. He's not thirty points, twenty rebounds a game, but he goes inside and . . . GRRRRRR-*OWWWWWW!* He has impact on the games, even now. To his teammates he's an idol; everybody respect him, everybody listen to him. Oh, he's a *totem*.

And a nice person, a very nice person. Always smiling, making jokes, very funny. He's the harmony of his teams.

FLAVIO TRANQUILLO: Meneghin has such charisma, he could be a TV star—just give him a mike for sixty minutes. One time I was traveling with Milano and we got stuck in the airport for four or five hours. But the time passed like that [snaps his fingers] because of Dino.

MIKE D'ANTONI: Dino's a joker off the court, even right after a game, which coaches might not like. But he gave so much on the court, *always*, that nobody could complain.

Dino's first pregame meal with Milan, he orders wine. Peterson steps in and says no way, no wine. Dino told him he wanted wine; he said he always had wine with meals. Peterson said, "Well, I guess we've got a new policy on wine." What was he gonna say? This guy was Italy's greatest player, he'd been doin' it for years, he knew how to be ready.

DAN PETERSON: Dino and the wine? I hardly recall that. Everyone else does, though. But I know myself. I adjust. I probably said something like, "New policy on wine." I never really made a big deal out of such things. To me, other matters are vastly more important.

ETTORE MESSINA: Dino has never had a problem with one of his coaches. These great superstars are always having problems with the coach because of their great egos. But Dino was always the guy who said to the others, "Hey, he's right, let's do what he says." Now the players in Trieste tell me that every time the coach gets down—because Tanjevic works them hard and yells a lot—Dino says, "He's right, let's work harder."

RUDY HACKETT: I know Dino, I've sat down and had dinner with him, and he's a great guy, loves to laugh and joke with you. But the minute he steps on the court he's different. He takes off the mask and he's no longer that laughing, joking, amiable fellow. He's a warrior, a soldier. He follows the lead—yet he's a leader too. He *wants* to be the leader, the example-setter. What you've got to do is find the people who want to follow him. That's what Dan Peterson did. He lined up the people who wanted to be soldiers right along with Dino, and they marched through Italy. They put ten Dino Meneghins on the court, and people didn't want to play that team. That's what Dino Meneghin is all about.

ETTORE MESSINA: In Varese, until he was thirty, he was the best center in Europe, along with Kresimir Cosic. He was scoring, playing excellent defense, rebounding very well, screening. Plus, all his charisma. But he had many injuries in his first ten years: broke his nose, I think, seven times, broke his arms two or three times, his hands a couple of times; he broke *everything.* Then when he was thirty, just sold to Milan, he had a knee operation. From that point on—playing with McAdoo, D'Antoni, great players who could do the scoring—he developed into a great passer, a pivot man who could read games, screen for other players, call the defense. He really changed his game.

He's special, surely.

MARK CROW: Could Meneghin have played in the NBA? Maybe. I wasn't over here when he was twenty-three, twenty-four years old, but from what they tell me, he probably could have played. He certainly wasn't afraid of anybody, and the fear factor is a big part of the NBA. The pussies get weaned out pretty quick.

MAURIZIO GHERARDINI (Benetton GM): Meneghin was Italy's greatest player. Italy has never since had a player on a par with the greatest in Europe, but Dino was the greatest. A great team player.

Yes, he was a dirty player—he used to literally throw people off the court, and rarely even got a foul.

Personally? [A lengthy pause.] I think he grew more as a player than as a man. But a funny guy, a nice guy, great charisma.

I think he should stop playing now. He can still put up a shot or scare a referee with his look, but that's all. I think maybe he needs the money. [Gherardini suggests Meneghin lost money in bad investments, notably some real estate in Sardinia.]

He should stay in basketball. Renato Villalta is now a *symbole* for the national team; Dino should be able to do that, he has much more charisma.

ETTORE MESSINA: He's playing about twenty minutes a game, scoring three points and getting four rebounds, but he's more important to his team than the coach. I think the team will surely want him back next season.

LARRY MIDDLETON: He makes that team go. In practice he *goes*, he *goes*. When he takes a shower, that's when Dino's done. The other guys look at him, forty-three years old and all fired up, and they've *got* to play hard.

PIERO PASINI (Telemarket Forli head coach): Stefanel must ask him back again. If not, I'll take him on the bench beside me in a second. He will straighten out the young players who don't play right. I think Messina should have him with the national team, as an assistant or something. The players respect him so much.

ETTORE MESSINA: People have said maybe he would make a good general manager. But the problem with that, to me, for both Dino and Roberto [Brunamonti], is that they are too much clean persons to be general managers. I don't like that job very much; they've got to be ice people, they must forget feelings. Neither Dino or Roberto could do that.

Being a team manager is not a special job. You waste your charisma if you have that job.

I think they would be great coaching young players, junior players—that would be very special. If I'm a father and my son wanted to go play for Dino Meneghin, I would *take* him there. Because he would learn so much about life *besides* basketball, he would surely grow up a special person.

PIERO PASINI: What else can you say about Dino? Words can't explain.

Dino, looking like anything but a wild man in tasteful loafers, slacks, and sweater, drinking a soda in the Jolly Hotel bar in Rome on the Saturday evening before Stefanel takes on Virtus Roma: "Dan Peterson and the wine, that wasn't so much. I tell him I'm Italian, I like wine when I eat, one glass. I don't like Coke or Fanta when I eat. It was no problem after that: I drank a glass of wine with my meal."

"Do you remember whacking Roberto Premier, a teammate in Milan, *during a game?*"

Dino smiles. "His first years were terrible. This was a guy, if you didn't stay with the knife on his ass all the time, sometimes he forget to play. It was only one time and not very hard," he recalls cheerfully—"just to wake him up, remind him he's on the court."

"Did you take liberties with Premier's Gatorade too?"

Dino grins like a naughty boy who's pleased to be discovered. "He was always making these cocktails with vitamins and Gatorade, so I would, you know, put my socks or my jock in it."

Only your socks or jock?

"Okay, sometimes something else went in. Give him a *real* vitamin, you know? The olive in the cocktail."

Not surprisingly, Dino's unable to shed any light on the warlike side of his nature.

"I always liked to play this way, very aggressive on defense, and give it my best all the time—for me, for my team, for the people who come to watch the game. When I was young, I had the big men who teach me how to play. When I make a mistake they were on my neck [he pretends to clamp an unfriendly claw on his neck], yelling at me because I didn't do this, didn't do that. That's why I learn to do these different things."

Sure, everyone wants to do well. But no one in Italy has ever been as ferocious as Dino.

Dino knows it, not that he can explain it. "You know what they say here, and they say it in America too: 'Some people has balls, and some people doesn't have them.' " Dino's smiling like a killer sixteen-year-old stud. "I think I have them."

That's why it's hard to understand his sitting out the second half of that playoff game in Pesaro in '89, even though the coin hit him and even drew a little blood. He could have played. Some say it was unmanly to win a playoff game, and in effect a series, that way.

"In Pesaro," Dino admits, "I wasn't hurt that bad. I could have played. I've taken worse hits than that. But I said to myself, 'That's enough.' Because that court was terrible since I was sixteen years old. Every time I come there they yell at me, spit on me, put bad names on me and my family, *every* time. And it was not the first time I was ever hit by a coin there. So I say, 'It's enough, I don't wanna play anymore.' Somebody has to give 'em a lesson. Even the newspapers in Pesaro don't write about when the fans throw coins, papers, ice cream, everything. Somebody has to do something so people can see what they've been doing here every game. [Pesaro fans are consistently at the bottom of the Coppa Disciplina ratings.]

"It's too much on that court. Even when I was seventeen and never play in the game they yell at me. Now they *really* don't like me." Dino laughs. "They hate me, I hate them."

How about next season? *Il Gigante* had a big story around Christmas with Dino promising this is his last year. But people tell me he's said it a few times before.

"The writers have to write something. If I give them something, they're satisfied. I tell them I will probably retire. But like every year, I will wait until the end and look back at how I played.

"Right now I don't think I can play next year. I had problems with my shoulder this season, and it takes longer to come back from injury every time. And then when I don't play so good . . . I don't like to stay on the court just for making the numbers. I don't need to be the most important player, but just an important part of the game.

"Sometimes I think it's better to retire now, because I don't want to have to stop when I'm down, when the team will tell me to stop. If I play next year and do nothing, I will think it would have been better if I had retired. It's respect for what I try to do in my career."

Coaches and players say Stefanel would suffer without the example Dino sets. He does still "give the team something special."

"Wellllll . . . yes, this is why they gave me a contract. Because I am a good player—*almost*—and because they think it helps the young players. I tell them when they don't practice hard or play like I like. When I was young, the old players teach me to practice hard, and they get mad and do stuff [pretends to twist his ear off] if I didn't do it. So it's just my way to practice. When I see somebody lazy on the court, when somebody doesn't jump on the ball on the floor, then I feel crazy, 'cause if I can do it, so old, he can do it too.

"I just like to win. I don't like to come out on the court just to participate."

Bob Morse strides into the hotel bar at seven o'clock. I had a glass of wine with Morse yesterday and asked him questions for a couple of hours. Tonight he and Dino are going out to dinner.

Dino stands up, breaking into a smile, when Morse appears. "Bob-*bee*," he says, and they hug warmly. They haven't been teammates since 1980–81 in Varese and have rarely seen each other since '86, when Morse retired; Morse has spent most of the interval in the U.S. before returning this season to do color on TeleMonteCarlo's NBA games. But there were those nine years together, from their early twenties to early thirties, with the championships, the travels.

I sit with them for five minutes, but I'm out of place now. They're beaming at each other, looking each other up and down: the two monuments of "mighty Varese" of the seventies, now in their forties.

As I'm taking my leave, Bob asks me what I'm going to write about Dino.

"I don't know what, exactly, but I want to make him famous in America."

"At last," Dino chuckles. "I pay you off later," he tells me.

Bob asks, "Do you have a title yet for a chapter on him?"

" '*Il monumento nazionale*,' I think."

Dino's shaking his head. "I never like this name. They call me this for many years and I always think, 'National monuments, they're all dead guys.' When I hear it I always see myself like this, a statue"—and he throws one arm up and freezes, like a statue of a general with a sword—"with pigeons on my shoulder."

On Sunday afternoon Bob Morse and I meet at Rome's Palaeur for the Stefanel–Virtus Roma game. Stefanel is only a game out of second place at 13–7—a bit of a surprise, considering that the big *pivot* Davide Cantarello and the seven-foot finesse player Gregor Fucka have been out of the lineup much of the time. One reason is that Dino has been playing twenty to twenty-five minutes a game, more than he'd been counted on for, and if he's putting up feeble numbers, he's also playing smart and aggressive ball—Meneghin ball—and the team has hung together.

Today he's matched up against Roma's Dino Radja, Celtics property, one of the league's top scorers. On Roma's first possession Radja starts a drive and Meneghin forces him to the middle, but no teammate steps in to help and Radja gets an easy dunk. Dino might not be the madman he once was, whacking teammates who displease him, but as the teams head the other way he's pumping a fist and either encouraging, instructing, or dressing down the guy who should have confronted Radja.

For the most part he sprints up and down the floor—more than you can say for Darryl, or even a kid like Rusconi—and he's surprisingly spry.

But he *is* forty-three years old, and a few minutes into the game he starts taking an occasional rest, hanging back when the action takes off the other way. Tanjevic gives him a breather, but with Cantarello still injured he can't keep him out long.

Sitting on the bench in the second half, Dino gets angry about a call and starts yelling and flailing a towel in disgust. Back in the game later, feeling he got hacked when an opponent stole the ball from him, he kicks over a courtside chair.

Yet when he plows toward the hoop and flattens a couple of opponents, he makes a point of helping them up and slapping five. Bob Morse shakes his head in disbelief: "Dino didn't pick guys up in the old days."

Roma leads throughout the second half and wins by ten. Dino Radja plays all forty minutes for Roma and scores 22 points, grabs 11 rebounds. Dino Meneghin fouls out with a minute to go after playing twenty-five minutes: 4 points, 2 rebounds, 2 turnovers, 2 assists. He was intense, concentrated, but no way wild. He wouldn't have scared anybody tonight.

After the game, Bob and I chat for a few minutes with *basket*-world fixture Franco Lauro, a friendly guy who does interviews on TV games and hosts the weekly half-hour highlights show. As we say good-bye, Franco points to Bob and tells me, "He's a legend, Bob Morse."

We wait for Dino in the hall outside the Stefanel locker room. Youthful, wet-haired Stefanel players head out to the bus with their gym bags. Finally Dino appears.

"We heard the radio man calling you *il monumento nazionale*," I tell him as we walk out, and Dino laughs and thrusts an arm in the air: "Yeah, with the pigeons on my shoulder."

Outside Stefanel's team bus, Dino and Bob embrace. Dino says something to him in Italian, ending in "Bobby," which he must have called him in the old days—before Morse became a legend in his own right and now a respectable TV man; he quickly corrects himself, "I mean, *Bob*." Laughing, he says, "Say something to me on TV, Bob. Say, '*Ciao*, Dino,' next time."

People are waiting, staring. A couple ask for autographs. Dino signs, then gives us a wave and gets on the bus.

I can't help teasing the proud but exceedingly modest Morse about Franco Lauro's comment. "That must have been some team you had in Varese, with a legend *and* a *monumento nazionale*."

Bob smiles and jerks a thumb back toward the Stefanel bus. "There are lots of legends," he says, "but there's only one national monument."

D'Antoni Floating

Some of these winter weeks in Riccione stretch a little long, when it's too stormy to get out much and no midweek Euroclub Championship games in Pesaro or Bologna to break up the time.

But then, I've got more to do now. I'm accumulating more and more material for my book, so I can sit cozily in my living room (in the cozy Telemarket sweat suit Lou appropriated for me) and work on that. I know more people around Riccione, so when the weather's not too rough I can walk Viale Dante toward the Center and find company not only at the Savioli and at Aldo's bar by the canal, but at Chantal's gift shop and Signor Estudienta's market and the sweet thumbless lady's always-deserted leather shop and various other places.

Sometimes I'll break up the week by meeting Mark Crow for a long lunch in Rimini before he heads up to the office in San Marino at two-thirty or so. Some days he's got his giggly five-year-old Jack with him and we go over to the house instead, where we eat cheese and bread and prosciutto and veggies and drink wine with the witty and delightful Lia, and afterward Mark pours me a generous shot of his "special" Scotch and eventually lets himself be persuaded to join me.

To puff him up (when the hoops dinosaur finds himself telling about his recent duels with Rudy Hackett in an *amateur* league), I tell him I can't leave without stopping in the den for another look at the framed photo of "the pride of Fabriano," back in his ten-years-gone prime, throwing down a dunk over a baby-faced Drazen Petrovic in some European competition.

Occasionally I'll train to Forli and meet Lou Colabello at "his" cafe near the great town square, where, as I like to remind him, he's as big as Jerry West at the Forum Club. Lou! they cry. *Ciao,* Lou! Lou! We stand at the counter and choose among the various sandwiches already prepared in hard rolls three feet long; you just point out approximately how much you want, the man in the apron hacks it off, you order a *birra* and you're set.

And there's always Bologna, where at the very least I can get some magazines and newspapers: it's ninety minutes on the train and ninety minutes back, but Proust or no Proust I need the occasional *Spy* and *Newsweek* and *Sports Illustrated.* There's a great newsstand in the *stazione,* a comparable one across the street, and the best I've found in Italy a mile or so away, across the street from the Palasport—they've got everything, including all the trash papers from England with the latest pictures of Di.

Then there's Feltrinelli's International Bookstore, a vast two-story affair near the two leaning towers and Roberto Brunamonti's restaurant. (Alberto says Bologna is known for "tits, towers, and tortellini.")

And there's Brunamonti's restaurant, Benso, at the end of the little alley. I've had lunch there two or three times with Roberto, falling in love a little more each time (as when we're leaving one day and I say, "I must pay for my lunch, I've never paid," and Roberto replies, pushing me out the door, "I'll play an extra season"). I've had long, wonderful lunches and conversations there with Ettore Messina, who'll get together any time I like and always suggests Benso and signs it off to a Knorr tab. (I don't know if *any* Italian has ever let me pay for a meal, or even for my part of one.)

And, of course, Bortolo, over at the *lega* offices on Viale Aldo Moro. Anytime he's not off on business he's happy to see me, and I'm always warmed not only by his high-five and the sight of my Christmas gift on his wall (a framed blowup of a photo I took of him the first day I came to the office, back in October, with the stick-on letters *VIP* on the glass) but by the reception from Daniela and Tiziana and Loretta out front and from *lega* VIPs who evince not even a mote of the arrogance of some of the pipsqueaks in the Trail Blazer PR department. Alberto and I go to lunch every few weeks, occasionally at his apartment where the angelic Annarosa has left something he has only to warm up.

I get by. And then it's the weekend again.

I don't need any distractions this week. After seeing Dino in Rome I hung out with Tom Federman, the lawyer, until Tuesday, and I've barely gotten home and transcribed my interviews with Dino and Bob Morse before it's Friday and I'm leaving on one of my rationed trips to Milan. "Rationed" meaning that though I talk to Mike and Laurel two or three times a week and feel as comfortable with them as with my own family, I'd feel guilty about taking advantage of their hospitality too often.

On Friday, February 5, I take the train to Milan and taxi to the apartment, where the landlady gives me a key the D'Antonis have left for me. I drop my bag upstairs, then walk over to the squash club to meet Mike for lunch.

"Hey, how's it goin', guy?" he says brightly, without a trace of the gloom-and-doom air of my last trip.

As it's turned out, the win in Treviso that last night, December 23, was *not* just a freaky reprieve in a disastrous season. Philips has been the terror of the league ever since: seven straight wins and counting. They're winning their Korac Cup games, everything.

"Aw, man, Jim, everything's different," Mike gushes. He's

absolutely aglow, and I recall him saying during my last visit, "As low as you feel when it's like this, that's how high you feel when you got it goin' good."

"It's fun to wake up in the morning," he says now. "Fun to go to practice. The guys are so close; it feels so good. No doubt about it, I'm psyched. I'm lookin' at a team that could win the championship, no doubt in my mind, even without Ambrassa [Fabrizio Ambrassa, starting forward, got hurt last week and is out for the season]. I'm not sayin' we will; I'm sayin' we *can*."

After seven consecutive wins Philips is tied for second with Panasonic at 14–7. They probably can't catch Knorr in the regular season, but could—should—finish second and have good position for the playoffs.

That's all Mike wants. Yes, they're thin with Ambrassa gone, but he *likes* his team. Everybody talks about unbeatable, ten-deep Knorr, but Mike thinks his six or seven little guys can play even with them.

Back at the apartment he plays the tape of Philips's Korac Cup win a few nights ago. *Damn*, he likes this small, quick lineup he's gone with since the win in Treviso!

How do you think we stack up against Knorr, Jim? he asks, but before I can give it two seconds' thought he's effusing about the matchups. First—this is how he begins the comparison between Philips and every other team—they can't guard Ricky Pittis at power forward. Ricky will go right around either Wennington or Binelli, Knorr's two big men. At center, Antonio Davis holds his own, or better, with either of the two. Yes, Danilovic is a problem, but Riva's been stopping Pace Mannion and the league's other big guards, and if he can just slow Danilovic down a little . . .

Mike talks, talks, talks about teams and matchups. Stefanel? Clear? Panasonic? Scavolini? Mike won't say it too loud, but he feels his team is better than any of them.

Benetton? Up and down all season with no point guard, but Terry Teagle hurt his foot and Benetton has just filled his spot by signing playmaker Chris Corchiani for four games.

Mike thinks they'll improve once Corchiani fits in. Teagle was great at what he did, but Corchiani is what they need.

But bring 'em on! Knorr too!

Laurel and I have a glass of wine in the kitchen while she grills chicken for dinner. Mike comes in, pours himself yet another Coke, makes a little small talk, then puts a choice breast on a plate and spends ten minutes hunched over the table dicing it into the tiniest, most perfect bites for the beloved cats, Lupo and Medea. He's more attentive to the cats than to us, a sign that he's locking in on tomorrow's game.

After dinner he lies on his couch in the living room watching more tapes, then a little TV. He's talking to Medea a lot, so I hang out in the den with Laurel, who's choosing music for the game tomorrow. When Mike wanders in, we titter about his game face.

He doesn't mind. All's right with the world.

Eventually we call it a night. Mike takes a cassette to put into the bedroom VCR. I finish a highball in the living room, jot some notes, finally turn out the lights and head down to "my" room. The lights are out in Mike and Laurel's room, but through the smoked glass doors, as I pass, I can see the game is playing, I hear the low commentary—a lullaby for a hoops junkie . . .

The Stefanel game has been moved to Saturday night because of a scheduling conflict at the Forum. They'll probably have a bigger crowd than usual, without the Sunday competition with soccer. It's hard to comprehend why the league insists on going up against almighty *football* every week, year after year.

Mike holds a shootaround in the morning. For the second straight day Milanese cars aren't allowed on the streets due to smog levels; Mike and the players pile into some friends' cars with out-of-the-region plates to get to the Forum. Laurel gets a ride out with someone too, to set things up for tonight.

Back at the apartment at mid-afternoon, Mike and I watch

part of an NBA game. The second half of Benetton–Scavolini is coming on in a few minutes; we'll watch that before we head to the arena, as Milanese cars aren't allowed on the streets until six o'clock. We both want to see the new Benetton, with Corchiani replacing Teagle; if they're better, as Mike suspects, they're a threat for the championship.

The television slot for the weekly Saturday TV game amounts to whatever is left after the weekly Saturday TV *volleyball* match ends. Mike goes back to the bedroom to change into a suit for the game, but volleyball ends earlier than usual and he reappears in his T-shirt and boxer shorts, pulling his chair up close to the TV.

Benetton is 20 points ahead in the first half, with Corchiani controlling the ball and getting in for short jump shots. "Terry Teagle is a great player," Mike says, "but three guys would stand around not knowing what to do. They'll be better this way."

Almost time to go. Mike seems to loosen up now, as if the worst—the waiting—is over. As the Benetton-Scavolini game winds down he's back and forth between the bedroom and the TV, bit by bit getting into his suit and tie and shiny shoes.

Bucky Buckwalter of the Trail Blazers is coming to the game tonight. "Maybe he's checking out coaches as well as players," I say. "Maybe Rick Adelman needs a new assistant."

"Yeah," Mike chuckles, "I'm sure Bucky's gettin' the contract ready right now."

We drive to the Forum talking about the game, the teams, the players. Mike's fired up. He likes his team, he *likes* 'em.

I meet up with Bucky Buckwalter in the press room and we watch the game together from the second row of the stands, near half-court. It's so nice to be with someone from home that I don't see much of the game: I'm asking questions, getting the gossip about the Blazers and the Portland writers and other friends and enemies of mine.

I do notice that Albert English is popping them in, and that Dino gets a few hoops and tops his scoring average early. But Philips stays out in front. Djordjevich, who's been the scourge of the *lega* since nearly getting released, is scoring a lot of points, and he barely breaks a sweat doing it. Once in a while he drives, but mostly he just drifts around three-point land, receiving passes and lofting them in.

Bucky, the professional talent hunter, manages to entertain me as well as absorb every detail of the game.

He's got some notes that he cups in his palm like a guy shielding his poker hand. He admits he's checking out English but I suspect he came mostly to watch Gregor Fucka (FOOTCH-KA), since Brad Greenberg has written to me asking what I know of Fucka and I saw Bucky's dismay before the game when someone nearby told us the kid is hurt again and wouldn't play tonight.

Having seen Fucka a few times, I venture the opinion that the twenty-two-year-old seven-footer could never play in the NBA. He's too scrawny to play inside and doesn't have any inside moves anyway; he's not a good enough ballhandler or shooter to play outside. He's a lower-case Brad Sellers, who hung around the NBA for several years with negligible impact. Fucka is talked up as a top young player, and I believe he is—on the rare occasions when he's not hurt—a top young player *for Europe, for Italy*.

In Europe, to say a guy does a little bit of everything is to say he doesn't do anything abysmally. In Fucka's case it means he's tall enough to get some points inside just by hanging around (at least in Italy, where he's not contending with bruisers); he can hit the occasional fifteen-foot shot (nice for a seven-footer, but it's not as if you'd want him shooting a lot of them); he "can handle the ball, for a seven-footer" (meaning he doesn't bounce the ball off his foot most times, but it's not as if he'll hurt the other team with his wizardry on fast breaks or his one-on-one virtuosity). NBA-wise, Gregor Fucka is a man without a position.

But in a land full of limited players, a Fucka stands out.

And if you had five Fuckas, you'd do well. The same goes for Philips's Ricky Pittis, who's been scouted by NBA teams. Knorr's Ricky Morandotti is 6'7" or so, a pretty good rebounder, pretty good defender, pretty good ballhandler, decent shooter—nothing remarkable, but this "little bit of everything," with no great weaknesses, makes him one of the better players in Italy.

Philips is in control all the way as Djordjevich scores 30, barely sweating. They play great team basketball, moving the ball briskly, finding the open man for three-pointers. Lots of three-pointers. The style is fun to watch; it's fun for the players. And it works.

Albert English scores 31 for Stefanel, but Bucky isn't impressed.

While I'm not looking, *il monumento nazionale* goes off for season highs of 17 points and 10 rebounds—to no avail, but it's great that he shows some of the old stuff for the Milan fans. Oh you Meneghin!

Dino's at the Torchietto when we get there, down at the far end of a long table in the back room with a group including the woman I recognize from the pictures in the D'Antonis' den as Caterina, the woman Dino calls "my wife" and who might actually become Signora Meneghin this summer. We all shake hands: "*Ciao*," "*Ciao*." I congratulate Dino on his big game.

"Finally they give me the ball, and you see what happens?" He laughs.

Bucky works. Just before Laurel introduces him to Dino, I mention that Dino's son plays in the league, and the veteran scout's antennae go up; after being introduced, then flattering Dino by saying he remembers watching him destroy so-and-so twenty years ago, Bucky turns the conversation to the only Meneghin who can possibly help him: How old is Andrea? How tall? What kind of player? At the table he quizzes Flavio Tranquillo, who knows every player on seven continents, about a 7'6" creature in some back country. While we're eating he tells Mike he'd like to ask Djordjevich about any young prospects in ex-Yugoslavia; when Mike calls Sasha over to our table, Bucky introduces himself as "the man who drafted Drazen Petrovic," congratulates Sasha on a great game, then questions him for ten minutes about young players back home. Djordjevich, twenty-four, knows a few twenty-one- and twenty-two-year-olds, but he's not up on the teenagers, who are the ones Bucky's interested in. Still, Bucky takes his name and address; you never know, someday this Djordjevich connection might lead to Bucky Buckwalter being the guy who drafts the *next* Drazen Petrovic.

Bucky, who's been making trips to Europe since the early eighties, remembers Mike's glory days with the great Milano teams.

"You know, Mike," he says, "I always loved Drazen [Petrovic] as a player, but I remember one game over here when I actually had some questions about drafting him." Bucky shakes his head as if still amazed, giving Mike a chance to be modest. "He had what, ten points?"

Mike plays modest, but pride shines through. "I'd heard so much about Petrovic that before we played 'em I went around telling everybody, 'I'll so-and-so if he gets fifty on me.' Well, he scored forty-nine, I think it was.

"The next time, I got ready for him. I did all I could. I think he got ten or thirteen . . ."

"I saw that game," Bucky says. "I wondered about Drazen then." He skips a beat, then grins, his own pride showing: "Still drafted him, though."

It's 2:30 in the morning by the time we drop Bucky off at the Hilton. He's flying to Paris in the morning, catching a game on Tuesday, then coming back for the Scavolini-Roma game next Sunday—to watch Carlton Myers, no doubt.

As soon as we're back in the car and heading home, "just family" again, Mike's abuzz about his team. It's obvious that it's been hard for him to talk about other things tonight in order to be polite to Bucky, who after all didn't come seven thousand miles to hear solely about Philips Milano. But Sasha is *back!* Antonello is *shootin' it!* They're playin' defense, they're playin' hard! Ricky Pittis is the best number four in Italy! And they're so consistent!

He *likes* what he's got, *likes* it. It's a small team, there's no depth with Ambrassa gone, they're overly reliant on three-point shooting—but it's working. And it's almost more fun this way, living on the edge.

Back at the apartment, Mike's still talking matchups at 3 A.M. He's so confident, it seems like a good time to point out the obvious: "No matter what the other matchups are against Knorr, *you'll* have the problem matching up with Danilovic. He's the best player on the court."

"Antonello [Riva] can slow him down," Mike insists. "And their big guys can't guard Pittis. And Brunamonti will be worn out in the playoffs—he always looks like someone dipped him in flour by the end of the season."

The last thing he says as he finally heads off to bed: "Ettore is a good coach, a great guy, honest, straightforward. I hope he does well with the national team. But"—he smiles—"I wanna *kick . . . his . . . butt* this season."

And he says good-night.

When I turn out my light a few minutes later, I can tell by the glow out in the hall that he's watching a ball game in the bedroom.

Two days later I watch a Knorr practice in Bologna and chat afterward with Messina, who says cheerfully, "Mike thinks we'll start looking over our shoulders if we lose a couple? No, no, no, no, no—he's thinking about how *his* team would react. We in Bologna"—and he makes the big-balls gesture—"have *grandi coglioni.* Tell Mike our game at the end of the season won't mean anything, because we'll have everything settled by then."

I tell him that Mike says the Knorr big men can't guard Pittis.

"No problem. I won't try to guard him with Wennington or Binelli; I'll use Morandotti. Tell Mike he'll have to think of something else.

"And he thinks Roberto will be exhausted by the playoffs? I know Roberto often gets tired, so I'm resting him as much as possible.

"Tell Mike what I say," Ettore reminds me. "Have some fun with him."

"*Fine*," Mike retorts when I relate Messina's plans to thwart Pittis with the 6'7" Morandotti instead of Wennington or Binelli. "Fine. Then we've got one of their big men out of the game. And Morandotti hasn't been playin' worth a shit anyway.

"And Roberto *will* be tired, you'll see."

Nyah, nyah.

"Welcome, Chris, the Future Is in Your Hands"

Hard to believe, as March approaches, that I've been here almost five months. Even harder to believe—or maybe just hard to accept—is that in only three months more I'll be gone.

I keep recalling my little exchange with Bucky Buckwalter when we let him off at the Hilton in Milan last week. As we shook hands Bucky said, "It looks like things are going real well for you over here. I'm glad."

"*Real* well," I told him. "It's still hard to believe this is my *job*, traveling around watching basketball games and meeting nice people and eating great meals."

"I know," Bucky said with a conspiratorial grin. "I've been getting away with it for twenty years."

A week later I'm on Knorr Bologna's team bus for the three-hour ride up to Treviso. Messina, the night we met last fall, said he'd try to arrange for me to travel with the team sometime if I wanted, and with Benetton newly threatening I decided a couple of days ago that this would be a great trip. Ettore cleared it with his bosses, and here I am. I'll ride up with the team, stay with them at the Hotel Al Fogher (where Philips put me up on the trip just before Christmas), eat with them, the whole thing.

I sit up front chatting with Ettore and his amiable assistant, Renato Pasquali, for the first hour or so. But Ettore is increasingly preoccupied with tomorrow's game and after a stop for snacks at a little store along the *autostrada* I walk back toward Bill Wennington, who's sitting alone playing games on a pocket computer. Ettore introduced us last month when he'd invited me to join the team for its pregame meal at a hotel in Pesaro. I wasn't overly interested in Wennington, except maybe as a guy who many people feel is *stealing* eight hundred thousand dollars a year, but I did try calling him one day soon afterward. He was gone to practice, his wife Ann said, but she and I had a fifteen-minute conversation that snapped me back to the reality I want to live in: meaning that Bill Wennington isn't the world's greatest ballplayer, but he does all he can, and then, what's important, he goes home to one of the nicest, brightest women I've ever talked to. I've had a whole new regard for him ever since.

For one reason or another I haven't called back, though Ann invited me to visit anytime, and now I don't know whether Bill even remembers meeting me in Pesaro. But he looks up as I approach his aisle seat, and after startling me for an instant by snapping, "Hey, get off the bus, man," he laughs and moves over to the window seat to make room for me.

We talk for the rest of the trip. Bill reviews his six uneventful NBA seasons and his decision to come to Italy ("I just wanted to *play*"). Last season was tough, he says, with Ann back in the States at the start giving birth to their first child and with the Italian writers trashing him, but it's much better now: Ann and their son are here, and he's so jazzed on fatherhood that he doesn't worry about what the papers say. Lowering his voice, he says he's not even bothered by Messina's constant screaming at him in practice: "I don't take it personally. I think he takes things out on me because I'm the type who never argues with my coaches. I just say, 'Okay, whatever, you're the coach.' "

A most friendly, easygoing fellow. I recall Dan Peterson's comment on him: "Ettore wanted a versatile and coachable player. Bill Wennington is that. And he blends well with the Italian players. That counts."

As we near Treviso I see that Ettore, up front, is reading several pages of Peterson's responses to questions I've faxed to him. Like me and many others, he finds Peterson brilliant and highly entertaining, and ever since he learned that I do these written interviews with Peterson, he's wanted to see them. I brought them along today, and now Ettore—occasionally laughing, occasionally tapping Renato on the shoulder to show him something—is absorbed.

Like virtually everyone else, he also finds the famous ex-coach one of the most egotistical people on earth, which turns out to be what's got him in stitches as we finally pull up at the hotel. I've never seen anyone laugh so hard for so long. As the players get off and get their bags out of the luggage compartment down below, Ettore is howling over the fact that after the three pages of answers Peterson sent me the first time, he had attached a self-glorifying *five-page* resume: AWARDS AND CITATIONS WON BY DAN PETERSON, DAN PETERSON'S 14-YEAR COACHING RECORD IN ITALY, DAN PETERSON'S PLAYOFF COACHING RECORDS, etc., right down to such minutiae as DAN PETERSON'S BOLOGNA CITY SERIES RECORD (he coached Virtus Bologna for five years before moving to Milan and putting together the eighties dynasty), DAN PETERSON'S ALL-STAR GAME RECORDS and BREAKDOWN OF DAN PETERSON'S 22 PLAYOFF ROAD WINS.

"Incredible!" Ettore splutters. "Big Dan! Little Big Dan! His ego's two feet taller than he is! Look at this: the TV Key Magazine Award for his Lipton Tea commercials—*the Italian equivalent of the Clio,* he adds! The TeleGatto Award for TV commentary—*the Italian equivalent of the Emmy!* Oh, my God! Oh, Peterson!"

I'm glad I could play a small part in keeping worrywart Messina loose, at least for a while, the day before a big game.

• • •

The green-and-white Benetton rooting section is packed into the upper deck long before game time, chanting filth about Knorr, the city of Bologna, and the Bolognese as a people. A small group from Bologna happily sings, "We're first in the league, la-la!" which only incites the Trevigiani further—which, of course, is the point.

The Treviso fans are charged up for this game. It's Chris Corchiani's first home game and there's new hope. Today Benetton can throw a scare into Knorr, which has already lost its aura of invincibility by getting knocked off twice in five days by Scavolini last month, in *lega* and then Euroclub play.

WELCOME, CHRIS, THE FUTURE IS IN YOUR HANDS, reads a big sign in the upper deck. Another, CHRIS: LIGHT OUR FIRE. There are lots of Corchiani signs.

Well before the players come out for warm-ups I find Messina standing at courtside looking around at the crowd and sort of just being alone. He admits he's nervous; he says he's nervous before every game. His concern today is that his team will look past this game. Benetton isn't a real threat to catch them in the standings and Philips, only a mild threat anyway, has a tough game today (Scavolini, on the road, with Scavolini in danger of missing the playoffs if they don't get tough). There's no obvious motivation.

And Danilovic, experiencing pain in his foot lately, isn't playing. Messina says, "I think Sasha is afraid now because the pain is in the same place where he once broke his foot." Meaning, another break and he'll be learning a trade before he ever gets into that Golden State Warriors uniform.

Corchiani is one of the first players out to loosen up, well before the teams appear. A roar goes up from the Benetton rooters, getting their first look at the player they hope can resurrect their championship hopes. Corchiani smiles and gives them a wave, but in a few seconds the smile vanishes into an American-style game face and I know, even if they don't, that he won't acknowledge them again.

Messina remarks that he hadn't known Corchiani was so

short. "But he's definitely smart," he adds. He's seen plenty of Corchiani on film. "We'll challenge him on his outside shot today."

Bill Wennington comes out for some early shooting, and I'm hoping he'll get his eight rebounds today. "I need to get eight rebounds every game," he told me on the bus. "Ten points and eight boards and Ettore is happy with me. Less than eight boards and he's pissed." Eight rebounds doesn't seem like so much to ask from a seven-foot center in a league of undersized and not overly talented centers, but more often than not Bill falls a little short; he's averaging around seven per game.

The teams come out. The Palaverde fills up. There's a big-game atmosphere.

The pale, lanky Kukoc, who has played in many bigger games, moves languidly through warm-ups. Due to the endless dance between Kukoc, Benetton, and the Chicago Bulls it seems he's been around forever, and it's always a bit of a shock to see him and be reminded how young he is: twenty-four, and with his smooth, open, almost innocent face he looks even younger. He's even got a cowlick.

Corchiani—he of the hard, square jaw, and short, thick legs—takes it all in, looking around at the crowd and down at Knorr warming up, everywhere, as if an undersized thinking-man's player needs to be in perfect tune with everything around him.

Terry Teagle, in blue jeans and a jean jacket, watches from the Benetton bench.

As the teams huddle at their benches and send their starting fives out, the Benetton fans are screaming and loosing a blizzard of green-and-white confetti and flinging dozens of rolls of toilet paper down on the floor and maniacally waving green-and-white scarves. The place is *throbbing*.

If the Knorr players weren't motivated before they took the floor, the crowd's emotion has gotten them pumped up. The best measure of the intensity of the game is that when Roberto Brunamonti gets called for a weird offensive foul in the opening minutes, he reacts. That is, he looks at the ref with his arms spread questioningly for about three seconds before heading the other way. Not a word, not even a *look*—almost no reaction at all, but extreme for Roberto.

Kukoc, whatever his flaws, can be dazzling. Today he's shooting well, which is hardly a given with him, and his passing is as usual—which is to say, the nearest thing to Magic Johnson. In the second half Knorr, the best defensive team in the league, double-teams Kukoc, and he starts zipping passes I can't believe; I don't dare take notes, out of fear of missing something.

He's freakish, a towering kid with the hand-eye genius of John McEnroe. He's got that rarest of gifts, the kind of vision and anticipation that lets him make several passes each game where you're saying "There's no one there, why did he do that?"—just as someone in Benetton green materializes, *another incredible dish!*, and you're left wondering, How?

The green-and-white scarves are going crazy. Corchiani's got the ball in his hands most of the time, and he's got an idea, as coaches used to say, as in "Have an idea out there!" Benetton looks as if it's got an idea, which hasn't always been the case this season.

They're singing in the upper deck as the last five minutes play out. *Who doesn't jump is Bolognese!* and *Bologna, Bologna, go fuck yourselves!* and *Don't be sad, Bologna fans, the important thing is to participate!* At the other end there's a hardy group of twenty or so Forever Boys—hardy, but not nearly enough of them to be heard over the tidal wave of sound from the Treviso end.

The final is Benetton Treviso 85, Knorr Bologna 74.

Besides running the offense without making a single turnover, Corchiani scores 20 points in thirty-five minutes and makes 4 steals. Brunamonti, his matchup, plays thirty minutes and scores 3 points only, with 3 turnovers and no steals.

Kukoc plays all forty minutes, scoring 29 points and passing like Magic Johnson.

Ten minutes after the teams leave the floor, no one has left the Palaverde. The end-zone group chants and sings and finally starts yelling "Toni! Toni!" as if they expect a curtain call. They're just hanging out, having a great old time, excited about Benetton again.

"The crowds here are unbelievable," the twenty-five-year-old Corchiani exclaims a half hour later outside the Benetton locker room, flushed from the game and a shower and probably from love, as his fiancee, visiting from Raleigh, North Carolina, is sitting beside him. Life's grand sometimes: you're a hero again, and your girl is there to see it.

"This is the wildest atmosphere I've ever been in," Corchiani says. "High school, college . . . I played in the ACC, and this puts Duke fans [the notorious "Cameron Crazies"] to shame. You don't see anything like this in the NBA, for sure. I like the idea of playing in this atmosphere."

I'm sure it beats the CBA, which is where Corchiani, recently cut by the Washington Bullets, was heading when Benetton called.

"I was gonna go back to the CBA and keep working on my game and just see what happened," says Corchiani, who's obviously nowhere near giving up his NBA dreams. "But this was a great opportunity for me, a real nice situation.

"I think sometimes you can make more money over here. In the NBA I'm a fringe player, but over here I'm called on to score and lead the team, a lot of things. It's a different kind of role, a key role."

So he expects Benetton to keep him for the rest of the league season?

Corchiani shakes his head: no comment. "I just leave it up to the team. I signed a contract for four games, I'm two-and-one now, so we'll see what happens and what they wanna do."

• • •

"I think we had too many alibis in our minds," a disconsolate Messina tells me as the bus pulls out of the Palaverde parking lot. "No Sasha, a big Euroclub game coming up on Thursday—then Binelli got hurt and we just said, 'Okay, that's it for today.' And Roberto played badly. When my best player [with Danilovic out] plays like shit, that makes it tough." An empty, faraway look in his eyes, he expels a long breath. "We always fall back when I think we're on the verge of becoming a great team."

He's miserable, and I leave him alone all the way back to Bologna, even after the news comes through someone's radio that Philips's nine-game winning streak ended in Pesaro today.

"Any messages for Mike?" I ask as we prepare to part in the parking lot outside the Palasport.

"No." Ettore is down. "Nothing."

"Well, Mike probably won't have much to say either."

"No. I think we both got a little high, and now we come back down to earth."

I wonder if he's thinking what I'm thinking: Benetton might kick both their butts.

Toni Wins

Back in Treviso a week after the Knorr game, I seek to solve the riddle of Toni Kukoc.

Everyone knows that Toni, drafted in 1990 by the Chicago Bulls and the eye of an international publicity storm ever since, *wins*. His Yugoslavian national teams won the World Junior Championships back in 1987 and the Goodwill Games in 1990; his club team in Spalato won three consecutive Euroclub Championships, '89–'91; last season, his first in Italy, Benetton won the *lega* championship. Last summer, Toni's Croatian team took the silver medal at the Olympics.

Everyone agrees Toni is too talented for this league. Most of the talk is about Toni and the NBA. Will he go? When? How good will he be? Will they break him in half?

Mike D'Antoni: "He's by far the best player in Europe. At one time I thought he would be the best European player ever, far better than Petrovic, Divac, Sabonis, Volkov. He's six-ten, six-eleven, with a point-guard mentality. He passes, shoots, rebounds. But I've heard he doesn't work hard in practice, and you can see his game beginning to deteriorate. How he'll do in the NBA depends on what he's got inside of him, and I don't know. If I said he's not a fighter, I'd base it on the fact that he's still here instead of in the NBA, not on how he plays."

Mark Crow (an interested observer, as Kukoc is IBC's prize client): "I think Toni needs to pick up his game a little. He's a great talent, but he needs to develop more of an attitude. Predrag [Danilovic] always comes ready to play. Toni's got so much ability . . . it's like people used to say about Kareem: he's got so much ability, he looks so effortless that you wonder, 'If he tried harder, would he be better?' "

Bob Morse: "What Kukoc needs is better competition and more physical strength. With that NBA schedule, he's going to need to be stronger and tougher."

Paolo Pressacco (Benetton team manager, a former player): "Toni cannot last in the NBA. Not strong enough. When we play two games in a week, he's tired."

Dan Peterson: "Toni Kukoc is not in physical condition and never has been. But get him in shape, put him in the NBA, wait two years, and you have a dominating NBA talent."

Nobody knows.

A few days before Toni goes after yet another trophy in the Italy Cup Final Four in Forli, I make a quick trip to Treviso to meet with him after Benetton practices. By the time we sit down in a couple of courtside seats in the deserted Palaverde he's had a shower, his freshly cut hair is brushed back and I'm struck, as always, by how young he looks, this guy who's been in the news for so long.

He's oddly passionless. With his droopy eyelids, diffident manner, and quiet, hesitant way of speaking (possibly due to uncertainty with English), it's hard to imagine him the headliner of all those championship teams.

He says he knew for sure that he wanted to try the NBA after Croatia's first meeting with the U.S.A. in Barcelona last summer, the game in which his prospective Bulls teammate Scottie Pippen tried not only to make Kukoc look bad on the court—which Pippen did, with plenty of help—but also, classlessly, to humiliate him with postgame comments to the international press such as, "He's playing in the right league [the Italian]."

"After that game," Toni says quietly, "I decided I must try to prove myself in the NBA. Then at the finish of my career they can say, 'He was a good European player, nothing else,' or, 'He was a good world player.' "

"Deep down," I ask him, "how good do you think you are?"

"I dunno. I really dunno. For Europe I'm good, sure, but for the NBA I dunno. If I go to the NBA, in two years I might be at the end of the bench or in the All-Star Game." Toni cracks a little smile. "No, I'm sure I'll not be on the end of the bench. Because in the middle of the season, if I'm bad like that, I'll leave: You don't have to give me the money, nothing, I'll leave, it's not the place for me.

"But I don't think I'll be bad like that."

He can't imagine failure, because he's known virtually nothing but triumph in his brief career. (He played well in the second Croatia-U.S.A. game in Barcelona, after which Magic Johnson told him, "You have to try the NBA," and Jordan said, "See you in Chicago.")

He simply seems gifted, in the rare sense that Magic and Bird and Bill Walton were gifted: physically talented, sure, but the real gift is more than physical. Court sense, vision, an almost extrasensory anticipation, a special unteachable understanding of what it takes not only to play well but to win games. Toni came to basketball late, but it was there.

He grew up in Split, Yugoslavia, on the Adriatic coast (directly across the water from my Adriatic coast in Riccione) and claims he didn't take up basketball until he was fifteen.

"People say that because I played four years table tennis, then four years soccer, I had . . . yes, hand-eye coordination. One day I was on a beach near Split and a coach for kids saw me and said, 'If you wanna come and try playing *basket* . . .' So I leave soccer and start coming to the gym because it was close, only about a hundred meters from my house. After three months I was on a team."

A couple of years later he starred on Yugoslavia's world-championship junior team. And he's won almost everything he's competed for since.

Gifted. Fortunate too, to have been the greatest player in Europe—and to have been drafted by the Bulls, which doubled his leverage—when the fantastically wealthy Benettons, two years ago, decided to go all-out for a championship. Already in that summer of 1991 they had purchased Stefano Rusconi, the brutish *pivot*, from Varese for a record $15 million. Vinny Del Negro, who had torn up the league in his first season, was already in place. Benetton sold its other *straniero*, Dan Gay, and paid millions to Pop 84 Spalato (Yugoslavia) for Toni's rights.

Represented by IBC (that is, Capicchioni), Kukoc signed an unprecedented six-year contract for some $20 million. He could have gotten a tasty deal from Chicago, but the war was on and bombs were dropping around his parents and sister in Split; it wasn't the time to go to America. Six years is a long commitment, but there was an understanding that Gilberto Benetton wouldn't prevent his golden boy from striking out for the NBA if Toni ever wanted to.

Some people say Signor Benetton wants to get rid of Toni, or at least Toni's salary. The Benettons are rich, but they still want to make something on basketball, and right now, like everyone else, they're not doing very well. Having the biggest payroll in the league doesn't help, and Toni's salary is nearly half of it.

Maurizio Gherardini, the Benetton GM, has told me the team does want to cut costs, but it won't start with Toni, Signor Benetton's pride and joy.

Nobody believes anybody when it comes to Toni, Benetton, and the Bulls. Toni says he hasn't talked to Chicago GM Jerry Krause for several months, and Bucky Buckwalter, when we met in Milan, said he's heard rumblings that Krause has decided Toni isn't worth it and will plead salary-cap restrictions to the media to avoid signing him.

Mark Crow says, "That would be Chicago's politics, of course, because they don't want to give Toni any money, but I think they're *very* interested in signing him. That's just Krause sleuthing. His nickname is 'the Sleuth.' He never says what he really means."

Everyone agrees it's time. Toni more or less concedes he's ready. Things are ugly in the former Yugoslavia but there's no fighting now in Split, so he's not so worried about his family.

He's even willing to play for less money than he makes now. "No problem. It's still a lot of money. In my opinion, if you have five million or seven million, it's the same thing."

He's not worried about adjusting to the States. "For me, it was a big change coming from Croatia to Italy, so another change would not be so big." He'd have his wife and baby girl with him, and Capicchioni will probably open an office in Chicago and spend most of his time there, handling what he expects to be a lot of Toni-business.

I ask Toni what he feels he'll bring to the NBA.

He apparently comes up empty. "I dunno. Nothing special, nothing the people in the NBA don't see all the time. Maybe I can give the Chicago team something they don't have at this moment—but then, they're world champions, they have everything."

The best part of his game?

"Passing game, assists, fast breaks."

He's right. He's wrong, or disingenuous, when he says he won't bring the NBA anything uncommon. Whenever he gets there, Toni's going to make a lot of highlight reels.

I ask him what he wants to be doing in five years.

"*Basket*. NBA."

In ten years?

"Boat," Toni says, scintillating as ever. "Family. Nobody else. I'll be satisfied."

• • •

For now, winning here is the thing.

Logically, the Italy Cup is the least prestigious of the titles to be won each year. Way back in September and October all thirty-two Series "A" clubs played a short elimination tournament to determine which would play the Final Four five months later.

That is, the Italy Cup isn't necessarily indicative of much, but don't tell an Italian fan it's insignificant. It's for the glory of Italia.

And this year, in Forli's Palafiera, it *will* be an indicator. Knorr and Benetton, two of the three realistic contenders for the league championship, are here, in opposite brackets, and everyone's psyched for a neutral-court showdown in the final tomorrow night, less than two weeks after Benetton rattled Knorr's cage up in Treviso.

First, they've got to survive the Thursday night doubleheader. First Knorr plays Stefanel, Dino's team, which was playing well last fall but has been struggling for weeks with injuries to Gregor Fucka, Davide Cantarello, and Albert English. Then Benetton plays Ticino Siena, Darren Daye's team from A-2—God only knows how Siena got in.

But this is the Coppa Italia, and two hours before the first game hundreds of kids, mostly from nearby Bologna, are clamoring outside. A few minutes later the doors open and they're inside, hanging banners and staking out their spaces. The chants start immediately, the Forever Boys singing variations of "Fuck off, Stefanel!" to various tunes, then turning merrily toward the Benetton rooting section with something along the lines of "All together against Treviso!" The Benetton contingent bursts into "Who doesn't jump is Bolognese!" The Forever Boys, with bigger numbers by far, laugh and then drown out anyone silly enough to taunt them.

I find Terry Teagle sitting alone in a corner of the lower stands, not very happy with his situation. A few days ago Benetton signed Corchiani as his replacement for the rest of the league season, including the Italy Cup. But Euroclub Championship rules prevent such a change, and so Terry will have to stick around and play in Benetton's last couple of qualifying games. Then, if Benetton survives, he'll have to wait around for three weeks until the Final Four in Greece.

"Yeah, it's a weird situation," Terry says. "Really, I'd rather play all the games or just go home." He says his agent is talking to some NBA teams about Terry signing for the rest of the season and the playoffs—when Benetton is finished with him, of course.

The Palafiera fills up. Everybody's here: agents, coaches, executives, journalists, Darryl Dawkins.

The sound is deafening as Knorr and Stefanel are introduced, and it keeps on at the same pitch.

Knorr starts fast. Danilovic slashes to the hoop on a break; Morandotti does the same; Roberto hits a three. In three minutes it's 10–0, Stefanel calls a time-out, and the place is rocking with the Forever Boys and the rest of the Knorr fans screaming "Veer-*toos!* Veer-*toos!* Veer-*toos!*" and then, frenziedly in all directions, accompanied by gestures, "*Vaffanculo! Vaffanculo!*"—"Fuck you! Fuck off!"—over and over and over.

Danilovic is outstanding. He hits an NBA-style fadeaway jumper from deep on the baseline. He backs in a smaller defender, then whizzes a pass by the guy's ear to a teammate underneath. He takes Wennington's outlet pass, weaves down the floor, powers in, gets fouled, and scores anyway.

In the second half Knorr's cruising by eighteen points when Carera swats a Stefanel shot out of bounds—except it never lands out, because Roberto Brunamonti flies after it and throws it back, starting Knorr on yet another fast break. When Messina takes Roberto out a minute later the Knorr fans behind the bench stand to applaud—singing, to the tune of "Guantanamera," one of their favorite songs:

> "*Un Brunamonti*
> *C'è solo un Brunamonti.*
> *Un Brunamonnn-ti*
> *C'è solo un Brunamonnn-ti.*"

"Big Daddy" Dino (who has won six Italy Cups, more than anyone else) doesn't have a chance. Five minutes into the second half Stefanel is cooked and, for all except Messina and his players, forgotten. For that matter, Ticino Siena might as well not exist. This Italy Cup is about Knorr-Benetton, and their fans are going at it. As the Forever Boys celebrate the imminent victory over Stefanel, the Benetton group gleefully reminds them what awaits tomorrow night: "To-ni, To-ni, KOO-coach! KOO-coach!" The Forever Boys' singsong reply: "Sa-sha-Da-NEE-lo-veetch! Sa-sha-Da-NEE-lo-veetch!" And so on.

Knorr blows Stefanel away as Sasha scores 25.

The second game looks like an upset. Siena gets 15 first-half points from Darren Daye and 14 from a guy named Vidili and leads Benetton by nine.

Nothing to worry about. As the second half opens, it's clear Toni Kukoc has made up his mind. He gets a couple of quick hoops, but mostly he's passing off and his teammates are hitting.

I've never seen him so demonstrative. I've seen him apathetic, I've seen him serious, but I've never seen him emotional. Maybe it's because there's a trophy at stake, but when Benetton fell behind early he looked anguished and even frantic—questioning the refs, shouting at teammates, flinging his arms up disgustedly when he missed a shot—and he's much the same even after they take the lead on a play that few guys in any league can make: Toni grabs a defensive rebound, covers the court with three or four ground-gobbling dribbles, splits two defenders in the lane with a nifty fake and sails in for an exclamatory two-handed hammer.

Three minutes later Benetton leads by ten and the remaining Knorr fans are leaving, yelling all kinds of things at the Benetton fans, who are shaking their fists and yelling back. It feels like it could get out of hand.

It's mad. These are *basket* fans, of all things, from two Italian cities a three-hour drive apart, but you'd think they were warring nations.

Benetton wins going away. Toni scores 19 and dishes out a bunch of assists.

Chris Corchiani scores 30. I feel bad for the gentlemanly Teagle, but Benetton looks better this way. Corchiani won't always score 30 points, but he's the playmaker Benetton needs.

I enjoyed the crowds more at my first few Italian games. Now I don't understand why the *lega* tolerates a lot of their behavior.

It's one more way the league shoots itself in the foot. Everyone tells me, "The NBA is our model, we want to do everything like the NBA," and okay, they'll go to forty-eight-minute games next season, six fouls instead of five, etc., but they don't do anything toward making the league a successful business.

The NBA strives to create a safe, pleasant environment. As Dan Peterson says, "You throw something in Boston Garden, you're in jail before it hits the floor." Here, though, a ticket apparently purchases the right to hurl toilet paper, trash, fruit, combs, lighters, coins, you name it. Players are at risk, games are delayed, it's ridiculous.

Every once in a while a game is called off in progress and forfeited to the offended team (Philips was given a game in Livorno back in January, after the home fans pelted the players with coins and garbage and spat on D'Antoni). More often, a club is penalized for its fans' behavior by having to play an upcoming home game or two on a neutral court instead. But since the club can buy its way free for about four thousand dollars, why even have such a penalty on the books? Why have any rules?

Earlier this season Varese had to play two games on a neutral court, then a while back they had an incident where a referee was hit by a coin and, while he was dazed and bleeding, got punched from the blind side. For the second offense

Varese was ordered to play four more games on neutral courts, making six penalty games for the season. But, oops, it turns out there's a rule saying that if you're penalized more than five games you automatically go to Series "B" next season. The *lega* doesn't want to lose Varese, one of the traditional clubs, so the four-game penalty was reduced to three. So much for sending a message.

I used to enjoy the cheering sections more too. I still think the rivalries between different cities and regions, many dating back to the ancient city-states, are interesting. At a Roma-Scavolini game I saw the Pesaro fans doing "Who doesn't jump comes from Bologna!" and later in Bologna, watching Knorr entertain a *Spanish* team, I did a double take when the Forever Boys launched into "Whoever doesn't jump is Pesarese!" "Oh yes," Alberto said, "Pesaro and Bologna are enemies. It doesn't matter that Scavolini isn't here tonight. Their coach is here announcing the game, their general manager is here, the PR man is here—that's enough."

I like some of the phraseology the feuds have spawned. *Better a dead man in your house than a Pisan on your doorstep*. I admit I'm amused when the visiting cheering section humbles the Rimini rooters by making rowing motions and singing, "You're all fishermen in Rimini!" I even like (all right, I especially like) some of the filthy wit. But too often it goes too far, all of it, and spoils a good thing.

D'Antoni thinks the league should do away with the cheering sections altogether. "They feed off each other. *You* think it's colorful because there's nothing like it in America, but if you hear it very long it gets old. For one thing, if I'm a parent I'm not gonna pay fifty bucks for my kids to go listen to people yelling 'Fuck you, fuck this, fuck that.' It's horrible, vulgar, often racist—slurs against southern [Italian] people, blacks, whatever. There's no call for it. In Milan we're trying to drown it out with loud music before the games and during time-outs."

D'Antoni also points out that it's easier to get away with throwing things if you're in a crowd. Especially if everyone else is doing it.

Of course, it's all irrelevant unless the league decides to stop the misbehavior—that is, throw the offenders out. Seems elementary to an *americano*.

But the league plays helpless. Alberto says, "It's impossible. You can't do that in Italy." I say, You've got *polizia* at the games with batons and machine guns and handcuffs, why is it impossible? "Impossible," Alberto says over and over.

For better or worse, the crowd steals the show on Friday night.

Again, they're going at it long before the game. The arena's dressed up with even more signs than last night. One, SOCMEL 3:16, is obviously a cousin of the JOHN 3:16 signs that appear at every NFL game. What, I ask, does SOCMEL mean?

Suck it, apparently.

The crowd is predictably crazed, and from the beginning I'm watching the fans as much as the game. They're producing that nonstop din that reminds me of the sound at a championship prizefight when the combatants are furiously exchanging punches—only here it doesn't abate after a few moments. It never abates.

Toni comes out looking as if he intends to dominate, but Knorr looks like the better team. Wennington takes a feed from Roberto and shakes loose for a dunk. "Beel!-Beel!-WENN-ington! Beel!-Beel!-WENN-ington!"

The noise is overwhelming. Sitting at a press table under one basket, I look behind me and see red-faced old men shrieking at the players and refs, looking as if they're about to stroke out. Withered old women scream and wave their umbrellas. Beautiful young women. Kids.

Sasha Danilovic, playing with supreme confidence, isn't fazed. A jumper, a couple of free throws, an unlikely floater in the lane. He's barely twenty-three, but his demeanor is all business, all pro.

Messina smolders, even with a lead. He's a smart, witty guy with big-picture perspective, and he's always personable right up until game time despite his nerves—but once the game starts he's ferocious, stalking the sideline, clapping his hands frantically, jabbering at the refs. Or quietly smoldering.

Knorr leads by ten at the half.

The second half is like the fifteenth round of a championship fight: this is *it*. They're fighting for every ball. The crowd is howling.

Suddenly there's a sense of unreality to the scene, when, in front of the Benetton bench, Roberto Brunamonti is in coach Skansi's face, pointing a finger and screaming at him—*Roberto, the sweetest man in the world!* And, shock of shocks, he doesn't back off after a few seconds and pardon himself but keeps tearing into Skansi until some of the other players, no doubt as startled as Skansi and I, pull him away.

Skansi, a Croatian, a former player around 6'5", is quirky, controversial, and frequently described as crazy. You can only wonder what he's been saying down there, to so incense *Roberto*. ("All the game," Roberto tells me weeks later, "he's saying everything to the refs: 'Your mother, your father . . .' They give him a technical, but they won't give him a second one. I ask them, 'Why don't you give him another *T?*' " And what did Roberto say to Skansi? He smiles sheepishly. "Aw, is not nice. I make a mistake, acting like him. But not," he assures me, " 'Your mother, your father . . .' ")

A couple of minutes later Messina's got him on the bench, and when Coldebella hits a three-pointer Roberto is on his feet with the rest of the Knorr bench, cheering. At least I thought he was cheering, but suddenly we're back in the twilight zone. Roberto's up, cheering Coldebella's three, pumping his fist—

And suddenly Messina's in his face, shouting something and pushing Roberto down onto the bench! What is going *on?*

("I have never seen Roberto lose his composure in ten years," Messina tells me much later. "But on the bench he was insulting the referees and yelling at Skansi. He was so wound up; he put so much pressure on himself for that game. I told him to sit down, that we needed him to help us keep our composure."

Roberto, much later, literally blushes when he's reminded that he chastised a referee.)

I look at the faces in the crowd. It's blood sport. A cluster of Benetton fans boo Roberto. Thousands are out of their seats waving fists, doing fuck-you signs. It's almost too much. It's *basket*, people! You're *not* warring nations!

Benetton fights back. The second half is back and forth, the place is going ape, the Italy Cup is there to be had.

And the crowd spoils it for me. Hundred-lire pieces heavy as silver dollars sail out of the upper deck, sing past my ears, and almost chip the tabletop two inches from my hand.

With five minutes to go and coins raining on the press table all around me, I give up my courtside seat to go stand in a corner by an exit. I'm pissed as hell. There's no excuse. I understand perfectly why Dino said fuck it and sat out the second half after he got hit in Pesaro a few years ago. If the *lega* doesn't like having playoffs decided that way, they should do something about it.

Studying the cops nearby, with their helmets and machine guns and batons, I realize most of them don't look old enough to shave. They look scared to death . . . by a bunch of punks at a basketball game.

Back and forth, back and forth. Tied. Benetton goes up by two with :09 remaining. Knorr scrambles downcourt and moves the ball around. Danilovic passes up a shot, gets the ball to Roberto in the corner.

Roberto's three-pointer at the buzzer is no good.

The place erupts—the Treviso kids, that is, while the Forever Boys and the other Bologna fans stream out of the Palafiera.

But getting out isn't as simple as just walking out. While hundreds of Benetton fans overrun the court, others in the stands lean over the railings, berating the Bolognese scurrying out; the Bolognese—grown men in suits—scream back, and both sides wave their arms and insult each other, and I keep thinking people are going to fight. One guy rushes down out of the stands after another; he'll never catch him, but I'm sure some of these nuts will willingly meet outside afterward.

I just try to stay out of the way and not make eye contact with anyone.

Down on the court Toni's wearing a funny hat and a big toothy grin, clowning and celebrating with his teammates, a far cry from the dry, deliberate, almost drowsy fellow he normally is. He pulls his wet jersey off and hurls it into the stands, then grabs a bottle of champagne and sprays everybody within spraying range. He can't stop laughing and embracing one person after another.

Corchiani, a crazy hat pulled low across his forehead, throws his shirt into the crowd, then holds the Italy Cup over his head. Things are working out pretty well for the kid who was on his way back to the CBA a few weeks ago. He could get big over here.

The Benetton loonies are still doing chants toward the deserted Forever Boys section. "Don't be sad, Bolognese, the important thing is to participate!" It still feels crazy.

The cops take it all in. They look too young to be carrying real guns. I wonder why the *lega* even bothers.

Now Toni's at the baseline, holding up the Cup for the fans. He points to it, then makes a sweeping wave, saying "It's for all of you." He's beatific. Another trophy.

He scored only 13 points tonight, but what can you say? Toni wins.

McAdoo's Back

Thursday, March 18, I travel to Milan for the Korac Cup final between Philips and Virtus Roma. Laurel's home for lunch when I get to the apartment around one-thirty. Mike, she says, is over at the squash club watching people play "just to escape."

She says Bob McAdoo might show up later. McAdoo has spent the past two months in Africa as an advisor on a basketball movie (*The Air Up There*, starring Kevin Bacon), and he's passing through Italy on his way back to the U.S.

I knew McAdoo was in Italy. Everybody knows. Apparently he got together with his old friend Micheal Ray a few days ago, a TV station showed a film clip of the two of them, and the word got out that McAdoo's here.

And McAdoo started getting calls. He's forty-two years old and hasn't played a game in a year, but teams started calling, asking him to finish out the season. I know, because Lou Colabello, along with Telemarket Forli GM Roberto Rozzi, met with McAdoo a couple of days ago about replacing poor Rob Lock. Laurel tells me that McAdoo has also talked with Robe di Kappa Torino.

Anyway, he's probably coming up this afternoon with a woman from Forli, where he played the past two seasons, to watch the game and spend the night. "We'll be one big happy family," Laurel says brightly.

I walk around the corner to meet Mike for lunch. Sure enough, he's sitting there watching strangers play squash.

He's nervous but confident about tonight's game. He talks again about how easy it is to coach his team, what a pleasure the guys are.

Back at the apartment (Laurel's gone back to the office) we've got all afternoon to kill. Knowing Mike is preoccupied, I sit on "my" couch in the living room reading magazines while he's sprawled on his, remote control in hand, watching weeks-old NBA tapes. Once in a while he exclaims, "Jim, *look*, you gotta see this play," but mostly he's self-absorbed.

Tonight isn't just another game. It's the Korac Cup final, and Mike might finally win something as a coach.

A couple of days ago he got a call from his former teammate Roberto Premier, who's playing out his career with Virtus Roma. Premier kiddingly asked if Mike had champagne on ice for tonight, and they joked about how, in the great eighties, the photographers had to tell jokes to get them to look happy or excited after winning something as trifling as a Korac Cup. Those teams rarely even played in the Korac Cup, which is for the previous season's runners-up from all over Europe; Milan was usually playing for the Euroclub Championship.

But that was the great Milan dynasty. No, the Korac Cup isn't the biggest thing going, but it's something. It counts.

The championship is two games, most total points wins—or as Mike says, one eighty-minute game, with the first half played in one arena and the second half in the other. It makes things interesting. If you lose the first game, on the road, by ten points, you not only have to win at home, you have to win by at least eleven; if you only win by nine, you lose. Win by exactly ten and you play an overtime period.

Philips is in good shape. Last week in Rome they won by five points, so all they've got to do tonight at the Forum is not lose by more than four.

Mike's nervous anyway. It's been a rough year for Virtus Roma, beginning with the Mahorn debacle, but they've battled this far and they've got enough talent in Radja, Niccolai, and Dell'Agnello to beat anyone on a given night.

Around five-thirty, Mike goes back to the bedroom and changes into a suit for the game.

A little before six the buzzer in the front hall sounds. McAdoo's downstairs.

A minute later Mike goes to the door, I hear their greetings and laughter in the hall, and then here's lanky Bob McAdoo himself, in the flesh. I rise from my couch and shake his hand.

He's with a voluptuous olive-skinned woman named Patrizia, somewhere in her thirties, who's wearing too much makeup and a supertight miniskirt. She speaks passable English and she's friendly, nice. I don't know the depth of her relationship with McAdoo, only that they knew each other when he played in Forli.

In the car on our way to the Forum, Bob tells us a little about his experience working on the movie in Africa, but the talk quickly turns to his new employment opportunities.

Torino (Turin) contacted him first. With three games remaining, they're simply hoping to stay out of the last two spots in A-1.

"But I think with the financial problems in Italy now, nobody wants to pay, and with my talent I'm not gonna play for cheap. That's it in a nutshell. I'd rather be home in New Jersey with my sons than to go back out and play for a little bit of money. [McAdoo's two sons have been attended by his mother and a family friend while he's been gone.] I didn't come to Italy thinkin' of playin', anyway."

I say, "You wanted about ten thousand per game?" I know that's the figure he discussed with Telemarket.

Bob doesn't say. "A team that gets me is paying for experience and a proven winner. I haven't had a bad season since I've been over here, and I've won. I mean, I shouldn't have to prove myself to anybody."

According to Lou Colabello, Telemarket was ready to pay McAdoo's price if he was in reasonable condition.

"Telemarket wanted to see what I looked like before we signed a contract, but I told 'em, 'Naw, I can't do that. I don't *try out*. You know what I can do, I know what I can do. If you want me to practice, you gotta sign me to a contract. If you want to *see* me, you pay me one thousand dollars a day to work out. Or, *arrivederci*.' They called the owner, he said no, so *arrivederci*. No sweat off my back.

"I'm not saying I could go out and play a whole game. But I could go out and score twenty points in twenty to twenty-five minutes."

Mike chuckles at McAdoo's bravado—not disparagingly, because he knows it's probably true. "I could play over here till I'm fifty," Bob snorts. "But they gotta make it worth my while."

He crows on. I think he's excited by the idea of playing a few games. This is Thursday, and he's not flying home until next Tuesday, so though he won't play this weekend there's plenty of time for clubs that want him for the last two games plus the postseason. "If someone wants to talk real money I'll consider it. If not, hey, I don't need this. I'm happy to get home to my sons. I've been gone two months now.

"But I can still play," Bob assures us once more. "Guys age differently. Philips threw Dino and Mike out three years ago so they threw me out too, even though I was averaging thirty points a game. I did it last year too [twenty-seven points per game in Forli, even as he traveled to the U.S. almost every week during the first half of the season as his wife Charlena wasted away with cancer]. I could play over here till I'm fifty!" he blusters, raising his hands into shooting position and giving us a few pump-fakes. "Give 'em this, give 'em a little of this—can't do *nothin'* about it!"

He entertains us in this vein until we reach the Forum. I remember Dan Peterson saying, "McAdoo? Greatest attitude of all time. He figures he cannot be guarded. Know something? He's right!"

McAdoo's remembered fondly in Milan. When he arrived in 1986, thirty-five years old, he was the biggest NBA name the people had ever seen, and they'd never had a shooter who compared with him. The club had won the last two league championships, but that '86–'87 edition swept *everything*—the Grand Slam—and is considered by many the greatest Italian team ever.

"Milan was one of the greatest experiences of my life," Bob tells me as we chat in the VIP room at the Forum. "Coming over here, I didn't know what to expect, but because I'd played for so many NBA teams I just looked at Milan as another city. Being out of the country didn't bother me. My family took to it well, and if your family's okay, you're okay. And being on a winning team helped. The first coach I had, Dan Peterson, was American, so we didn't have any communication problems. Mike was here, a veteran in Italy. So it was like home to me.

"Me, Dino, and Mike were here together, all of us about thirty-five years old, and everybody was sayin' the team was over the hill. But the three of us have a lot of pride, and we ended up winnin' everything. That's something that hadn't been done in a long time. It was quite an accomplishment for the whole organization.

"Then, after four years my wife got sick, and after a two-year bout with ovarian cancer she succumbed to it in December of '91 [a little more than a year ago, on Christmas Eve], which was a very big loss for me."

The words make a strange effect, as if Bob hasn't gotten used to the loss but has explained things in this medical-journal way a million times: "After a two-year bout . . . she *succumbed*."

By then Bob was in his second season in Forli. "I had a chance to come back to Milan to play later last season, and the fans gave me a standing ovation. They had a big sign for Charlena saying they remembered her—she was the one that started the cheerleaders here. It was just nice, comin' back home. People treated me like a king here, and it's something I'll never forget."

Though he still had the incredible McAdoo shooting touch and scored big in Forli last season, he wasn't offered another contract. Corbelli bought the club and brought in Lock and Dawkins as his *stranieri*. Late last summer McAdoo was still talking with a couple of clubs, but nothing was definite and when the movie offer came up, he took it.

But no, he hasn't ruled out the possibility of playing again. In a couple of months he's coming back to Europe on an NBA Legends tour with Magic Johnson, George Gervin, etc.; who knows, maybe he'll be back in the *lega* next season.

The game is a great scene. The thirteen-thousand-seat Forum is nearly filled, by far the biggest crowd I've seen this season. The PA announcer is the first one I've heard who jazzes up his pregame introductions. The Philips rooting section, though not so wild as the Forever Boys Virtus or Scavolini's bunch, is jacked up tonight, lots of "*Vaffanculo! Vaffanculo!*" and "Who doesn't jump is a Roman!"

And Philips is cooking. They trail in the first few minutes but they're quick and active, moving the ball sharply as always, and it's only a matter of time until the shots start falling.

Inevitably, Djordjevich starts busting. He lofts in his first three-point attempt—I've never seen a softer shot—and then *boom! boom! boom!* he's puttin' 'em down—*threes!*—then a couple of shorter jumpers, then a couple of free throws. The PA man does his "*Sa*-sha *Jorrrrrr*-je-vitch!" so many times that he finally starts adding, "from Portaluppi" or "from Davis" just so we don't forget the others.

Philips takes the lead. Mike gets forgotten forward Davide Pessina into the game early, which is unusual but feels like a good move to me too, somehow. Philips keeps running and whipping the ball around and hitting from the perimeter: Djordjevich, Pittis, Riva, Portaluppi. Antonio Davis sweeps the boards, intimidates Roma's shooters, and gets a few hoops himself. Pessina, glad to get into the big game after being buried for three months, plays hard and then exhorts the crowd when Roma, getting blitzed, calls a desperation time-out.

Mike's low-key. He's been particularly calm tonight—on the outside—as if he wants this Cup so badly he doesn't dare let his emotions out.

Of course, it's easy to be cool when you're twenty points ahead.

In the second half Philips experiences the inevitable letdown, the lead is cut to seven, and Mike isn't so cool anymore. He's red-faced, screaming, stomping his feet at questionable calls.

But he barely gets started before Djordjevich and Riva score on circus layups and Philips bumps the lead back up. When Djordjevich sticks yet another three, Roma's finished. The crowd is howling. And Mike is Joe Cool again.

At the end the mood is happy, not rowdy. The Philips cheering section sets off some fireworks and smoke bombs as the jubilant players hug and laugh and lift each other off the floor and Flavio Tranquillo interviews Mike near the bench. Laurel, up in the booth, cues the theme song from *Chariots of Fire*. Olimpia Milano, the most illustrious *società* in Italy, has its first title of the post-dynasty age!

It's a long time before people start leaving the Forum. They hang out, sharing the moment, well after the players leave the floor.

Finally I head for Mike's office. He's just getting back from the press room, where he did the obligatory media session after a locker-room celebration with his players in which they threw him into the shower, fancy suit and all. The two assistant coaches are whooping and high-fiving. When Flavio Tranquillo comes in the three of them start teasing Mike, in Italian, about being a championship coach now; Mike says something back that gets them all hooting at him, which Flavio kindly translates as, "I don't know why the guys threw me in the shower—it's *only* the Korac Cup."

Mike's glowing. I think the coach's son really and truly feels like a coach himself now.

Finally McAdoo shows up with Patrizia, Laurel finishes her duties, and we depart the now nearly empty arena for the Torchietto.

McAdoo, knowing Mike is excited about his first title as a coach, congratulates him and compliments the team, but he can't keep the conversation off himself. After praising Antonio Davis he adds, "Of course, *I'd* kill him." He puts his hands up, does a couple of pump-fakes. "I'd have him up in the air like a helicopter," he chortles.

"Yeah, yeah," Mike razzes. He loves McAdoo, but tonight he loves his player more.

"Like a *helicopter!*" McAdoo squeals, showing us more fakes before finally pretending to release a shot.

"Yeah, yeah. Antonio'll throw that back *at* you," Mike exults. "And then all you'd see is Antonio beatin' you down the court every time."

"All he'd get is a few dunks," McAdoo insists, contemptuous but also a little defensive. The age thing.

" '*All* he'd get!' " Mike roars. "But he'd be gettin' 'em every time! No way you could keep up with him, no way, no way . . ."

"I'd have him up in the air like a *helicopter!* Like a helicopter!" McAdoo head-fakes. "Nothin' he can do!"

Mike just laughs. He doesn't care. "Did you see Ricky Pittis tonight?" He raves about Pittis. Then about Djordjevich, who scored 38 in one of the hottest shooting displays I've ever seen. Then about Riva, his unlikely defensive ace. All of 'em. He likes this team, *likes* 'em.

As we walk several blocks from the car to the Torchietto, Mike is hailed by happy Philips fans and stopped several times to sign autographs. He's happy to accommodate.

He's one of these Southern gentlemen who always hold doors open and enter buildings or rooms or elevators last of all, but in this case we all stand back and make him go into the Torchietto first, alone, and as he does we hear the cheers go up from the crowd in the big front room. Beaming, he's waving and shaking hands as he makes his way toward the back room. Finally Laurel and I go in. A moment later there's another spate of applause for the gone-but-never-to-be-forgotten McAdoo, who comes in behind us with Patrizia. Bob smiles and waves, loving it.

Beyond the open grill and the glass cases full of five-star desserts, beyond the jammed and celebratory middle room, we find the back room packed too. The players and their women and friends fill the table that runs the length of the back wall. *Lega* big shots and dressy people I don't recognize, probably sponsors, fill up the rest. We stand for a while, jammed between a couple of tables, squeezing back to let the waiters pass. McAdoo nuzzles and whispers with Patrizia.

Although Mike is reveling in his Korac Cup, it doesn't do him any good in the *lega*, and I know he's already thinking about Sunday's game. Catching Knorr still isn't out of the question. And if Philips takes first and gets the home-court advantage in the playoffs . . . as Mike says, Fer*git* it. Knorr is reeling. Mike's convinced Benetton can't beat his guys. There's nobody else.

At last our table opens up. McAdoo, Patrizia, and I take one side. Enzo the GM and his wife sit down. Flavio Tranquillo. Laurel, though she has produced a little video camera and repeatedly gets up to go film people. Finally, Mike.

Vino, bread, pasta, vino (except for Mike, who drinks Sprite), sirloin, salad, vino, fruit salad, *sorbetto*, espresso. We joke about the night back in December when we ate here after the overtime loss to Knorr and Mike, having decided the season was lost if Philips didn't get rid of Djordjevich, asked Flavio to come back to the apartment and discuss possible replacements. Hours pass. Almost everyone is gone by the time we finally shove back from the table at 2:30 A.M.

Out in the streets, people still shout to Mike: "*Bravo*, D'Antoni! Yo, Mike!" I hear *scudetto* a few times, meaning the league championship—that's what they really want.

As we drive home, McAdoo, up front with Mike, carries

on about how he'd have Antonio Davis up in the air like a helicopter. Trying to convince himself, I think.

The phone starts ringing early the next morning. First, Ettore Messina calls Mike with his congratulations. They chat for a few minutes. Ettore says he thinks Knorr is bouncing back, he's feeling good about things again.

Dan Peterson calls. This is a nice one for Mike. "Thanks, Coach," he says—then says very little else until "good-bye" ten minutes later, which reminds me of my own conversations with Big Pete. But Mike's happy. "It was nice of him to call." Having Peterson respect his coaching means a lot.

Laurel comes in and tells us that one of many messages on the recorder is the unidentified but unmistakable voice of "Dino Lino"—*il monumento*—simply shouting "Coach! *Campione! Campione!* Coach! Coach!"

As always, Laurel makes instant coffee for herself and me, and the three of us stand around the kitchen talking for a last few minutes before I go. We take the elevator downstairs, where the landlady kisses Mike and effuses about the big win, and say good-bye out in the sunshine as the taxi driver puts my bag in the trunk.

We're thinking *scudetto*.

Looks Like Curtains for Philips

Two days later—Sunday, March 21—I see McAdoo and Patrizia at the game in Forli. McAdoo gets a great ovation when they enter the gym; he smiles, waves. Rob Lock spots him and comes over to the stands. I hear Bob say he's flying home on Tuesday, and Lock, who still thinks he might be replaced any day, says, "Save me a seat on the plane."

On Monday afternoon McAdoo, on his way back to Milan to spend the night at the D'Antonis' before flying home on Tuesday, gets a call on his cellular phone. Larry Spriggs has pulled a hamstring and is out for the season, and Teamsystem Fabriano, desperate to avoid dropping to A-2 next year, wants Bob to play the last two regular-season games for about seventy-five hundred dollars each. They offer twenty-five thousand for the month-long ten-game playout if the team makes it.

Easy. This is Monday, and the regular season wraps up with two games this week, Thursday night and then Sunday. All Bob has to do is practice for a couple of days, play two games, and then he's probably on his way home, fifteen thousand dollars to the good. (Teamsystem has to win both games to make the playout. Maybe they'll beat improved

Marr Rimini—*maybe*—but the finale is against Knorr. And it might well be important for Knorr.)

Lou Colabello tells me that Telemarket not only failed to sign McAdoo, but the Andre Spencer deal is off too: Spencer, after two ten-day contracts with Atlanta, signed with Golden State for the rest of the season.

Rob Lock, after all, will finish the season in Forli. Midnight Friday is the deadline for roster changes for the playoffs.

Messina tells me that Bill Wennington, who was in some danger a few weeks ago, has given him the "little bit more" he wanted and is likewise safe.

Il monumento nazionale played his eight hundredth league game on Sunday. Though it's the equivalent of only ten NBA seasons, it's by far the most in Italy. Dino has also played nearly three hundred games for the national team.

He started at *pivot* against Clemon Johnson and played thirty minutes, with 11 points (on 5-for-5 shooting), 10 rebounds, 3 steals, and no turnovers, and held Johnson to 7 points on 2-for-10 shooting, as Stefanel hung on to fourth place by beating Bialetti Montecatini.

Thursday night, March 25, I'm in Bologna for the big Philips-Knorr game.

Philips can turn the whole season upside down. Knorr has been on top all season, but they've been reeling for a month.

Then again, maybe Knorr has just played a few bad games. "Reeling" is newspaper talk, like "*in crisi*." I'm sure Roberto Brunamonti, with his wife still unwell, isn't reeling over a few bad basketball games. Tough-kid Danilovic isn't reeling.

Most of all, Messina isn't. I remember what Dan Peterson said about him: "Forget the wins, forget the national team.

Ettore is one of the few coaches that transmit character to his team. No court is too tough for them. No lead is too big to overcome. I respect that."

Sure enough, Knorr plays tough. Their league-best defense, Messina's trademark, is as feisty as I've ever seen it. From the start, it doesn't look like Philips's night.

Brunamonti, more determined than I've ever seen him, plays thirty-five superb minutes. I remember D'Antoni saying, a few weeks ago, "Roberto is wearing down, but he's the one guy I worry about, the only one who can take Knorr to a higher level. Coldebella can't do it. Morandotti, Binelli, Wennington—no. But if Roberto plays well, they all play at a higher level."

In the second half, Knorr's Ricky Morandotti and Philips's Antonello Riva get thrown out for pushing and woofing, which pretty much seals it: eight-deep Knorr brings in Paolo Moretti, a twenty-three-year-old national-team sharpshooter, while Mike can only signal for a quivery kid I don't even recognize. Knorr wins by eight and clinches first place and the home-court advantage through the playoffs. They'll be tough to beat.

The real bad news for Philips comes the next day: Antonio Davis broke his hand near the end of the game and is finished for the season.

Mike talks optimistically in the *Gazzetta* (I'm told), but his season is over.

Mark Crow watched Teamsystem play in Rimini last night and says McAdoo was "magical." Forty-two years old, idle for a year, he didn't miss a shot until midway through the second half. He was puffing by then, but he finished with 28 points in thirty minutes. Even better than he promised he could do.

Teamsystem, however, lost. If they don't beat Knorr on Sunday, they'll probably go to A-2 next season.

Sunday, March 29, McAdoo is unremarkable with 16

points and 4 rebounds as Teamsystem falls. But hey, he's forty-two, what do they expect?

A few extra days with Patrizia, two ball games, fifteen thousand dollars, and Bob's outta here, *arrivederci*.

Teamsystem and Robe di Kappa Torino, finishing at 9–21, will go to A-2 next season.

I call Mike on Monday. Amazingly, Philips defeated Benetton yesterday with former St. John's University reserve Marco Baldi at *pivot*. Benetton needed the game, with second place at stake, but they were playing in Milan, and Ricky Pittis bounced back from his poor game in Bologna with 34 points, 12 rebounds, and 7 assists.

"I gotta admit," I tell Mike, "I had written you guys off."

"I told the team everyone would write us off. But I guess we're just not ready to die yet. I know we don't have any margin for error now . . ."

"You didn't have any before."

"Yeah, but now we *really* don't. But we'll see. I still think we can beat Benetton in a series. They look disorganized again. Kukoc and Corchiani overlap each other. They both need the ball. Neither one can come off a screen and hit the jumper, which Teagle could do."

But I'm pretty sure he knows that with Antonio Davis gone, Philips will have a hard time with anybody.

He doesn't even bring up Knorr.

Getting Very Near the End

Ever since my first day in Italy, despite all the wonderful people and unforgettable times, a part of me has pointed toward the day I'll board the plane home. Now, though, when the beginning of the *lega*'s brief playoffs lets me know the day is nigh, I can hardly imagine leaving.

Friends are arriving from the States, having waited for the nice weather, and showing them around I feel virtually Italian. Casey and Twink come first (Casey a great old friend, Twink a vague acquaintance who invited himself along), and without me to meet them at Malpensa in Milan they might as well have landed on another planet. But with me on hand, hey, no problem catching the shuttle bus to the train station, and buying tickets, and changing in Bologna later, and finally buying bus tickets and getting on the #11 in Rimini for the hop down to Riccione.

I've never stopped feeling embarrassed for not learning more Italian, but these guys are impressed because I can order an espresso. Yeah, this is *my* country.

I'm going to be following the first part of the playoffs largely through the newspapers. These guys want to see a little of Italy and at first, anyway, they're not about to go anywhere alone. Which is fine, really. Just so I see the finals.

I do catch the first game of the Scavolini-Bialetti series down in Pesaro, which Scavolini loses, putting themselves in a dire situation; all playoff series here are no-margin-for-error two-out-of-three sets until the final, which is best-of-five.

Tonight coach Bucci keeps out-of-control Carlton Myers on the bench for much of the second half, and Myers, when finally called upon, angrily snaps off his warm-ups and slings them on the floor on his way to the scorer's table. I feel sorry for Messina, who's leaving Knorr after the season to take over the national team—Myers, Rusconi, Gentile (one of the "complete idiots" who can't get the ball to Cadillac Anderson), and no Brunamonti . . .

Scavolini, however, wins game two a couple of days later over in Montecatini. Then they win the third game, back home, and move on to face Philips in the quarterfinals.

I read about it the morning after in the *Gazzetta*, which I purchase at a newsstand near the Spanish Steps in Rome.

Casey and Twink have a hotel room a couple of blocks away; I'm staying over at my friend Raphaela's place, downstairs from Tom Federman's office. I meet them at the hotel this morning, we have coffee (and I read the *Gazzetta*) at a bar near the Steps, and then we spend the day seeing the sights.

It's my fifth trip to Rome but my first time seeing the fabled Colosseum, though it's not a half mile from Tom's office and the Steps. I'm just not a big sightseer. But even I'm blown away by the sight of one ancient ruin we pass on the walk over, right in the middle of bustling modern Rome—huge toppled pillars, it looks like, down in a vast dug-out area that apparently used to be a meeting place—and the moment the Colosseum comes into view I get the willies such as I've experienced only on Civil War battlefields. Right up to the entrance you've got T-shirt stands and trinket vendors and every evidence of modern times, but suddenly you're inside the great amphitheater, feeling like the minuscule grain you are in the sands of time, speaking in hushed tones just like the little clusters of French and Japanese and Swedish gaping at the tiers of seating and, *give me the willies*, the mazelike tunnels down below where, two thousand years ago, the leopards and lions and tigers were starved before being turned loose on Christians and war criminals and each other for the amusement of fifty thousand bloodthirsty Romans. In the stillness of the beautiful spring afternoon you can almost hear the echoes, down through time, of the roaring crowd and the shrieking human sacrifices.

There must be a dozen cats, which apparently live here, lazing in the sun. (Who feeds them? Or, like the bigger cats of distant times, do they feed on other living creatures down in those tunnels?) Some Japanese tourists ask us to take their picture. A couple of teenaged English guys ask us if we know where they can buy some hashish. (We don't. Twink, who's had the heebie-jeebies since he got off the plane, must have asked every hawker and caricaturist around the Spanish Steps.)

Heading back, we stop to marvel at other ruins. I don't know the names—it doesn't matter to me; it's enough to soak up the sense of the ages and contemplate my own wee place in the scheme of things. I realize why they call Rome "the Eternal City."

Evening: Tom and his lawyer friend Anthony, the one who calls me "the Dinosaur" because I'm nearly forty, cook dinner for us over at Tom's filthy studio apartment. Casey can't believe we're three blocks from the Vatican and St. Peter's Square; *he's* got the willies.

Twink is in heaven when, after dinner, an amusing fellow named Irving, who teaches at the American School and lives downstairs, drops in for a while and eventually asks if we'd care for hash. I'm not so interested when Irving pulls out a pouch of tobacco and sprinkles a few crumbs of hash into a huge cigarette—*why not just put it into a pipe and get to the point?*—but I go along after he chides me: "It's the European way, Jim. How about a little cultural open-mindedness?"

After two hits I quit, already dizzy from sucking down tobacco smoke. Even Twink doesn't want any more. Then Casey drops out, leaving Irving (the lawyers stick to Scotch) smugly puffing away.

A minute or two later I note with amusement that he seems to have had enough, in fact he looks a little pale. A little queasy. Finally he asks Tom to open the window, but as he starts to move his chair over near it he abruptly takes off for the bathroom instead.

He's a whole lot more humble when he comes back fifteen minutes later, white as paste and a little shaky on his feet. I can't resist a little joke about cultural open-mindedness.

Two days later, after a superficial, but mind-boggling taste of St. Peter's Basilica, the Sistine Chapel, and some of the museums in the Vatican Palace, Casey and Twink venture to Florence alone while I, after a stupendous dinner at Raphaela's, take the night train to Milan to meet another Portland friend at Malpensa. We'll regroup back in Riccione and go from there.

Tuesday, April 6, Scavolini's at Philips in the quarterfinals, Philips having advanced on its first-round bye. And Philips wins! Twenty-six points for Djordjevich, 23 for Pittis, 21 for Riva. (For Scavolini, Carlton Myers comes off the bench to score 6.)

Elsewhere, Clear Cantu beats Stefanel, although Dino scores 10 points and the next day's papers put him on the *quintetto ideale*. I'll mention it to Messina, who told me on the phone a few days ago that he doesn't consider Stefanel a threat in the playoffs because they lack experience. When I pointed out that *il monumento nazionale* has more experience than any four Knorr players, he chuckled and said, "Yes, but he still has to run and jump. Monuments tend to stay in one place."

Benetton uses balanced scoring to beat Panasonic.

Knorr stomps Kleenex Pistoia.

Tonight's attendance: 4,200 in Milan, 4,000 in Trieste,

2,800 in Treviso and 6,200 in Bologna. For the playoffs.

I read about it all the morning after in the *Gazzetta*, in a roadside *rosticceria* on the way to Venice with Casey and Twink and my newly arrived friend Kim in a little rented Fiat, and don't feel I missed a thing. Just so I see the finals . . .

Casey and Twink head to Milan for their flight home after two days of rides up and down the Grand Canal, walks through miles of narrow alleys, slow meals in inexpensive restaurants, quick drinks in bars, indigestion for Twink and—for us other three—increasing irritation as a result of his shameless belching and farting and wheezing and complaining. I have to remind myself I'm Mister Mellow these days.

Kim and I stay one more day to do St. Mark's Basilica and the Doge's Palace, then take the train home on Saturday night. Dipping briefly into *basket*world, we make it down to Pesaro on Sunday afternoon, April 11, where we witness Philips's pathetic performance in their second game with Scavolini.

They look hopeless without Antonio Davis. They still move the ball smartly around the perimeter, but snappy ball movement doesn't amount to much when there's no inside threat at all and the defense can fearlessly get out in your shooters' faces. There's no rebounding. And the pressing defense doesn't work without Davis back there to swat away shots when Scavolini breaks it down.

The deciding game won't be played until next Sunday, a week away. Benetton, which has to play a third game with Panasonic, is playing in the Final Four of the Euroclub Championship this week, so the *lega* playoffs go on hold.

Philips is lucky to have the deciding game at home. I don't know if it will be enough.

• • •

On Monday I check in with Messina on the phone, who tells me he threw Danilovic out of practice and fined him last Thursday for verbally abusing Renato Pasquali, one of the assistant coaches, who was officiating an intra-squad scrimmage. It seems Danilovic didn't like a call, exploded at Renato, and kept escalating until he was bellowing, "You can't treat me like this! My people [Serbs] are special people! I have friends who could come and shoot you in the legs!"

"You can't let your most important player do that," Ettore says, "or the assistants think you don't support them and the other players think the big player can do whatever he wants. Sasha, all year, has been such a wild kid sometimes. I should have drawn the line early in the season, but I figured he would settle down with the influence of the team."

I remark that it's a tough call for a coach, disciplining a testy young star during the playoffs.

"I had no choice. And I knew Sasha would respond well. He had very good practices Friday and Saturday and played very well yesterday—not just shooting, but passing and defense."

Knorr beat Kleenex on the road yesterday to take the series 2–0. Danilovic, typically economical, scored 29 points on only 14 field-goal attempts: 9-for-10 on two-pointers, 2-for-4 on threes, 5-for-5 from the line.

"Now he won't talk to me," Ettore says. "He's very professional about the job, but he doesn't talk to me. But that's okay."

As Messina says, Danilovic is a wild one. He's got a strikingly mature game for a kid recently turned twenty-three, but all the while he's throwing cheap elbows and cursing opponents in Italian, English, Serbo-Croatian, French, or whatever language fits. He speaks a few languages and swears in all of them.

He's been civil but far from pleasant the few times I've met him. Roberto Brunamonti says Danilovic isn't really as hard as he puts on, he's just playing the role of the professional ballplayer, but I don't know. I remember Messina, a while back, making a fist and telling me, "He's like this: closed, tight." You see the on-court behavior, you hear about him blowing off kids wanting autographs—not very appealing.

And I know this: at home, Ann Wennington always lowers her voice when she says his name, and cautions me not to say it much above a whisper. Danilovic and his girlfriend live in the next-door apartment, and Bill and Ann both think he's a little crazy.

And this is before Ann tells me that she was leaving the building with little Robbie and encountered Danilovic getting back from practice the morning Messina threw him out; she said hello, then was startled when he launched into a tirade about the incident, including, "My people are special, you don't treat us this way, I know people who could shoot you!"

Even after Kim leaves and I figure it's just me and *basket* from here on out—and though I see a game every few days, and follow the box scores in the *Gazzetta* and read *Super Basket* as always—somehow the playoffs and the playout are passing me by.

The weather is changing. We get some beautiful days at the coast: not quite warm enough for shorts yet, not nearly warm enough to go in the water, but most days are sunny and mild and hinting of days not far off when I'll be out in the sea or lolling on the sand. Dozens of restaurants and shops and hotels that have been shut since October are opening up. Tourists are coming on weekends. Flowers are blossoming. More than that, as Mark Crow says, *people* are blossoming. Not only in Riccione but everywhere I go, people are smiling, strolling, sharing conversation and laughs and long meals at open-air restaurants.

Basket seems more secondary than ever. Part of it, for me, is that so few clubs have a chance to win the *scudetto* (which doesn't mean "championship," it turns out; the *scudetto* is the little tricolored patch that the championship players wear on their jerseys the next season). Knorr and Benetton are clearly the best teams now, and while upsets are always fun as they're happening, we as fans are often sorry afterward because we're deprived of an anticipated matchup farther on. It might be exciting if someone knocks off Knorr or Benetton on the way to the finals, but who except the fans in Reggio di Calabria or Pesaro wants to see a Panasonic-Knorr finals, or Scavolini-Benetton?

Maybe the lack of *gravità* about the playoffs has to do with their brevity. There's nothing of the brutal, interminable, last-man-left-standing-wins nature of the NBA postseason. I catch a couple of early games, then when I look up after a couple of short trips with my friends the playoffs are half over.

But the biggest difference is in my own attitude. I'm getting Italianized. *Basket* isn't a religion here. It seems more natural to be out living your own life than watching other people. You start thinking of basketball games as *games*, amusements, entertainments you might partake of if *you* don't have anything better to do. *Games*, and if one is televised at all (and few are, because people don't tune in) the network simply shows *the game*. Imagine, they come on the air and just start the game: no melodramatic music and voice-overed story-line intro to reinforce what a momentous matter it is, with reputations at stake and even "character" determined! Over here it's a bunch of guys playing basketball, and on any given day some will do better and some worse, but in any case the citizens will go out for a leisurely dinner afterward and drink a little wine, it's over, it killed a couple of hours, and next time other guys will be up and others down. And eventually there will be a champion, and that's great—for that town—but life pretty much goes on. None of it is a big deal.

It feels healthy, it feels right.

• • •

Thursday, April 15, I eat lunch with Messina at Brunamonti's restaurant, then spend a few hours at the Wenningtons' place. I've seen them a few times now. Bill's a good guy, Anne's a jewel.

This evening I plan to take the 8:30 train so as to get home in time to watch a replay of tonight's Euroclub Championship final from Athens, but Bill invites me to stay for dinner (we'll get Chinese takeout) and watch the game live on a satellite station he picks up.

After trailing at halftime on Tuesday night, the "old" Benetton, with Terry Teagle playing his first game since the qualifying game against Scavolini three weeks ago, beat the Greek club PAOK (Cliff Levingston, Ken Barlow) as Toni Kukoc took over down the stretch. Maybe the Final Four is Toni's show for as long as he stays in Europe. Maybe everything is. He won those three straight Euroclub Championships with his Yugoslavian club, then came over here and won the *lega* last year. This hasn't been the greatest season for Benetton, and Toni has come in for some criticism, but they did win the Italy Cup, they're within a game of the Euroclub Championship and should at least reach the *lega* finals—a possible Grand Slam. Say what you will about Toni, he always seems to be around when they're handing out the trophies.

Lately more than ever, everyone's talking about Toni and the Chicago Bulls. Is this his last appearance in the Euroclub Championship? Does all the talk disturb him and the team?

I don't know about the team, but from everything I've seen, all the publicity swirls *around* Toni, *outside* him. While Capicchioni and Benetton and the Bulls negotiate, and the international press and millions of fans speculate about his future, Toni's this young, pleasant, unassuming guy living in little Treviso, Italy, hanging out with his wife and baby girl and shopping at Kmart-type stores like anyone else.

Teagle, who played only twenty-five minutes and scored 9 points on Tuesday, comes out smoking tonight. Still, Bill and I laugh when, less than ten minutes into the game, the broadcaster, an Englishman, says tonight's MVP can't possibly be anyone but Terry Teagle.

The French team Limoges plays tough defense, slows the game to a crawl, frustrates the opposition. They trail by only six at halftime, 28–22.

Teagle, though he winds up as high scorer for both sides with 19 points, doesn't do much after the first few minutes, doesn't even play a lot of the second half. Even Kukoc can't get off against Limoges's prickly defense.

Yet, phlegmatic as he can be at times, Toni seems desperate to win. After Limoges goes ahead late in the game he tries to do it all himself in the last few minutes, and I've still got the feeling it's his game. The crowd is howling, millions are watching all over Europe, the Bulls' Jerry Krause is there, but Toni won this thing when he was twenty, and twenty-one, and twenty-two; the pressure's nothing new.

It gets tight, then *tied*. Limoges scores to go up by two, and Benetton's got a last possession. Toni brings the ball up and dribbles around, looking, looking—he's not about to give up the ball until he either shoots or passes to a teammate under the basket, nothing less.

He gets stripped. A Limoges guard takes the ball, gobbles up the wide-open court, and lays in two as time runs out.

The crowd—which has been rooting for Limoges, because Benetton knocked off *their* team, PAOK—goes nuts. The Limoges players act as crazy as a high-school team. Toni sits on the Benetton bench amid the bedlam with a towel over his head. Rusconi, the brute, openly bawls, a strange sight. Petar Skansi, Benetton's spooky coach, tells an interviewer that Limoges's winning with their ugly grind-it-out style is the death of basketball, or something.

A few minutes later, Toni glumly accepts the Final Four MVP award.

Now the *lega* is all that's left.

Benetton has to play the deciding game with dangerous Panasonic on Sunday afternoon.

• • •

Saturday afternoon, I watch on TV as Philips exits the playoffs. For most of the game it looks as if the home crowd is going to pull them through, but their shooting goes cold late in the game, which spells doom when they don't have Antonio Davis to help keep Scavolini from scoring. It ends with Haywoode Workman weaving the length of the floor to score and give Scavolini the lead with ten seconds to go, and Ricky Pittis, miscalculating the time, putting up a long, rushed jumper with six seconds left instead of looking for a better shot or driving to the hoop to draw a foul. Even at that, Philips rebounds and misses again and rebounds and misses *again* before the buzzer sounds.

It's over for them. For Mike. Even for me, in some little way. I feel like I went through it all with them.

When I call Mike the next afternoon he greets me with his usual, "Hey, what's happenin'," but lifelessly. When I ask how he's doing he says, "All right—I don't think anybody ever died from this," but it's easy to tell he's in acute suffering, at least.

"We just didn't get any breaks," he says. He cites the ball's bouncing out of Walter Magnifico's hands near the end—but right to a Scavolini teammate; Philips shooters getting hit on 4 three-pointers, with no fouls called ("That's twelve free throws"); and Pittis, one of the *lega*'s three or four best players since Christmas, "getting brain-lock" and casting up the prayer with plenty of time remaining.

But more than anything, they missed Antonio Davis. "I think we won the first game on emotion," Mike says, "pulling together after we lost Antonio. Then we lost down there, and in the long break before this last game the team really started having doubts. In practice all week we had junior players going down the lane and dunking. I think the guys knew they couldn't do it without Antonio."

I ask how late he stayed up last night watching the tape.

"Till three or four. And I've watched it two or three times today."

No doubt he'll watch it two or three times more. Today.

"You going to go to any playoff games?"

"Nah. They don't have much interest for me now." He and Laurel are leaving in a few days to visit his parents in West Virginia for a couple of weeks; then he comes back for some clinics and some Philips planning for next season—whom to sell, whom to buy. The club has big financial problems. Pittis will have to be sold just so the organization can pay some bills, meaning Mike will essentially have to start from scratch next season.

We'll be in touch.

Benetton, after squeezing past Panasonic in their deciding quarterfinal game, cruises past Scavolini in the first game of the semis.

On an idyllic Saturday, April 24, Mark Crow picks me up in Riccione and we drive down to Pesaro for game two.

With the notorious Red-and-White Hell going berserk in the upper deck, Scavolini wins to force a third game up in Treviso. Workman and Jim Farmer score 20 points each, Carlton Myers 18. Corchiani scores 24 for Benetton, Toni 23, but big Rusconi gets only 8.

Mark drives back alone. Alberto, always happy for an excuse to come to the coast and "eat feesh," showed for the game and wants me to ride up to one of his friends' apartments in Rimini to watch the Knorr-Cantu game on TV, then go out to dinner. It sounds great: in these sweet days and nights, I can't imagine anything nicer than eating out and socializing with some "blossoming" Italians.

It's always fun too, watching Knorr with Alberto. Yes, he works for the *lega*, but as Laurel D'Antoni said after meeting him, he was born with a Virtus Bologna *V* on his chest. I think he gets more nervous than anyone except Messina.

Tonight he's more than usually so. He's been crowing all week that Knorr will become the first team ever to roll through the playoffs undefeated, but tonight's game might be the toughest of all—up in Cantu, where Brunamonti says he's won only once in ten years.

With Bortolo sitting on his hands in his friend's living room, Knorr falls behind by ten at halftime. But they're right back in it when Bill Wennington, who scored only 2 points in the first half, opens the second with a few baseline jump shots. It's close down to the wire, but Knorr finally inches ahead and then hangs on to move into the finals. Undefeated.

At dinner at a nice Rimini restaurant with his friend and the friend's wife, Alberto is a glad man. We're all feeling good, for our various reasons. Alberto's friends don't speak a word of English, and the guy gives me a hard time for picking up so little Italian in seven months, but we're there for two hours and with the help of vino and rampant goodwill a splendid time is had by all. Wine, *piadina* with prosciutto, stuffed tomatoes, tortellini, salad, and "feesh"; *sorbetto* for dessert; espresso; and a short glass of grappa at the end, which is served ice-cold but nevertheless heats you up all the way down and then through and through. *Yes!*

They drop me off on the Via D'Annunzio, where I'll catch the bus down to Riccione. It's a balmy, dreamy midnight. People are out, people are happy. I'm happy.

It's hard to believe it's almost over.

Up in Treviso, Benetton jumps on Scavolini early, leads by twenty at halftime, and cruises into the finals against Knorr. Toni scores only 13, but Corchiani gets 20 and Massimo "Yakko" Iacopini throws in 33 by shooting 12-for-16, including 7-for-10 on threes.

I make a call to *il monumento nazionale*. Stefanel got knocked out of the playoffs three weeks ago, but Italian players' contracts run ten months a year and coach Tanjevic, a noted slavedriver, is still working his club out—sometimes twice a day!—for some meaningless tournament in Spain late next month.

Dino's good-natured as always. He says he hasn't talked to the owner about next season, but he's pretty sure the club wants him back (*everyone* knows Stefanel will want him back) and pretty sure he'll oblige. A twenty-eighth season, during which he'll turn forty-four!

"I didn't play great this year, but I was satisfied, and we played well even though three important players were injured much of the time." He laughs. "Besides, I don't know what I would do if I didn't play basketball. Even today, our one day off in the week, I don't know what to do. I would like to have practice."

I like it. In the U.S. we hear, "I won't stay when my skills drop off. There's much more to me than basketball." As if the guy is going to write a novel, or take over General Motors. In fact, most do stay after their skills diminish; few leave on their own terms, and fewer still find second careers as fun or satisfying or remunerative as their first. Dino's far from what he used to be, but he loves to play and they like having him around, so why not play on?

Dino talks about maybe doing something for the national team someday—team manager, assistant coach—or working for Stefanel in some capacity, or going back to Milan and working for Philips (assuming Morbelli would have him after Dino broke his door three years ago). He could probably do a lot of things. People say he could be an entertainer if you just turned him loose with a mike, and I don't doubt it.

But for as long as he can, Dino Meneghin plays *basket*.

The Kiss

The Palasport in Bologna is dressed up for the first game of the finals: signs to the players everywhere, VIRTUS PRIDE signs, flags, a sheet of black or white construction paper on every seat in the house (to be waved as the starting lineups take the floor).

This is it. Danilovic, the headstrong Serbian kid with the *grandi coglioni*, the most consistently productive player in the league all season, and Kukoc, the sleepy-looking Croatian, certainly the most brilliant player over here at his best. Wennington and Corchiani, the last two Americans left standing. Brunamonti. Rusconi. Morandotti. Iacopini. Moretti. Messina, with his last chance to win something in this season when people half expected him to win *everything*, making his last stand in Bologna after ten years ("What happens now will determine how I'm remembered here"). Skansi, the unpredictable but peculiarly charismatic Benetton coach.

Alberto, beside me, clings nervously to his prediction that Knorr won't lose a playoff game. To make him more nervous than he is, I predict Benetton will take the series. I half believe it. I half believe in the Kukoc mystique.

After Brunamonti opens the finals with a three-pointer, Toni dribbles out most of the shot clock—looking, looking—before whipping a mind-blowing assist inside.

Danilovic, meanwhile, looks tight. With Iacopini dogging him he's reduced to trying his weak behind-the-back move to get off his first shot, which misses everything and sails out of bounds.

Rusconi, the Benetton brute, keeps getting fouled—and missing one free throw after another. "Cry for us, Rusconi!" the Forever Boys taunt, referring to the aftermath of the Euroclub Championship final.

Kukoc, handling the ball virtually all the time as if set on controlling his own fate, keeps Benetton in the game with his amazing passing. Knorr leads by only four at the half.

But the second half is a rout. Corchiani doesn't do much. The referees, particularly on the road, no longer send him to the foul line every time he drives the lane, as they did in his first few games, and Corchiani isn't big enough or athletic enough to finish many plays inside. At the other end, he can't handle Brunamonti or Coldebella. "Send him away!" a Treviso journalist behind us shouts repeatedly, holding his nose.

Knorr leads by sixteen with a couple of minutes left when the crowd leaves off tormenting Benetton's Nino Pellacani, whose crime is that he once played for the *other* Bologna team ("Pellacani's a son of a whore!"), to break into song: "It's over, it's over, it's over!"

Knorr's depth and balance weigh in: 19 for Danilovic, 18 for Morandotti, 17 for Brunamonti, 16 for Wennington, and 15 for Coldebella. Kukoc scores 29 for Benetton.

Attendance for the first game of the finals is 6,325—not even capacity, not even in *basket*-mad Bologna. It's springtime in Italy.

Early every morning I walk on the beach—the sun just coming up, the all-night fishing boats coming in. Then it's over to the bar by the canal where Aldo, who speaks no English except for calling me "Cleeen-ton," pours me two espressos and tries to make something of my feeble Italian. Cool, clean, salty air wafts in as I walk back to my apartment. Riccionese are opening their shops, hosing and sweeping the sidewalks in front. Everyone smiles and says *Ciao, buon giorno*. Old and young alike pass by on their bicycles, going to work or to market. I make my daily stop at Amici di Riccione to see Cinzia and make my calls, then put in a couple of hours of work before walking over to the open-air Savioli to look at the *Gazzetta* and josh with Fausto, Silvano, and Maurizio while having my *fornarina*, pasta, and *birra*. Afternoon finds me back on the beach, though I rarely go far before simply dropping down on the warm sand for an hour or two. It's shorts weather now, no-shirt weather (though, as the locals say, the only people who'll go in the water yet are German tourists).

It's easy to understand why even the championship series draws less-than-capacity crowds. I skip the second game myself.

They're playing it up in Treviso on Wednesday evening, May 5. Alberto's got my pass arranged, a front-row seat in the Palaverde. I had planned to take an early train up, spend the afternoon in Venice, then go to the game. But the morning was so fine in Riccione, I couldn't leave. *I'll go after lunch, and just skip Venice*.

But having lunch over at the Savioli (where Fausto and Geo have all the guys wearing matching flowered shirts), I'm thinking how nice the evening will be here, and how nice it's been to stroll over to the Nicolettis' hotel, the Hotel Gambrinus, late every night since they opened up and have a couple of shots of ice-cold lemon vodka with Signor or his son, Luca, whoever is working the bar.

When Fausto tells me he'll show the game on the Savioli TV this evening, it's good enough for me. (By now, knowing I can read the results in the *Gazzetta* tomorrow would be enough.) I call Alberto and tell him I don't need the pass—realizing, as I do, how inconceivable it would be to skip a life-or-death NBA championship game. But here, tonight, what's inconceivable to me is the idea of passing up these sweet, simple pleasures for a ball game, *any* ball game.

Bleary from too much sun but chilling with a beer, I relax in a booth at the Savioli at six o'clock. I couldn't be happier. *Basket* is only a game. As if I need reminding, this "crucial" game doesn't even come on TV for a while. There's news or something, talking heads, though it doesn't seem like anything pressing. The score is already 23–21 when the network takes us to Treviso.

I don't even mind.

By halftime, in the game Benetton needs to win, Knorr leads by thirteen. Benetton looks discouraged.

I start with *piadina* and prosciutto, then move on to pasta, then fish, with a couple of glasses of wine. The sea breeze drifts in. Happy groups come into the Savioli to drink toasts, eat long, leisurely meals, talk boisterously, laugh uproariously.

Benetton never begins to solve Knorr, but who cares? It's a ball game. I'm pretty sure no one would care much more, even here in Knorr country, if it were a Benetton romp.

Afterward, after Fausto has Silvano bring me samples of three liqueurs I didn't even ask for, I stay around for a while talking with my friend Chantal, who has just closed her gift shop across the street and dropped in for a pizza with her little girl, Rebecca. I'm heading home at last when Elio pulls up with the kids, and after a stroll down to the Center for gelati we treat Stefano and Janis to some video games at the *sala giochi*.

Around eleven I amble over to the Hotel Gambrinus. It's quiet, no one around except Luca and his girlfriend minding the desk and the bar until Signor Nicoletti shows up to relieve him. Finally Signor shows up, my *patrono*, looking drained after yet another sixteen-hour day but brightening as always when he sees me—less because of my sparkling personality, I think, than because he gets such a kick out of what a kick I get out of the way he always exclaims "*Ciao*, Jeemy!" and whacks me with that high-five.

Luca and his girl stick around for a quick lemon vodka; then it's the *patrono* and I, though we're still virtually unable to communicate, sharing another glass or two and immeasurable good cheer until well past midnight.

It's amazing how you can start missing people before you've even left.

The third game is the strangest I've seen all season, maybe ever.

It's Saturday afternoon, May 8, a warm, blooming day in Bologna. The Palasport is decked out with signs and trembling with a bloodlusting din. The Bolognese feel a sweep. Even the experts are saying Knorr cut the heart out of Benetton by staying with them in the early part of Wednesday's game in Treviso and taking that thirteen-point halftime lead. The papers are saying Skansi has lost control of the team, he's feuding with players, etc. Capicchioni, who watched Benetton practice when he went up to Treviso to see Toni on Thursday, says it was the worst workout he's ever seen.

The game is a rout from the start. Knorr comes out swarming on defense and scores time after time off egregious Benetton turnovers. Benetton looks frustrated, confused, and dispirited. Brunamonti saves a loose ball and the fans are singing: "*Un Brunamonti/C'è solo un Brunamonti./Un Brunamonnn-ti/C'è solo un Brunamonnn-ti . . .*"

The bizarre part is that as Knorr's lead quickly mounts, Skansi does nothing. He not only does nothing in the way of substitutions or time-outs, but *literally:* he takes his seat at tip-off and remains virtually motionless until halftime, creepily impassive as his club gets overrun in the final game. I've never seen anything like it. This is the guy who's usually so hyperactive and abusive on the sideline that he incited *Brunamonti* to bad language in the Italy Cup final.

The nearest Alberto can come to an explanation is that Skansi has occasionally in the past tried to motivate his teams by giving them free rein, or something like that. But no matter what you're trying to accomplish psychologically, you eventually call a time-out when you're getting blitzed, you make substitutions, you change assignments. Even when Rusconi is called for his third foul midway through the first half, Skansi sits there like a guy watching in his living room; all he needs is a footstool and a *birra*.

It's obvious that what the embattled Skansi is saying, for whatever reason, is *vaffanculo*. Fuck off and die. See what you can do without me.

He's publicly giving up, and flaunting it. Certainly he's cutting his own throat, unless there's something here I don't understand. But no one else understands either.

Alberto isn't amused. "This looks very bad for the league, this kind of show in the finals. It looks like they're giving up." A moment later, as Knorr's lead swells: "I'm worried about our TV ratings. People will turn this game off."

Knorr just plays ball. Messina rotates eight players, utilizing the depth that has set his club apart all season. Danilovic continues his torrid playoff shooting with a 7-for-9 first half, 17 points.

Five minutes into the second half it's 67–40 and even the Benetton players have all but quit. Kukoc keeps trying to make something happen every time down the floor, but he's out of whack along with the rest.

The Forever Boys Virtus unfurl a huge sign: TREVISO, THE IMPORTANT THING IS TO PARTICIPATE! Another: BLACK-AND-WHITE SCUDETTO!

With eight minutes remaining they're serenading Roberto again: "*Un Brunamonti/C'è solo un Brunamonti . . .*"

Then they're singing "*Grazie*, Ettore!" It's Messina's last game here.

It's a lovefest. And the moment that puts a perfect cap on the season for me comes with seven minutes left, when Messina removes Roberto to a huge roar . . . and the one and only Brunamonti, instead of going to the bench, jogs the opposite way instead, leans over the railing behind the basket and kisses his wife Carla, who seems as surprised as everyone else in the place.

The place goes nuts.

It's so simple, yet so perfect. So *Roberto*. Anyone could do it, but who else would even think of it? I can imagine some publicity-conscious NBA jock contriving some such thing ahead of time—say, Magic Johnson and Isiah Thomas with their little kiss-kiss before each tip-off in the 1989 finals—but this is so clearly spontaneous, so unself-conscious, so real, so *right*, like everything Roberto does, that people are just looking at each other and shaking their heads: *Roberto*. I'm reminded of Anne Wennington saying that even if you hardly know him, you can't help thinking of him as a man first, then as a ballplayer.

"All the wives were jealous when he did that," Anne tells me later. "Everyone just went, 'Awwwwww.' "

I even hear later that the TV announcers, choked up, told the audience, "You must excuse us," and couldn't speak for a minute.

Part of it is that everyone knows Carla spent part of the winter in the hospital with a nasty unexplained illness and still isn't well. But mostly it's just Roberto, who seems to make some simple but sublime gesture every time I see him. As Piero Pasini said of *il monumento*, words can't explain.

All I know is that I'm one of many with a tear in my eye as Roberto turns from Carla and jogs to the Knorr bench. Messina hugs him, the assistants hug him, his teammates do, and Roberto's beaming his rare smile. When the game stops for foul shots, Benetton's Iacopini comes over and hugs him. Ettore comes down and hugs him again.

I want to hug him, but I'll settle for the one more lunch we've agreed to share before I leave.

With five minutes left and everyone having fun, Bill Wennington takes a long pass in the open court, approaches the hoop for an uncontested big-man jam—and slams the ball down *on* the rim, so that it bounds twenty feet in the air. The fans groan. But an instant later they remember that Bill, who's taken a lot of abuse in two years, has become one of the good guys with his excellent playoff performance; all is forgiven, with Knorr on the verge of the *scudetto*. "Beel!-Beel!-WENN-ington! Beel!-Beel!-WENN-ington! Beel!-Beel!-WENN-ington!"

And Bill makes up for the missed dunk with twenty seconds left when he takes a pass in the open and, with the euphoric crowd egging him on, shoots and *makes* his first three-pointer of the season. Bologna goes bonzo!

Knorr wins, 117–83, for a three-game sweep and the *lega*'s first-ever undefeated playoff run. Danilovic scores 28 points on deadly 11-for-14 shooting. Wennington and Morandotti score 18 each, Coldebella 14, Carera 13.

Roberto provides superb playmaking and the high point of the day—probably the high point of the season, for me. Along with a bunch of other things he's done.

The fans flood the court and engulf the players; the players are hugging and celebrating and trying to get to the tunnel, but there's no way, they're mobbed. A few pull off their jerseys and fling them into the crowd, others are getting theirs torn off. I catch a glimpse of Roberto: they've got him on their shoulders forcibly and they've got his *shorts* down; he's thrashing around, then disappears. Huge Italian flags are waving above the throng. Music plays. Carla Brunamonti and Anne Wennington and Danilovic's girlfriend and the other women stand, applauding in their front-row places at the end opposite the tunnel the players are trying to get to.

The *polizia* finally get the players and coaches out, but that doesn't quell the pandemonium a whit. I want to get down to that tunnel in a few minutes and go downstairs and hear the coaches, but there's no point in trying for a while.

Eventually I try, and I end up regretting it. After shoving my way as close as I can to the tunnel, I've got waves of humanity pressing in on me from all sides, all going nowhere, just *there*, so I can't move; my press pass ain't gonna get me in, and it's gonna be a bitch even to get *out*.

A few days ago, Messina, anticipating that today's game would be the last, invited me to the team's celebration dinner at Roberto's restaurant afterward. I've arranged to ride over with Bill and Anne. I don't expect the players to be able to get out for a while yet, but when I finally fight my way out of the mob on the court and go down to the pressroom to ask someone how I'm supposed to get downstairs, I unexpectedly run into Bill, who's asking an usher to bring Anne back here so he can sneak out or something (ha). I go back out and retrieve Anne, and then, with the usher and a security guard, we're ducking out a back pressroom door and hurrying down halls I've never seen, headed for some exit or other. Bill's not even going to go back to the locker room for his bag and gear—until it occurs to him that he wants that championship jersey, and then we're reversing through the labyrinth, down some back stairs I never imagined, emerging finally in the dingy Palasport downstairs. Bill takes us into the locker room for the minute or two it takes him to gather his stuff. It's nearly deserted: a couple of players left, a couple of young attendants. And Roberto, sitting between two middle-aged reporters on a bench in the back corner, earnestly answering questions. On *scudetto*-day, the day people are going to be taking pictures (as if it would enter his mind), he's wearing the usual blue jeans and sensible shoes and, charmingly, the most unhip shirt imaginable: green with yellow stripes, something a sixth-grade nerd would wear with a pencil holder on the pocket. It's perfect. Roberto's unhip because Roberto's beyond hip; hip never occurred to Roberto. As Messina said, Roberto doesn't live in this world of ours.

We're back out of the locker room, back upstairs, running through the maze of hallways. For what? Bill's going to sneak out? Outside, singing and cheering and chanting fans have the Palasport surrounded.

Who cares? Bill's having a great time, we're gonna brave it.

"Beel!-Beel!-WENN-ington! Beel!-Beel!-WENN-ington!"

It starts as soon as Bill appears at one of the side exits. They mob him as soon as we step outside.

It was never like this in the NBA. Signing autographs and shaking hands, Bill looks as if he wouldn't escape even if he could.

He's still surrounded as we move across the street on the other side of the arena and into the park by the apartment building, where Bill stops to sign and high-five until the last fans are satisfied and gone and there's only the three of us and some neighborhood people left in the park.

A few minutes later, after checking in with the baby-sitter upstairs, we're back into it, driving to the restaurant: it's gala in the streets anyway, and when people spot Bill they wave and honk and shout and flash *V* signs. Bill laughs, waves. Anne and I giggle. *He's a star!*

Getting out of the car, we can hear the crowd in front of Benso from two blocks away. A roar goes up when we come around the corner and they spot Bill. He's engulfed, swallowed up, and it's ten minutes before some cops get us inside.

Benso is filled to overflowing, and they're cheering Bill as we squeeze between tables behind a waiter who leads us to a big private room crowded with Knorr people—the owner, Cazzola, and players, wives, girlfriends, sponsors—plus a couple of busy photographers, since Cazzola also owns *Super Basket*.

Messina, having changed into jeans and a button-down shirt after being thrown into the shower after the game, is greeting people just inside the door. He looks immensely relieved and a little dazed.

Shaking hands, I congratulate him on the *scudetto:* "You're right there in the record book with Big Pete now as a championship coach. And even Big Pete never went through the playoffs undefeated."

Ettore, not missing a beat, cracks back, "Yes, but no matter what, I will never, ever have the Italian equivalent of the Emmy."

He says he doesn't have a clue about Skansi. Yes, it was bizarre, but Skansi's bizarre.

But who cares? That's Skansi's problem. For two weeks, Ettore says—until he takes over the national team—*he* doesn't have any problems.

Sasha has even been talking to him. "I think it was crucial when he was fined. He's been perfect since. He was mad for a while, but he was okay after I congratulated him after the second game against Cantu. He started talking to me during the first game with Benetton, when I took Roberto out with six minutes left; he said, 'Coach, I don't think you should take Roberto out now.' I didn't take his advice, but I knew he was fine about me then.

"I think now I understand what he was going through, feeling a lot of pressure all season to be the next Toni Kukoc, to win. He's been much different the last few days, when he knew we were going to win."

I sit with Bill and Anne, and Goose and Sylvia Binelli. Someone brings us a bottle of champagne. We take pictures. All around us people are celebrating, laughing, accepting congratulations over cellular phones.

Roberto and Carla come in, and on the way to their table Roberto stops to introduce Carla and me. She understands that I'm the *americano* who's called their home asking for Roberto a few times, but she doesn't know a word of English and we can't communicate—except that she radiates the same warmth, humility, and serenity as Roberto. She's got long, straight black hair and perfect posture, and she stands there looking perfectly self-contained, a beatific expression on her face (suggestive of Mona Lisa, except Carla's smile is big and brilliant) as Roberto chats with us for a minute. I wouldn't call her beautiful, but she's luminous. They seem perfect together. Not of this world of ours.

I ask Roberto, Now what? People are saying Ettore must call him for the national team.

"No, no. Ettore knows I'm finished with it." He lights up as they start toward their table. "For three months I do nothing."

This was his seventeenth season in the *lega*, and since he first made the national team fifteen years ago he's played *basket* all but two or three weeks of every year. No wonder his body is broken down. No wonder he lights up thinking about three months off.

Heads turn when a loud, obnoxious horn starts quacking over by the door. Sasha's entrance! With the pressure off at last, he's grinning, cutting loose, being a kid.

He sits at a back table with a couple of the other young guys and some slinky girls, including his fiancee, and laughs a lot and acts cool, playing the star. Feeling good: *he* won the *scudetto*, not Kukoc. No one knows how he and Kukoc will stack up in the NBA—veterans of the League such as Pace Mannion and Wennington think Danilovic will have a hard time against American two-guards and small forwards, the most athletic of players—but that's another year off in the future for Sasha. Tonight, and this season, he's the man.

Every so often I turn my head for a glance at the Brunamontis. When no one's occupying Roberto's attention he gazes at Carla like a moony teenager. Maybe Carla's illness has something to do with it, but you sense they've always been this way.

You sense they'll always be this way.

We stay past midnight.

A little later there's a get-together at a disco across town. We go back to the apartment and consider it; Bill and Anne talk it over with the baby-sitter. It's fine with her; Robert William is asleep, she's happy to stay and watch a movie.

There's shouting outside, down below; it sounds like fans. "Beel!-Beel!-WENN-ington! Beel!-Beel!-WENN-ington!" But Bill recognizes the voices and walks out onto the balcony. It's Goose Binelli and Flavio Carera and a couple of others. Come to the disco!

Then: "Sa-sha-Da-*nee*-lo-veetch, ohohohoh*oh!*" Sasha comes out onto his balcony next door, laughing and spewing invective down at them. His motorcycle buddy, Coldebella, roars up on a big bike. They're all whooping back and forth.

We finally head for the disco. Horns are honking, Bolognese celebrating Virtus's first *scudetto* in nine years. People spotting Bill honk and wave and call out. Bill's loving it. As Anne says, he's gone from goat to god in a few weeks.

The disco interlude is uneventful. A few people dance; most just sit on a couple of long couches off to one side. Roberto gazes at Carla. Everyone is rapt when a few minutes of NBA highlights play on a TV hanging from the ceiling.

We leave after an hour or so. It's 3 A.M. when we get back to the apartment. The baby-sitter is asleep on the couch. Bill takes her home, then he and Anne flip a coin to see who gets up with little Robbie in a few hours. *Anne*. Exhausted, she brings me sheets, blankets, and a pillow to use on the fold-away couch, then heads off to bed.

Bill and I stay up a little longer. He's still high from the game, the long-time-coming glory. It's been a tough couple of years in Bologna, despite the mitigating factor of an eight-hundred-thousand-dollar salary. The press has given him a hard time, and he's been Ettore's favorite whipping boy, but now he's triumphant: not just the championship *pivot* but the surprise star of the playoffs. They can't say, as many people said all season, that Knorr's on top in spite of Bill Wennington.

Though he doesn't turn in until sometime after four, and though Anne lost the coin flip, a few hours later it's Bill who gets up when Robbie starts bawling. I don't know if it's because this is Mother's Day or if he's simply energized, but by the time Anne comes out he's not only got Robbie dressed but he's set the table and started on a big American breakfast for all of us: coffee, scrambled eggs, a tall stack of toast.

Then again, he's a professional ballplayer, a guy who wants to use basketball to put away money until he's thirty-five, and the end-of-game buzzer that officially made him a champion last night also made him a guy without a job. His two-year contract is up.

Now what?

Bill says no one else knows this, but Knorr's owner, Alfredo Cazzola, took him aside a few weeks ago and said that both he and Alberto Bucci, who'll be coming in as Messina's successor, like Bill's game and are interested in having him back next season. And Bill's agent back home recently told him a few NBA teams have expressed interest and might even offer a three- or four-year deal.

He'll have to wait and see. If Knorr makes an offer, it's likely to be much less than eight hundred thousand dollars a year. The salaries over here, after the wild spending of the past few years, are expected to go down, down, down now. Benetton GM Maurizio Gherardini has told me that players signing new contracts now, both Italians and *stranieri*, will be lucky if offers are only thirty to thirty-five percent less than what the players could have expected before.

Bill's thinking about security. He'd sign with Knorr tomorrow for six hundred thousand dollars if he could get it for four years. For only a year or two he'd want more, because he's pretty sure he'd never get a long-term deal after that, certainly not in the NBA. "It's funny. When you're thirty, like I am, NBA teams look at you as in your prime and will give you a long-term contract. When you're thirty-one or thirty-two, most won't; they think you're slipping."

His best guess is that he'll be back in the NBA next season.

For now, he's a hero in Bologna. You're a hero, Bill!

He chuckles. "Not a hero. I'm just a guy playin' ball, havin' fun." And he adds, on this morning after having had half of Bologna shouting his name, "It's hard to believe we get *paid* for this."

Loose Ends and Endings

A few hours after leaving the Wenningtons on Sunday morning I'm in Forli for the Telemarket–Phonola Caserta game. Today is the real end of the season: the last round of playout games, with a few positions for next season still undetermined. Phonola, with a win, will stay in A-1 next year. Telemarket's only chance to move up is to have things break right in a couple of other games while they not only win this one but, in order to move up via tiebreaker, win by at least twenty-one points.

Unlikely—but what do these guys care anyway? Darryl Dawkins will probably be back with Telemarket, but Rob Lock will surely be elsewhere, and Bonaccorsi, the wild but talented guard, will probably be sold too.

Phonola's not likely to be fighting to the death either. Cadillac Anderson is sure to be gone next year. Tellis Frank, who's had a weak season, probably won't be back. And the talk is that Stefanel Trieste is set to pay millions for Nando Gentile, the flashy, temperamental guard.

The game is not an artistic success. Darryl slings a couple of the pointless long-bomb passes he's prone to, which seems to annoy Lock. When Lock throws a bad pass, Darryl is openly peeved. On the Phonola side, Nando Gentile is launching hopeless threes from five feet behind the line and squawking at his coach during time-outs.

Telemarket, after starting out as if they might actually win by twenty-two, plays more in character and leads by only five at halftime. They wind up losing by five as Gentile sticks to his strengths in the second half, going to the basket and then dishing to open teammates.

Telemarket will stay in A-2 next season.

At the team's last dinner, Darryl, whose weight dropped from 305 to 265 over the course of the season, tells Corbelli he'll show up in August at no more than 277. No way, Corbelli says, but there's twenty thousand dollars in it for you if you do. Now you're talkin', Darryl says . . .

As everyone says good-bye, Darryl slips five one hundred thousand lire notes (about four hundred dollars, "for college") to Lou's son Chris, who worships Darryl already. Little tough-guy Chris has to pull his baseball cap down over his eyes to hide the tears, and Lou and Silvana are likewise choked up. Darryl reminds them to call him before they pass through New York this summer, and he'll have a limo pick them up and bring them out to his spread in New Jersey.

Darryl's leaving Forli at 4 A.M. He'll be home tomorrow afternoon.

Everybody's gone.

Soon I will be too. Sometimes I still can't believe any of it has really happened. I think back on all the places I've been, the people I've met. Lots of the *basket* people, I wonder about.

I remember a forlorn J. J. Eubanks telling me his sad story in a Rimini pizzeria on a drizzly night last fall, then taking me over to see the mold on the walls of his apartment. Things didn't look promising for him, but he wound up in Greece and averaged 21 points a game.

I remember the fans down in Fabriano going crazy over Sky Walker, former NBA lottery pick and dunk champion, and Teamsystem beating Benetton. Unfortunately, Teamsystem lost the other three games Walker played, though he averaged a respectable 15 points and 9 rebounds, and the club let him go when his four-game contract was up. "I think I represented myself real well over here," Walker told me before flying home, "so I accomplished everything I set out to do." He caught on in Spain soon after and finished the season with about the same stats he compiled here. And for Sky, coming back from the Achilles injury, simply getting through the season healthy was the major triumph.

LeRon Ellis, who signed for six games with Hyundai Desio the same week that Walker signed, missed the first game due to the snafu in the ABA-USA office, then played in four games with numbers identical to Walker's: 15 points and 9 boards per game. But Hyundai, in first place in A-2 when Ellis arrived, was tied for fourth a month later and chose not to have him play the last game he'd signed for, reactivating Hansi Gnad instead. Mark Crow says Ellis went back to the CBA and is still trying to collect what Hyundai owes him.

I finally get Paolo Di Fonzo's story. Di Fonzo was Il Messaggero Roma's coach when Rick Mahorn blew up last fall. Though even Rick's self-serving version of events was enough to convince me the club had sufficient reason to fire him, I always wanted to know what really happened.

Di Fonzo, who was fired himself in December after the Ferruzzi Group sold the club, admits that Rick is "a strong personality who must be accepted for what he is." He says Rick didn't hesitate to criticize his teammates but had a hard time accepting "reproachment" himself.

Still, Di Fonzo says, the other players respected him. Rick was a winner; sometimes he didn't get up for lesser competition and ended up getting outplayed, but he was always tough against big players in important games. "For instance, in the Cup of Cups last year against Arvidas Sabonis, he gave a lesson to Italian players on how you defend against a super talent who also happens to be much bigger than you are."

As for the fateful scene after the Korac Cup game back in

October, Di Fonzo admits that Rick cursed his teammates for not giving him the ball enough.

As for the chair he threw, "It's not important *what* he threw," Di Fonzo says. "In light of what I know now, I'm certain the Ferruzzi Group, which was secretly trying to sell the club, wanted to dump Rick's contract, and what mattered was that he did this in front of some management people. It was a gross tactical error on Rick's part to force the issue right then and there. A good night's sleep would have refreshed his perspective and allowed him to reason in a whole different way."

Di Fonzo proposed fining Rick and suspending him for two practices. Fining him never entered his mind. But the Ferruzzi Group saw its chance to unload a $2 million salary and make the club a much more attractive proposition. (Someone saw the chance, anyway. Di Fonzo suggests that the prospective buyer nudged Ferruzzi to drop Mahorn: *Lose that $2 million albatross and you've got a deal.*)

Anyway, Rick was gone. The sale of the club was consummated a few weeks later. The new ownership shortly replaced Di Fonzo with Franco Casalini and cleaned out everyone else connected with the old regime, including assistant coach and longtime NBA forward Greg Ballard.

Back home, Rick played in seventy-four games with the New Jersey Nets, averaging about 4 points and 4 rebounds in fifteen minutes per.

In Rome, Tom Federman of Dobson & Sinisi keeps working on Rick's lawsuit against the club.

Carlton Myers is home in Rimini, waiting for Messina's national-team camp.

At lunch a few months ago, Messina stated the obvious about Myers: "He could be very important to the national team, because he's so talented." On the other hand, Ettore doesn't have stars in his eyes. "He might not last the first practice," he joked at Benso after the championship game.

• • •

A week after I awoke in the Wenningtons' living room—when Bill was a hero—the *Gazzetta* says Arvidas Sabonis is leaving Real Madrid and joining Knorr next season. That is, replacing Bill as the center and the second *straniero* along with Danilovic.

"That's not gonna happen," Mark Crow assures me. "The guy they really want is Cliff Levingston." Levingston played this season with the Greek club PAOK, one of the Euroclub Final Four teams.

I call Bill, knowing he and Anne are leaving in another few days and that he had expected to talk with Cazzola about next season.

"We talked," Bill says, not nearly as exuberant as when I last saw him, "but not about specifics. We're supposed to talk again before we leave. But there's no place for me here next year."

But the NBA is interested, right?

Bill isn't sure.

I get together with Messina in Bologna one sunny afternoon during my last week. He's getting ready to leave the city where he's spent the last ten years, virtually his entire adulthood—he arrived as an assistant coach at twenty-three. He and his wife and little Lucy are moving to a house they've bought in the country up near Venice.

"The greatest thing," he says, "is to leave Bologna with the championship. Now I know I can come back and go to the games, maybe watch practice once in a while, and things will be fine, people will say 'Hello, how are you?' I couldn't stand it if, after ten years, I felt I couldn't come back because I didn't win the championship. That would be a disaster.

"Now I have fifteen days until people bust my balls again. We start national-team workouts, then Chris Webber and the Americans come here for an exhibition game, and when they kick our butts I will be the asshole not only for Bologna but for all of Italy."

One last lunch with Roberto Brunamonti. This time Alberto's coming along, as we've planned for weeks, because I've always been a little frustrated knowing that Roberto's elementary English prevents him from communicating more than a fraction of what he's thinking; I want him to speak in Italian, tell everything, and Alberto can translate.

I never do get any deep answers from him. He gives some lengthy answers; it's Alberto who condenses them into two lines of English.

No matter. As always, it's just pleasant being around Roberto. It isn't so much what he says as the way he says things, his sweetness and sincerity and unself-consciousness.

The kiss?

"I never thought about it before. I just did it. No, I've never done it before."

What was he thinking?

"I'm thinking, 'I can't do it after the game because of the crowd, so I must do it now.' "

Simple.

How's Carla's health now?

Roberto sighs. "Patience. It's five months now. It's better now—she's tired, she has some pain, but she takes less cortisone. We're hoping it will go away this summer."

As always, he's inexplicably a little nervous about the future. I never get over it: he's this icon, admired and adored and still a great player to boot, with two years left on his contract, but he can't even see past next season—as if he's *not* that good, and as if Knorr might try to stiff him out of the last year of the deal. (Him! I will never forget the sign, C'È SOLO UN BRUNAMONTI, or the song, or the fans chanting after one of his belly flops for a loose ball, "ROE-BEAR-TOE! ROE-BEAR-TOE! ROE-BEAR-TOE!" as if there could never be another.) He repeats, as always, that he doesn't expect anything from the club after his playing days are over.

He really imagines he could be out looking for a sales job in a year or two.

The *Herald Tribune* quotes "Lucky" Luciano Capicchioni as saying he and Toni Kukoc are flying to Chicago next week for contract negotiations with the Bulls.

The next day, Bulls GM Jerry Krause is quoted as saying there's no meeting scheduled, nothing, he's focussed on the Knicks-Bulls Eastern Conference finals.

I spend my last week saying good-byes close to home. I realize I'll head back to the States having seen very little of Italy—I've never been farther south than Rome, and even north of Rome I spent only a night in Florence and never saw the great ancient walled cities of Tuscany or the lakes and mountains up near Switzerland or many other great things—but it will all still be here when I come again.

The friends I've made here are more important than any historic site or breathtaking sight I have or haven't seen. One reason I haven't traveled more is that I've been so happy hanging out with the people I know, and no matter how close I feel to the Nicolettis, and Elio and Roseanna, and Maurizio over at the Savioli, and Lou up in Rimini, and Mark in Rimini, and Alberto and Ettore and the Wenningtons over in Bologna, they're still *new* friends. We're still breaking new ground; I haven't gotten nearly enough of them, and since I don't know when I'll ever see them again I haven't wanted to give up much of this precious time traveling around simply to look at different landscapes or churches or museums—*things*. Every time I've missed a Monday morning cappuccino-and-chat session with Lou up in Rimini I've felt as if I've missed something that means more to me than seeing the Tower of Pisa.

The week passes in a flash. I meet Lou in Rimini on Monday morning, and though we make a quick stop for coffee, you don't spend Riviera mornings like this sitting in a cafe. We go down to the beach, bury our sandals, and walk for a half hour, our feet in the surf, then walk back and simply flop down on the sand for another hour. We talk, but mostly I'm recalling our times together and wishing there were a way to thank Lou for kindness I'll never forget.

On Monday evening Elio picks me up and takes me out to Roseanna's family's fast-food restaurant. After we eat, as usual, Steffie and Janis go outside and make faces at me through the window until I come out and chase them around the building a few times, and then Elio and I go across the street for a shot of Jack Daniel's and an espresso, and then we drive back to Riccione and take the kids to the *sala giochi* before finally saying good-bye. Elio, who lived in the U.S. for a while and loves it, says he'll see me there within two years.

So it goes. On Tuesday I'm up in Rimini again for lunch at Mark and Lia's place. Afterward I train on to Bologna, where I meet Alberto at the *lega* office (so I can say good-bye to Tiziana and Loretta and the redoubtable Daniela) and then go home with him for dinner with Annarosa and little Francesca. This one's tough; I've known for months it would be, because since the week I arrived Bortolo has done more for me than anyone. There have been times in the past few months, with my departure still a long way off, when I've gotten tears in my eyes thinking about his great openheartedness and knowing how much I'll miss him when it's all over, and now that the time is here—even though Bortolo says he and Signor Nicoletti want me to join them for lunch in Riccione on Thursday—it's all I can do not to start bawling when he drops me off at the *stazione* late at night.

Heading down to the beach around noon on Wednesday I run into Luca Nicoletti, who's on his way over to the hotel. I walk along just to chat and end up sharing lunch with him and Mariagrazia and their eighty-four-year-old grandparents and the half-dozen kitchen staff in a big room behind the hotel kitchen, before all except the grandparents go to work serving lunch to the tour group of forty Germans staying in the hotel. Pasta, vino, vegetables, everything, and though no one but Luca and Mariagrazia speak any English at all and my Italian is still negligible, I'm welcomed, and somehow we're all joking and laughing and I'm marveling yet again about the Italian way. I know a little of it, at least, has rubbed off on me; I wonder how much will stay with me once I'm back in the States.

Lunch on Wednesday is more true Italy. Ever since I used my immense pull to get him a pass for the two nights of the Italy Cup back in March, Maurizio from the Savioli has wanted to have me out to the house in the country where he and his brother and sister live with their mother. He drives into town and picks me up at noon, and we travel fifteen miles or so west to where we're on a dirt road winding through rolling hills, past farms and old estates whose hillsides are covered with vineyards. Maurizio's family's place is a vast old stone house on top of a hill from which you look back across a beautiful valley to more hills, farms, and—barely visible in the distance—the tops of Riccione's seaside hotels. Maurizio's got vineyards too, and a garageful of bottles of his own product. His mother, in her sixties, has never met an American in her life and can't speak a word of English (nor can his twenty-two-year-old sister, who has an office job in Riccione and arrives for lunch soon after we do), but she's gone all-out on the cooking: pasta with a spicy sauce, home-baked bread, broccoli, salad, and the main course, rabbit, which is a treat for me. Plenty of Maurizio's wine, of course. I'm overwhelmed, as I've been so often, by the welcome I get from people who don't even know me—and pleased that I'm able to put together enough Italian words to communicate, minimally, with Maurizio's mother and sister.

When I get home there's a note from Mariagrazia saying that I'm invited to join her father and Alberto at one o'clock tomorrow for lunch over at the Fino oceanfront restaurant.

Bortolo's family had a summer place in Riccione when he was a kid, and his late father was a good friend of Signor; Signor remembers "little Alberto" and has wanted to see him ever since he found out I'm friends with the grown-up version, but it hasn't happened until now. I figure I should let them visit for a while, so I walk over to the Hotel Gambrinus and tell Mariagrazia to tell her father, in case I don't see him tonight, that I'll come over to the Fino at two-thirty or so tomorrow and just join them for coffee.

But I should have known that's not the Italian way. It's not even one-thirty the next day when Mariagrazia shows up at my door saying Signor had phoned home from the Fino and asked her to try to find me and bring me over there as soon as possible. And as soon as we get there, of course, we're all eating and drinking wine and laughing and Signor is telling me (through Bortolo, as he so often tells me through a translator) that I must come back to Italy and marry an Italian and stay; and I'm thinking, as I often do, *I'd think about marrying this lithe daughter of yours with the big brown eyes, who still gives me those long looks, if she wasn't tied up with this wholesale-grocery salesman she's constantly arguing with.* Bortolo keeps ordering "feesh," of course—"Always when I come to the shore I tell them, 'Just keep bringing it' "—and finally there are cakes for dessert, and liqueurs, and coffee at the end.

Saying good-bye outside, I know it's the last time I'll see Bortolo; he won't be at the all-star game in Forli on Saturday, and I'm riding up to Milan with Mike and Laurel afterward for my last two days in Italy. Fortunately, we're all very much in the moment—I'm just happy, not choked up—and Alberto's got to drop off Signor at the Palazzo de Turismo and get back to Bologna. We say *ciao,* I tell him I'll call him before flying out of Malpensa on Tuesday, and we go our separate ways.

My brother-in-law Chuck, in Italy on business, shows up on Thursday. He's brought along a notice from the IRS that's been forwarded to his and my sister Sarah's place in Tennessee; addressed to me and Jenelle, my ex-wife, it says they audited our last joint return and we owe $746.

I never thought I'd be glad to hear from Internal Revenue, but my heart leaps at the idea that I've got an excuse to contact Jenelle again. Maybe, I'm thinking, everything has happened for a reason. I had to lose my marriage to learn some lessons in humility that would make me a better husband, a better stepfather, a better person. I had to be alone so I could pursue my writing and bust out of the wretched jobs that caused the frustration I took out on Jenelle and Jenny. I wound up in Italy not only to write a book on *basket* but to learn the Italian way: how to live in the moment, to appreciate people and the little parts of life that we so often take for granted, to savor the spring sun and the sea air and my good friends instead of fretting over the purposeful tasks that, just a few months ago, seemed far more important than such things.

And I've learned. People have been so generous here, I've felt so *loved*, that I feel infinitely more capable of generosity and love myself. Maybe now things can all work out.

Even as I spend a lovely day showing Chuck around and telling him about my Italian experience and hearing about Sarah and my nieces, Katherine and Elizabeth, I'm thinking about Jenelle. On Friday, spending my last day in wonderful Riccione after leaving Chuck at the station, I'm thinking about her.

But it gradually dawns on me that I'm all wrong in looking at my Italian experience as the means to an end. Like love, like any exhilarating or enriching experience, it's an end in itself. Things *have* worked out for me. The other day Rosita remarked that I seem infinitely more relaxed than when I arrived, and I know it's much more than the fact that I was in a strange country where I didn't know a soul back then; Casey, when he was here, said I seemed much different from the guy he knew in Portland all those years.

These are the days, as Van Morrison says, and I realize

that even when I get back to Portland, life won't be about redeeming the past. This is Italy's gift to me: live, enjoy, be. Get on with my life.

I get up early Saturday morning and walk down to the balmy beach, recalling the winter storms that I feared would blow my windows out. I stop at Aldo's bar by the canal for an espresso, where Aldo comes out into the middle of the room and does a feeble but hilarious imitation of Michael Jordan floating to the hoop. I walk over to the Hotel Mon Pays (*everyone* operates a hotel in season) to say good-bye to Rita, Rosita's sister, and her daughters, Rafaella and Daniela. After strolling the surrounding streets once more I go back and spend a last little bit of time in my dynamite apartment. I sit on my balcony taking a long last look at the Adriatic, already missing people: Lou, Mark, Ettore, Dino, Roberto. Bortolo. Mike and Laurel—even though I'm going to spend my last few days with them, I already miss 'em.

I walk over to the Hotel Gambrinus, the sun shining bright, shopkeepers out sweeping their sidewalks. A bunch of tourists are milling around the hotel, but I've got to have a last coffee with the Nicolettis. I don't want to leave.

But it's time, finally. It seems like only a few days since I landed in Milan—frightened of leaving the airport alone—and drove the old guy I met on the plane all over the countryside, down past Florence, and then drove until nearly midnight to make it to this place called Riccione and called Marina and was directed to the Hotel Vittoria, where I sat in the bar very late writing postcards to friends and family and wondering what awaited me.

I take my thousandth and last (for now) train ride to Forli, my last bus ride from the station to the Palafiera.

They call this game an all-star game, but it's really a showcase for players who might be up for sale in the player-movement period that starts in a week or so. *Il monumento nazionale* is here, and Roberto, and several of the *lega*'s better players, but you've also got guys like Davide Pessina, the soft Philips power forward Mike benched at mid-season and whom the organization is looking to sell. A true all-star game would probably attract more of a crowd, but the Palafiera is only half full, and half of these seem to be coaches, executives, and agents, evaluating talent and talking about deals.

Mike and Laurel show up just before game time. Laurel sits in the second row near midcourt with her old friend Caterina, the de facto Signora Meneghin, while Mike watches from the near-empty stands down at one end with his assistant coaches, considering players for next season. The papers are full of talk about big changes in Milan; after Philips sells Pittis they'll have to buy at least one player and probably make other moves. Without Pittis, Mike's going to have to restructure the team.

The game is unremarkable: high-scoring, run-and-gun, like any exhibition. I wander around socializing, saying good-byes.

At the end, Dino and Roberto are named co-MVPs. Roberto actually played well and scored 20 points; Dino merely participated, but that's enough. You could hardly hold the game without him.

They accept little trophies at midcourt, little kids swarming around them. Dino, light as always, jokes with them and signs autographs. Roberto laughs along with everyone else (even he turns into something like a fan in the presence of *il monumento*); typically, he tries to hang back, but the kids are after him too for autographs and pictures and high-fives.

A half hour after the game, the D'Antonis and I stop to pick up their bags at the hotel where the league has put everyone up the last couple of days. There's a big dinner tonight, but Mike and Laurel want to get home.

Before hitting the road we stop for cold drinks in a pleasant screened porch near the front of the hotel.

Mike, a few days back from the States, is feeling better. Yes, it was tough having the season end the way it did, but it's over. "I wish next season started *now*," he enthuses.

We're sitting there, the evening sun laying a warm orange glow on the woodsy surroundings, when who should appear but Dino and Caterina—a saucy, busty, forty-fivish blonde in a short skirt and fishnet stockings—with an aging German shepherd. Dino and Caterina sit down; the dog (diabetic, it turns out) lies at Dino's feet. Dino orders beers for himself and Caterina and insists I have another one.

Yes, he tells Mike in answer to the obvious question, he's probably going to play another season.

He recalls coming to Milan back in '81, when everyone except Dan Peterson thought he was washed up. "I thought I'd play two years, maybe three, and be finished with basketball. But Peterson immediately talked to me about how I must play in the '84 Olympics, to become the first to play four times, and I started to think about playing longer. And it was easy in Milan. We had a great team, and Peterson said 'We don't need twenty points or twenty rebounds, just play for the team.' "

I ask him about leaving the team three years ago. He's never told me the story Mike told me about how he broke the president's door on his way out.

"Awwwwww." It's the same mischievous, happy-to-be-found-out smile that appeared a few months back when I asked him what he used to do to Roberto Premier's health drinks—another anecdote passed on by Mike. "It was nothing; I did nothing much . . ."

Mike bursts out laughing. "Oh, man! I saw that door—that door was never the same again!"

"Wellllll," Dino allows, "I closed it very hard, let's say." He explains: "I wasn't mad because they don't want me anymore. I'm mad because of how the president talks to me—talking real loud and putting his hand on the desk [Dino brings down a fist on the arm of his rattan chair, mimicking someone pounding on a tabletop]. I stopped him—I tell him, 'You can talk this way to someone else, maybe, one of the younger ones, but not to me.' "

"Aw, you split the door," Mike chimes in.

Dino grins again. "I close it very hard, okay. But I think this door is not very strong."

Not strong enough, anyway.

Right about now, idly watching the people coming up the walk from the parking lot, I spot Roberto with his arm around Carla, their nine-year-old son beside them. A few minutes later Roberto pokes his head into the porch and spots us, and he and Carla, sans little Brunamonti, join us. Carla looks serene and radiant. Roberto comes around behind my chair, puts his hands on my shoulders, and says something in Italian about the *libro*, my book. I tell him I still don't understand enough Italian. "Who will read this book in America?" he asks in English, as he always asks me. "They no care about us." I tell him I'm not sure, but a big American publisher thought it was worth a shot.

The setting sun plays on the big trees outside. Summer's here, the *basket* season's gone, I'm going home, and what better way to end my adventure than sit here with these three "columns," as people say, of Italian basketball? All so relaxed, so normal. Imagine sitting around with Kareem, Magic, and Michael.

Roberto acts as if he's just glad to be included—listening, laughing, letting others entertain. I'm reminded of what a Bologna photographer told me recently: "I go to photograph Dino and he's always laughing, joking, saying 'Come on!' Roberto is just the opposite: 'Oh no, why me? Take *his* picture!'—the guy next to him, or *anyone*."

Small talk. Dino, petting his feeble old dog, tells Laurel yes, he and Caterina really might get married this summer.

Maybe, he adds.

It's time, Dino Lino, Laurel says.

Carla leaves to check on little Brunamonti and dress up for the big dinner. By the time she returns, resplendent in a black velvet dress, it's dark outside, time for Mike and Laurel and me to head for Milan and for everyone else to eat. The big hotel lobby is filled with players, agents, coaches, and journalists. Carlton Myers, sitting on a couch, sees me and waves, though we never got together again after our interview back in December. The tireless Antonio Ricciotti of IMG, looking as if his collar's too tight and he needs an Alka-Seltzer, is still working the room as he was when we arrived, schmoozing twenty-three-year-olds, and I can only think, What a life.

Messina's here, happy—as he said before, he's got this brief time to savor the *scudetto* before he's back in the fire with the national team.

Il monumento walks his creaky old dog around.

Finally, having said exhaustive good-byes, Mike and Laurel and I are out on the *autostrada* heading to Milan.

As always when it's "just family," as Laurel once said, Mike starts musing about his team. He's proposing different lineups for next season, depending on what personnel changes Philips makes over the summer.

"Let me try this team out on you: Schonochini ["the gaucho," an exciting kid from Argentina who played for Panasonic this season], Dean Garrett [Panasonic's center], Djordjevich, Ambrassa, and another forward we'd buy, with Portaluppi comin' off the bench."

I like it. But how?

"Only Benetton, Knorr, and Scavolini have the money to buy Pittis. We tell 'em, 'You get the rights to Garrett and Schonochini from Panasonic,' then when they buy Ricky Pittis we've got the money to buy those two and pay some debts besides."

All the way to Milan, Mike's proposing combinations. For that matter, it goes on all weekend; you'd hardly know the season is over. Occasionally Mike distracts himself by watching *WKRP* (singing the theme song at the beginning) or reading a few pages of a crime novel, but usually he's watching *basket* tapes or reading *basket* stuff.

Louis and Betty Jo D'Antoni's baby-faced All-American

has made quite a life for himself over here, but as we watch part of an NBA playoff game I'm reminded how much he wants to get back to the League as a coach. He'd have to be an assistant, and he wouldn't earn a fraction of what he earns in Milan, but he'd gladly do it. It's the League, after all.

On the screen a Bulls player gets whacked to the floor, then stepped on by a couple of guys, the kind of rough stuff I didn't see in Italy and didn't miss at all. I mention to Mike that aside from the vast talent gap, I enjoy the *lega* much more than the League. "I like it when a guy gets knocked down and the other one gives him a hand up."

Forget it, Mike says. "I think that's a weakness. I never picked guys up."

"How do you account for Roberto, who's competitive *and* gentlemanly?"

"I can't say about one guy, but I'll say that Italians in general don't have our mentality. To them basketball is fun, it's 'How ya doin'?' They would never push things to the point of fighting during a game. They'd be offended. Whereas we can fight during the game and be friends afterward.

"I wasn't a nice guy on the court," he reminds me, and smiling at the memory he tells me he once smacked *Roberto* in the mouth with an elbow. "I thought he was someone else. I apologized afterward."

I don't know whether this Sunday afternoon exchange has anything to do with it, but on Tuesday morning, when we're down at the bar having cappuccino one last time before I catch the shuttle bus to the airport, Mike comes up with the most interesting suggestion yet for next season's team. "What would be the pros and cons," he asks me, "of bringing Dino back?"

I love it. It's a natural, Dino back in Milano.

"It would depend," Mike says, "on whether he could accept playing only five or ten minutes a game, unless there's an emergency."

I think Dino's ready for that. I think he was ready for it

this season, before Fucka and Cantarello got hurt.

"I think enough time has passed—the link with the old team is broken. And I think I'm confident enough now in my identity as a coach to handle Dino."

It's perfect. Fun for Mike and Dino too, not to mention Laurel and Caterina. And for me, when I come to visit next winter.

"Dino would have to go along with no wine at pregame meals. That's just one of my rules."

Do it, I say. Meneghin & D'Antoni, together again in Milano. Bring him back to play five minutes a game and just *be there*, just *be Dino*. It's good karma. I see a *scudetto*.

"I'll tell ya, Jim," the D'Antonis' forty-two-year-old boy says excitedly, three days after the season is finally put to rest, "I can't wait to get goin'."

I don't know how he's going to make it until training camp.

Afterword

I flew away knowing that on Sundays next season I'll be wondering how Milan did, and I'll wish I could spend that postgame hour or so in Mike and Laurel's living room before going to the Torchietto.

I'll miss watching Roberto Brunamonti applaud during the opponents' introductions before Euroclub games, and the way he shakes the other coach's hand after games (unless it's Skansi, in which case I like the proof that Roberto's human enough to get fed up like anyone else; he's *not* a saint).

I'll miss *il monumento nazionale*, who, even though he's a national monument, can't begin to compete with Charles Barkley or Clyde Drexler in the arrogance department.

I'll miss Ettore, the brilliant coach who, talking *basket*, casually refers to San Sebastian and the Greek mythological heroes.

I'll miss my daily phone conversations with Alberto, my Monday meetings with Lou Colabello up in Rimini for cappuccino and gossip.

Hanging out with Mark Crow: riding to games, eating lunch in Rimini (though *not* dinner at the raw-meat place in

Bologna), getting advice on clubs, being shown a club or two. The important stuff.

I'll miss not only *basket* people. There's Elio, and Maurizio, and the Nicolettis. I'll miss *Italians*, and the Italian way of life. In eight months I heard precious little of therapists, counselors, encounter groups, or divorce. I heard nothing of the "natural" phenomenon of teenagers rebelling against their parents and moving out as soon as they can; on the contrary, I saw dozens of people in their twenties and thirties still living with their parents, and enjoying it. *Dino* lived with his parents for years after he was a national hero (if not yet a *monumento*).

I'll remember families walking on the beach in Riccione. I'll remember how people hang out on Sundays at the Center in Riccione, and at the Piazza Maggiore in Bologna, and at the Duomo in Milan, to see their friends and make new ones and talk sports, politics, whatever.

I'll remember, every time I'm eating with friends and realize they're nearly finished when I've barely started, how much more Italians seem to enjoy life than we do—eating, drinking, talking, simply *being*—and how much less concerned they are with getting done and getting on with the next thing. I'll remember Twink, the fast-talking real-estate salesman, putting down a country where people take three-hour lunch breaks: "No wonder we're the greatest country in the world." Are we? And if we are, will Twink be around to gloat about it after age fifty?

I flew away knowing I'd miss the people and the lifestyle and the cuisine, but I didn't know how much I'd miss the *lega* until I was back in Portland watching the NBA finals on TV. That is, the capital-F (copyrighted) *Finals*.

NBA basketball, of course, is great. The *game* is. But all the surrounding stuff is too much, too much, *too much*. TV everywhere: at courtside, outside the locker rooms. No end to bombastic ads promoting the games and trying to make personalities and even philosophers out of the jocks. A national debate over whether Charles Barkley and jocks in general are "role models"—a question that would never even occur to anyone in Italy, or probably anywhere else on the globe.

Send me back to where *basket* gets a half page at the back of the papers, and where nobody cares if the network doesn't cut to a championship game until the score is 23–21.

Sure, the *lega* would like to be big. The NBA, a slick, zillion-dollar business, is the model, all the big shots tell me. Fortunately (as far as I'm concerned), the *lega* will never be anything like the NBA.

First, *basket* will never be big enough in Europe. Don't pay any attention when Al McGuire tells an interviewer, "I'd say that within three years basketball will be number one in the world. It's going to knock soccer out." Al knows what he likes, but he obviously hasn't spent much time in Europe.

Second, the way the *lega* is run it'll never be half of what it could be.

The NBA makes itself customer-friendly. No fighting in the stands, no throwing things on the floor, no trashing of arenas. Dan Peterson, now an advisor to the *lega*, says something has to be done, but the reality is that Alberto reflects the Italian mentality when he says it's impossible to curb the misbehavior.

The *lega* can't support so many teams. Thirty-two Series "A" teams in a country three-quarters the size of California? Six in the Milan area alone? Who's going to go to all these games? And where are the players to stock so many teams?

The *lega* can't keep going up against soccer. Why play virtually all games on Sunday, which is soccer day, almost a national holiday each week? Eighty thousand people go to soccer matches, while half the people at the *basket* games (including Alberto!) are listening on transistor radios and wishing they were out at the stadium instead. As Roberto

Brunamonti said, "Soccer is like spaghetti in Italy." Scheduling *basket* on Sunday is like putting horseshoe-throwing up against the World Series and expecting people to come.

Tradition, I'm told. But it's inconceivable that the NBA—supposedly the *lega*'s model—would cling to such a self-defeating tradition.

There's simply no leadership. The clubs aren't in it together to make the league a successful enterprise for everyone. The new president, Mulgara, is on seven boards of directors; this little gig with the league is just one more thing he'll fit in when he can. I think they should just put Peterson in charge and do whatever he says—which would include, right away, crowd control, better uniforms, a marketing office, fewer teams, and twice the number of games—but it will never happen. The little clubs will never give up what power they have, lest they find themselves dissolved.

So things career on, the *lega* and various clubs repeatedly shooting themselves in the foot. As Peterson once wrote to me, "Mismanagement is destroying the league from within. How can a team like Fortitudo Bologna [Bologna's second team, which played in A-2 this season as Mangiabevi] be fifteen million dollars in debt? How can Varese spend ten million dollars to expand its old arena when they could have built a new one with nine thousand seats for five million dollars and had the old one for their youth teams? How can Pavia take the final two years of Fernet Branca sponsor money and spend it all at once, making them stone broke going into that third and final year of sponsorship? How can Livorno, just two years ago, have two teams with three thousand season-ticket holders each and, today, have just one with fifteen hundred season-ticket holders? There's more, but you'd need another book."

The *lega* keeps itself small.

Which is what I like about it. My favorite thing about the Lega Pallacanestro Italiano is the scale of everything. That is, normal, not outsized, not bigger than life and more important than war. Ballplayers are ballplayers; most know it's *not* a real job, and a Brunamonti might even be a tad embarrassed about what he's doing. Coaches are *basket* coaches, not geniuses. If you call somebody, they'll usually talk to you. If they're not there, they'll return your call.

It's small-scale enough so that, though the players earn considerably more than ordinary citizens, none are zillionaires, and even guys like Dino and Roberto have to think about what they'll do when their careers are over. It keeps them human.

You can have the NBA publicity monster; give me the rough edges of the *lega*, where there are no manufactured heroes, where everyone is accessible, where people—because they're not going to be covered exhaustively—are free to be real people. Where the game might or might not be shown on TV. Where players might or might not get paid. Even the crowds—I hate the mayhem, but I love the fervor. It's loud and it's real; there aren't many cheerleaders, and no MAKE NOISE! messages flashing on any scoreboards.

I miss it.

I'm already wondering who's going to be playing for whom next season.

Who will be the new *stranieri?* Who *won't* be back?

How will Benetton do without Toni? Can Knorr repeat without Messina? Can Darryl top this year's *.822* field-goal percentage? Will Carlton Myers mature? Will D'Antoni get his *scudetto?*

I'll be wondering. And as I polish off this record of my trip, I know I'm going back.

I knew I was going to miss that hour or two at Mike and Laurel's place after Philips home games, before going to the Torchietto—a few people over, champagne, camaraderie, Mike running the tape of the game—and since talking to Mike a few days ago, I know I've *got* to be there at least once or twice next season.

Because, after giving it some more thought, Mike decided

to bring *il monumento nazionale* back to Milan. Dino is bought and signed, and undoubtedly he and Caterina will be in the D'Antonis' living room on some of those Sunday evenings. It doesn't get any better than that.

Apparently Dino's been forgiven for smashing Morbelli's door.

Postscript

More than a dozen players from the 1992–93 *lega* made the NBA in 1993–94. Rick Mahorn, though rarely a factor on the floor, remained on his old pal Chuck Daly's New Jersey roster and is apparently headed into coaching. Kenny "Sky" Walker signed with the Washington Bullets and had some double-figure rebound games as a reserve. Greg "Cadillac" Anderson came back with the Detroit Pistons and wound up starting at center for much of the season. Cadillac's pal from Phonola Caserta, Tellis Frank, returned to the Minnesota Timberwolves, with whom he had spent a few weeks in 1991. Chris Corchiani's perseverance paid off when he signed with the Boston Celtics. IBC client LeRon Ellis played in 50 games for Charlotte. Ron "Popeye" Jones was a part-time starter in Dallas. Eric Leckner made Philadelphia's roster.

Dino Radja was the Celtics' second leading scorer.

The Chicago Bulls won a surprising 55 games as Pete Myers moved into Michael Jordan's spot, Bill Wennington surprised people off the bench, and Toni Kukoc indeed made the highlight reels with his brilliant passing and last-second shots, proving he can rise to the occasion against any competition.

Haywoode Workman started at point guard as the Indiana Pacers went to the seventh game of the Eastern Conference finals. Antonio Davis, who signed a three-year contract with the Pacers after spending two seasons in Greece and last year in Milan, was a key defender and rebounder. Davis credited Mike D'Antoni for a big part in his development. "That's right," D'Antoni says. "Make sure people know I taught Antonio to run and jump."

John "J. J." Eubanks, though he scored well in Greece after Marr Rimini cut him loose in October 1992, didn't get an offer for 1993–94. As of June 1994, his agent is trying to get him a summer job in the National Basketball League (formerly the World Basketball League), and Eubanks hopes that someone, somewhere, will sign him to play for pay in 1994–95: "The videotapes are out there, and you're always waitin' for that call."

Oscar Schmidt, now an IBC client, went to Spain, where he led the league in scoring and his team was mediocre.

Bob McAdoo went home to New Jersey after his two-game stint with Teamsystem Fabriano, but returned to action for an NBA Legends tour and again for Magic Johnson's European tour. Presently engaged to Patrizia, McAdoo hopes to get back into the NBA in some capacity. That is, coaching or scouting or something—his playing days are finally over. Probably.

In the *Lega Pallacanestro Italiano*, Predrag "Sasha" Danilovic enjoyed another excellent season, as Virtus Bologna—formerly Knorr, now Buckler Beer—won another *scudetto*. The trash-talking sharpshooter, who remains Golden State property, signed for one more season in Bologna and plans to try the NBA in 1995.

Darryl Dawkins had a typical season, according to Ettore Messina: "Shot 89 percent from the field, 99 percent from the line, and his team played like shit." Darryl stayed in shape but was again criticized for playing it safe; in shooting .855 over 38 games, including the playout, he averaged only nine shots per game. Darryl's contract expired after the season, and with salaries dropping way off in the financially troubled *lega* he might not find many suitors. Perennial Euroclub contender Maccabi Tel Aviv and a couple of Greek teams, however, are said to be very interested. Darryl's peripatetic afterlife continues.

Rob Lock, no longer mismatched with Darryl, had a good season in Montecatini, including a 51-point game in the playoffs.

Aleksandar "Sasha" Djordjevich was better than ever in Milan, leading the *lega* in both scoring and assists: "Just like last year," D'Antoni says, "but without the eight-game slump in the middle."

Benetton Treviso lost Kukoc and Corchiani to the NBA, and though Ricardo Pittis and longtime *lega* star Pace Mannion appeared to be sound replacements, Benetton's season fell apart: They won the two-day Italy Cup, but fell to eighth place in A-1 and didn't threaten anyone in the playoffs.

Micheal Ray "Sugar" Richardson had another mercurial season in Livorno. Some weeks he played great, some weeks not so great—although a few of the bad games came when Micheal hadn't gotten paid and so hadn't practiced all week. In any case, IBC is job-hunting for him and he'll undoubtedly play again somewhere.

Carlton Myers, by all accounts, tore up the *lega* in 1993–94. D'Antoni says Myers almost singlehandedly led Scavolini Pesaro to the finals—going left as well as right, sharing the ball, you name it. In the *lega*'s first-ever MVP voting he was the winner in a rout.

Lou Colabello put in another season (the first on a two-year contract with Giorgio Corbelli) doing everything but selling popcorn for Telemarket Forli. After the season, the unpredictable Corbelli traded franchises with the owner of Virtus Roma, and since the new owner is bringing his own front-office people to Forli and Corbelli hasn't offered Lou a job in Rome, as of June 1994 Lou is out of work. He's just hoping Corbelli will make some kind of settlement on the second year of their contract—which was only a verbal contract, meaning Lou will probably wind up with nothing. If nothing comes up in the *lega* he's bringing Silvana and ten-year-old baseball stud Chris back to the States, which is good, but he'll be looking at the same jobs that drove him away in the first place, which is bad. Any NBA organization would be lucky to have him in PR or community relations.

Mark Crow continued living the good life in Rimini with Lia, she of the saintly patience, and their kids Jack and Erica. He put in a little more time at the IBC office up in San Marino last season, as "Lucky" Luciano Capicchioni was frequently in Chicago with prize client Toni Kukoc. Playing in an amateur league, the former *lega* star found his three-point percentage mysteriously dropping off.

Legendary ex-coach Dan Peterson was the color man (to rave reviews) on TeleMonteCarlo's weekly TV games. He continued earning millions of *lire* writing outspoken columns for newspapers and *Il Gigante* and making award-winning Lipton Tea ads. Carlton Myers's agent, IMG's Antonio Ricciotti, said that part of Myers's spectacular 1993–94 traces back to a straightforward piece Peterson wrote early in the season, laying out exactly what Myers needed to do.

Lega PR director and world's nicest guy Alberto Bortolotti continued living happily in Bologna with the lovely Annarosa and four-year-old Francesca, enjoying his job and his friends and soccer on Sundays and *feesh* at the shore as often as possible. Scavolini making it to the finals meant a couple of bonus seafood bacchanals in Pesaro.

Ettore Messina, the new national team coach, spent the season watching games on all levels, working with young players and having occasional workouts with prospective members of the 1994 team. He sometimes misses the day-to-day life and relationships he had as a coach in the *lega* but enjoys the challenge of returning Italian basketball to its former prominence. In any case, he's still just thirty-five years old; he'll be back in the *lega* one day.

In Bologna, Virtus played in a brand-new arena, former Scavolini coach Alberto Bucci replaced Messina, Cliff Levingston replaced Bill Wennington (and was ultimately replaced by Russ Schoene), and Claudio Coldabella replaced Roberto Brunamonti in the starting lineup. But a few things remained constant. The same old fans sang the same old song—*Un Brunamonti, c'e solo un Brunamonti*—and Roberto was always on the floor at the crucial times. "Unbelievable," Mike D'Antoni says. "He took Bologna to the finals, then won the opening game in the last second." The *scudetto* was especially meaningful to Roberto because it guarantees the team will be in the Euroclub Championships next season, which is almost surely the last he'll play. Maybe Roberto's great career will end the way Messina once said it should—with a big ovation at a big game in front of all of Europe (winning shot optional).

Carla's health, apparently, is fine.

Dino Meneghin, back in Milan, remained Meneghin, albeit the aged version. *Il monumento nazionale* turned forty-four during his twenty-eighth professional season and played about ten minutes per game, providing leadership and emotion and Meneghinian physicality. "He was responsible for turning the tide in three or four games for us," D'Antoni says. "And he didn't drink wine at pre-game meals." Dino will apparently play yet another season if someone in the reeling *lega* will pay for what he can still provide. (In Varese, twenty-year-old Andrea Meneghin broke out in his third season and showed signs of becoming a top player.)

In Milan, the big event of Mike and Laurel D'Antoni's year was the appearance of Michael Alexander, their first child, on March 3.

Meanwhile, Mike coached Recoaro Milan, formerly Philips, to a fifth-place finish in A-1, despite having lost Antonio Davis and Ricky Pittis. Shortly after the end of the season, Benetton Treviso made Mike an offer too good to pass up, considering that Olimpia Milano was a financial disaster and up for sale. He and the family will move to Treviso in July, after the annual summer trip to the States to visit parents and check out the NBA summer leagues.

In May, after reading a galley copy of *Il Basket d'Italia*, D'Antoni called the author to say he'd noticed only one mistake: "Knorr was not the only team ever to go through the playoffs undefeated. Look it up."

Duly noted, Coach: the first team ever to go through the *lega* playoffs without a loss was Tracer Milan '85, coached by Dan Peterson and featuring Meneghin, D'Antoni, Russ Schoene, and Joe Barry Carroll. They swept through their three rounds 2–0, 2–0, and 2–0.

In the sweet little town of Riccione, on the Adriatic coast, the bad news was that Italo Nicoletti—Signor—required surgery that kept him hospitalized in Milan for part of the winter. Since the family opened the hotel in the spring he's been putting in an hour or so a day at the desk or the bar, but he's cut way back at the Palazzo de Turismo. Everyone else in the Nicoletti-Fabbri clan is fine.

Back in the States in 1993–94, the author completed the current volume, fretted about money, fretted about what to do next, pined for Italy and his friends there, pined for his ex-wife (but less), went broke, then just in time found something to do. Of course, he knows it won't match eight months in Italy. Probably nothing ever will.

Sometimes he still can't quite believe it really happened.

Jim Patton
Signal Mountain, Tennessee